Social History in Perspective

General Editor: Jeremy Black

Social History in Perspective is a series of in-depth studies of the many topics in social, cultural and religious history.

PUBLISHED

Please note that a sister series, British History in Perspective, is available, covering key topics in British political history.

Social History in Perspective
Series Standing Order
ISBN 0–333–71694–9 hardcover
ISBN 0–333–69336–1 paperback
(outside North America only)

You can receive future titles in this series as they are published by placing a standing order. Please contact your bookseller or, in case of difficulty, write to us at the address below with your name and address, the title of the series and the ISBN quoted above.
Customer Services Department, Palgrave Ltd
Houndmills, Basingstoke, Hampshire RG21 6XS, England

BRITISH WOMEN IN THE NINETEENTH CENTURY

Kathryn Gleadle

palgrave
macmillan

First published 2001 by
PALGRAVE MACMILLAN

Palgrave Macmillan in the UK is an imprint of Macmillan Publishers Limited,
registered in England, company number 785998, of Houndmills, Basingstoke,
Hampshire RG21 6XS.

Palgrave Macmillan in the US is a division of St Martin's Press LLC,
175 Fifth Avenue, New York, NY 10010.

Palgrave Macmillan is the global academic imprint of the above companies
and has companies and representatives throughout the world.

Palgrave® and Macmillan® are registered trademarks in the United States,
the United Kingdom, Europe and other countries.

ISBN 978-0-333-67629-5 hardback
ISBN 978-0-333-67630-1 paperback

This book is printed on paper suitable for recycling and made from fully
managed and sustained forest sources. Logging, pulping and manufacturing
processes are expected to conform to the environmental regulations of the
country of origin.

A catalogue record for this book is available from the British Library.

Library of Congress Cataloging-in-Publication Data

Gleadle, Kathryn.
    British women in the nineteenth century / Kathryn Gleadle.
       p. cm.—(Social history in perspective)
    Includes bibliographical references and index.
    ISBN 0-333-67629-7
       1. Women—Great Britain—History—19th century.
    2. Women—Great Britain—Social conditions. 3. Feminism—
Great Britain—History—19th century. I. Title. II. Series.

HQ1593 .G58 2001
305.4'0941—dc21
                                       2001019438

Printed in Great Britain by the MPG Books Group, Bodmin and King's Lynn

CONTENTS

PART III WORKING-CLASS WOMEN, 1860–1900

PART IV MIDDLE-CLASS AND UPPER-CLASS WOMEN, 1860–1900

INTRODUCTION

Over the last 20 years, a myriad of conflicting narratives have been
constructed detailing the history of nineteenth-century British women.
The feminist revival of the 1970s, combined with the growth of social
history and the left-wing desire to recapture 'history from below', led to
a wave of historical interest in the lives of Victorian women. The
influential work of Sheila Rowbotham, for example, sought to bring
to light those women who had remained 'hidden from history', yet who
were of vital significance to both industrial and political protest and
early feminism. Such a project was informed by the politics of the 'new
wave' feminism of the 1970s which sought to consider afresh women's
role within society.[1]

During this period, pioneering works, such as the volumes of essays
edited by Martha Vicinus, were indicative of the enormous creative and
intellectual potential of women's history. Research into women's cultural representations; the discursive construction of women in medical
and scientific languages; and the attention to 'real' women's efforts to
forge independent lives, whether through employment or emigration,
highlighted the many diverse and fruitful fields of enquiry. A common
thread which often wove these stories together was the careful attention
paid to contemporary ideologies of femininity – and, in particular, to
the pervasive nineteenth-century rhetoric of 'separate spheres'. The
language of separate spheres was seen to embody the contemporary
perception that women were innately affectionate, loving and religious,
whilst men were perceived as naturally more robust, quick-witted and
pragmatic. This demarcation of gender attributes was typically mir-
rored, it was held, in a physical separation of the sexes. Men were to
engage themselves in the worlds of business, work and politics; whilst

1

women were consigned to the home and family. Although it was recognised by the new women's historians that the ideology of 'separate spheres' was a prescriptive dialogue which did not necessarily reflect the reality of nineteenth-century women's lives, such rhetoric was none the less constructed as a central starting-point in evaluating women's experiences.[2]

The attention thus paid to the influence of patriarchal ideologies in shaping women's lives was not without its critics, however. As Gerda Lerner was to insist in the early 1980s, such an approach reified women as victims and tended to detract from the ability and determination of women to shape their own lives. It was also recognised that merely 'adding' women into history would fail to offer a radical challenge to the conceptual foundations of male-dominated history.[3] Without such a theoretical basis, insisted Joan Kelly, women's history would continue to be marginalised within historical studies. Kelly argued that women's history, in fact, had the potential to disrupt the essential tenets of mainstream history. It called into question fundamental issues of periodisation (e.g. 'Did women have a Renaissance?'); it introduced new categories of social analysis (i.e. the role of gender); and finally, women's history posited alternative theories of social change (by looking, for example, at the significance of alterations in male/ female relations).[4]

By the mid-1980s, many of these concerns had developed their own creative momentum, as the concept of 'gender history' gained ground. This is an approach which shifts attention away from the study of women to the consideration, more broadly, of social structures. One of its most brilliant, if controversial, exemplars was Leonore Davidoff and Catherine Hall's 1987 work, *Family Fortunes: Men and Women of the English Middle Class 1780–1950*. This innovative book demonstrated the fundamental significance of gender and gender relations in the emergence of the English middle class.[5]

The application of poststructural techniques to the practice of gender history marked a further intellectual departure of the late 1980s. Through studying the proliferating constructions of 'woman' across a range of cultural discourses, ground-breaking works by Joan Scott, Denise Riley and Mary Poovey argued for the recognition that the category of 'woman' is an unstable one, its meanings shifting and diverging in different historical and cultural contexts. This insight, it is argued, brings into stark relief the multifarious ideological strategies which facilitates the patriarchal subordination of women. The deconstruction of the category of woman, its practitioners insist, also points to the dangers of constructing a new canon of 'women's history'. Such a project, it is argued, threatens to essentialise 'woman' and to elide and obscure the myriad of cultural, sexual, social and racial differences which actually comprise the term.[6] Whilst women's historians have replied that women's history was always sensitive to differences in class (and increasingly to differences in sexual orientation and ethnicity as well); the poststructuralist insistence on the existence of multiple identities has proved a stimulating field of enquiry.[7]

Nevertheless, many women's historians continue to insist upon the importance of studying women's as well as gender history. There is a danger, it has been argued, that women will become reduced to cultural or discursive pawns in the hands of poststructuralists; or once more marginalised and subsumed in a meta-narrative of gender history.[8]

Clearly then, women's history must be contextualised within the framework of broader historiographical developments: such as the rise of social history and, more recently, the impact of poststructuralism and cultural history. Women's history has also been strongly influenced by other intellectual currents within the discipline, such as the attention lately paid to empire, ethnicity, and regional and national identities; and the importance of consumerism. However, the field of women's history has equally been enriched by vibrant internal debates, many of which have drawn upon opposing theoretical models. In particular, socialist feminists and radical feminists have drawn swords over the comparative impact of patriarchy and capitalism in shaping women's lives. Within such debates, disagreements over the role of the family have often been centre stage. Broadly speaking, socialist feminists have tended to focus upon the seemingly iniquitous effects of capitalism upon women. Within such schemas, in which notions of social and economic change are paramount, the family has often been presented as a necessary bulwark of the working classes against economic and class oppression. Radical feminists, on the other hand, point to the enduring force of patriarchal relations throughout history, and so for them, women's history is better presented as 'standing still'. As a consequence, these scholars have been extremely sceptical as to the benefit of such strategies of the 'family wage' for working-class women, seeing it as a project to further extend women's dependence upon their higher-earning menfolk.[9]

Much recent research has tended to shift attention away from these debates of 'continuity versus change'. Many women's historians are now focusing to a greater extent upon the possibilities for female agency and the complex construction of nineteenth-century femininities, within broader narratives of historical explanation and gendered discourses. This 'new revisionism', as we might call it, has strongly influenced the writing of this book. By examining specific areas of women's experiences in detail, a mounting body of work has illuminated the processes whereby women were able to contest and subvert seemingly powerful gender constructs across a range of socio-cultural contexts – in the law, economy, family and literary discourse. Much of this work therefore recognises the fact that the actual implementation of gendered discourses and practices varied considerably. In the cotton and chain-making industries, for example, it has been shown that gendered ideologies were not a monolithic construct, but rather a mutuable and varied phenemona whose impact differed greatly in different contexts.[10]

While seeking to remain sensitive to the continuities of gendered discourses and patriarchal relations, *British Women in the Nineteenth Century* aims to construct a nuanced account of the precise ways in which such factors impacted upon women's own identities. Such an analysis is complicated by the need for a holistic approach to women's lives. As feminist historians have been at pains to stress, women's subordinate position in the economy cannot be understood without reference to their subordinate position in the family.[11] Equally, women's political and public activities, as philanthropists, Chartists, feminists and so on, were closely woven into their own subjectivities concerning their roles as wives and mothers.

A consideration of the construction of women's own subjectivities necessitates a revisionist approach to the language of 'separate spheres' – that ideology which, as we have seen, has so dominated historical enquiry into nineteenth-century British women. In recent years, the historical significance of 'separate spheres' has been greatly problematised. The burgeoning interest in nineteenth-century masculinities has enriched our understanding of the dynamics of contemporary life; whilst advances in our knowledge of middle- and upper-class women's role in consumerism, property-holding, philanthropy and politics have questioned the orthodoxy of women's confinement to a world of child care and domesticity. In her important essay, Amanda Vickery suggested that far from being a reflection of prevailing cultural practice, the language of separate spheres may be read as a backlash against the increasing public presence of women.[12]

However, 'separate spheres' cannot be understood purely as a reactionary doctrine. Historians of Victorian feminism have emphasised the importance of such language to the discourses of contemporary feminism, where it had empowering potential. By privileging women's caring and benevolent natures, feminists were able to argue for the importance of women's contribution to the polity. It is important, then, to consider the reception and impact of cultural discourses upon women themselves, and to assess the varied significance they had in constructing nineteenth-century femininities. The book is informed by a similar approach towards women's economic activities. In the eighteenth century, a woman's financial contribution to the family was taken for granted, but by the end of the nineteenth century, married women faced considerable public criticism for working. Consequently, Ann Oakley has presented the Victorian age as the period in which the very concept of 'housewife' was born.[13] However, in this book an emphasis is placed upon revisionist analyses which seek to understand the subjectivities and personal motivations of women themselves. Joanna Bourke, for example, insists on our understanding women's embrace of the role of 'full-time housewife' as a rational and sensible strategy for improving the quality of life for many working families.[14]

Indeed, throughout the book, attention is drawn to the need to look beyond cultural proscriptions of womanhood to understand how women themselves interpreted, judged and perceived their capabilities. Moreover, in stressing the potential for female agency, the book attempts to consider the many strategies which enabled women to undermine official barriers to their personal capacity for assertion and fulfilment. For example, although barred from property ownership under common law, revisionist work has pointed out that married women remained active as consumers and legators.[15] Furthermore, whilst the socialisation of nineteenth-century girls is often considered in purely negative terms – such as the role of an inadequate education, popular literature and family dynamics in creating subordinate, dependent women, the book will also hint at the potential for empowering aspects of girls' socialisation – such as the personal impact of their involvement in politics, philanthropy and the family enterprise.

Another recurring theme of this book is the extent to which generalisations concerning the nature of women's lives mask significant and substantial regional variations – a factor which problematises narratives of continuity and change. This becomes particularly apparent when the experiences of Irish, Scottish, Welsh and colonial women are taken into account. Women's lives were marked as much by diversity and difference as they were by uniform patterns of oppression.

The book is split chronologically into two parts, the first dealing with the period 1800–60, the second considering the years 1860–1900. This divide was chosen, rather than the precise mid-century, so that adequate attention might be given to the many rapid developments which occurred during the second part of the century, particularly in the areas of education, employment and political organisation. To aid its accessibility and utility, the book is cut thematically into sections upon work, politics and the family. However, as the following chapters indicate, a study of women's experiences actually requires substantial renegotiation of such key terms as work, politics and philanthropy. Women's work extends far beyond the classic definition of paid employment; whilst, as already mentioned, women's engagement with politics was often inextricably linked to their activities as wives and mothers. Consequently, chapters on work include such subjects as unpaid domestic labour and mothering; whilst discussions on politics and community affairs also incorporate material relating to industrial activity, and the centrality of the family. It is by stressing the interdependence and connectedness of their experiences that the complexity of women's lives, and their efforts to shape their own destinies, emerges most clearly.

I am extremely grateful to Sarah Richardson and Clare Midgley for their support, encouragement and practical assistance. Rowan Rogerson Gleadle and James Rogerson Gleadle kindly endured a paper-strewn house and provided a welcome source of distraction throughout. Many thanks are also due to the British Academy for their financial assistance during the closing stages of writing this book.

PART I

WORKING-CLASS WOMEN, 1800–1860

1

WORK

Introduction

Our story opens in 1800 – a critical juncture in the labour history of working-class women. The coming years were to witness an intricate tapestry of change and tradition, as new employment practices and technologies became woven into the work experiences of labouring women. For an older historiographical tradition (as in Alice Clark's *Working Life of Women in the Seventeenth Century*, first published in 1919), the nineteenth century represented a pernicious departure in women's exploitation as capitalism began to fracture the harmonious patterns of pre-industrial production. However, more recent commentators have noted that gender had played a critical role in the workplace in the pre-industrial period also.[1] This chapter will consider the ways in which gendered ideologies variously interplayed with economic advances to produce a highly diverse labour market for working women. In many industries, definitions of skilled work became increasingly codified by gender – a development which had complex and divergent implications for the self-perceptions of women themselves; whilst enormous regional and sectoral variations in both employment practices and customs of gendered labour division forewarn against simple analyses of female exploitation in the workplace.

Furthermore, although certain aspects of women's employment (most notably factory work) became the subject of impassioned debate amongst both the reading public and their own communities, more typically, women's labour was clustered in less socially visible occupations: such as home-based manufacture and domestic work.

This ubiquitous labour frequently eluded the census, making it extremely difficult to construct quantitative analyses of women's labour. Indeed, despite increasing cultural pressures for women to privilege their domestic role, for the majority, work remained central to their identities. This is not surprising: the widespread labour of children, whether informal (through assisting their mothers in agricultural tasks or home manufacture) or formal (through their employment as servants, factory and mine workers), meant that work formed a significant aspect of the socialisation process of working-class girls.

Agriculture and Service

Historians have pointed to a serious decline in women's contribution to the rural economy by the turn of the century. The ongoing process of enclosure and the incorporation of common land was having a catastrophic effect upon the survival strategies of the rural poor. It deprived women of their traditional role in exploiting common land resources through such activities as grazing animals and gathering wood, work in which their children often assisted. Meanwhile, landowners had become increasingly intolerant of the harvest practice of gleaning, which had previously enabled women to provide their families with bread for the winter. The loss of these opportunities led to the proletarianisation of labouring families as they became increasingly dependent upon money wages for their survival.[2]

At the same time, in many regions farmers, largely for social and cultural reasons, were increasingly employing labour on a wage basis, rather than housing servants in husbandry. Young women thus lost vital opportunities for agricultural training and socialisation away from home. They were increasingly relegated to the lowest paid and least-skilled jobs of the agricultural year, such as stone picking and turnip cleaning.[3] Moreover, the greater use of the scythe during harvesting, which many communities deemed to be too heavy for women to manage, greatly limited their employment opportunities during harvest time. Women's agricultural employment, particularly in the south of England, was further hit by the bitter agricultural depression which followed the ending of the Napoleonic Wars in 1815.[4]

Nevertheless, the experience of female agricultural labourers diverged considerably across the country. Certainly, in many areas, women's agricultural work was increasingly seasonal and sporadic, but the nature of their labour diverged considerably across the regions, as did hiring arrangements. Women continued to reap crops, sometimes in travelling bands, in areas such as Northumberland, and Scotland; whereas in York, an Irish immigrant explained to Arthur Munby, 'After taters comes turnip pulling; and then we are idle all winter and live on what we've earned in summer.'[5] Many urban women migrated to the countryside in the summer to pick up casual employment in market gardens and hop fields.[6] By contrast, East Anglia, with its large farms and scattered population, became notorious from the 1840s for its 'gang system', whereby large groups of women and children tramped long distances to work excessive hours in appalling conditions. Female labour should not be automatically associated with oppressive drudgery, however. 'Bondagers' (female farm workers provided by male labourers in south-east Scotland and north-east England as a condition of their employment) seem to have prided themselves on their physical endurance and independence.[7]

Indeed, in most areas of Scotland, Wales and Ireland, women appear to have felt no shame in undertaking all aspects of farm work.[8] In southern England, however, attitudes were beginning to shift. Parliamentary commissioners discovered in 1843 that young women there had become disdainful of performing the hard, physical labour of which a previous generation had boasted.[9] By the middle of the century, women in many rural areas were choosing to improve their family's lifestyle by concentrating upon household labour, rather than performing paid employment (see Chapter 7). This development may have made them more likely to concur with gendered notions concerning women's physical inferiority to men, as it validated their own choices. This is an indication that in some areas women's own subjectivities, and their perceptions of what their bodies might do, were changing.

Women did not necessarily embrace discursive shifts concerning their capabilities, however. In dairying, as attempts were made to reconstruct the industry upon scientific grounds, women's traditional dairying skills were increasingly seen as retrograde. By the middle of the century, although localised pockets of tradition persisted (as in Wiltshire), dairying had become a largely male-dominated occupation on the larger farms; and the Royal Commission on Women and Children in Agriculture (1843) could pronounce women to be ill-suited to the patience, skill and strength dairying required. Yet, as Deborah Valenze notes, there are clear hints that rural women themselves dissented from the various establishment views as to the decline in female dairying.[10]

For those displaced from agricultural work, domestic service became an ever-more likely option. Under the earlier practice of servants in husbandry, servants had been treated as one of the family. However, increasing class differentiation, combined with new standards of domestic comfort, came to necessitate a greater emphasis upon the services of a subordinate, *domestic* servant.[11] It should be pointed out that calculations as to the decline in women's agricultural work and their increased employment as domestic servants have been greatly skewed by the fact that census data often classified female farm servants as domestic servants. Nevertheless, domestic service remained the single biggest employer of women: 40 per cent of all working women were recorded as domestic servants in the 1851 census (although this figure also included many women assisting in the homes of relatives).[12]

Servants in larger establishments, (upper servants, in particular) might expect a reasonable degree of job satisfaction. It has been found, for example, that children's nurses tended to be motivated and affectionate towards their charges.[13] Feminist historians, however, have pointed to the ritualised subjection implicit in domestic service, in both the rural and urban contexts. Employees in the largest households were not permitted to turn their back in the presence of employers, and might even be given new names. Of course, such subservience was not necessarily internalised by the servants. As Davidoff shows, there were ways of asserting one's own identity – time-wasting, deliberately mishearing or, in one example, urinating in the gravy! Yet she also cites the pitiful case of a young girl working in a lodging house in Southampton in the 1830s who, according to one sympathetic guest, was 'worse off then [sic] an Asiatic slave'.[14] The overwork and isolation experienced by this poor girl were far from atypical. In 1851, half of all domestic servants were the only resident female servant at their place of work.[15] Such 'maids-of-all-work' might carry out not just domestic work, but assist in the family business too. Many working-class households could afford such assistance by taking on a girl from the local workhouse. Vulnerable girls such as these were particularly prey to physical and sexual abuse at the hands of their employers (the right to punish servants through beating was not legally abolished until 1861).[16]

Pamela Sharpe, however, emphasises the variable nature of domestic service, pointing out that in areas which boasted a wealthy genteel class, opportunities for servants could be good. Certainly, there was a strong current of female migration from rural villages in order to obtain positions in domestic service and the more fortunate might form a mobile work force, changing positions in order to better their own situations and to acquire new skills.[17]

Women in Trades and Rural Industries

Working-class women engaged in a wide variety of trades, although this was often dependent upon stages in their life-cycle. It was still common for widows to adopt their late husband's occupation, even in trades such as plumbing and ironmongery. Women were similarly much in evidence in the manufacture of chains and nails in the Black Country and in the Birmingham metal trades. In the latter, gendered assumptions concerning women's fine motor skills meant that they were most commonly found in button-making or piercing. Women's early instruction in domestic needlework may have accounted for such abilities – but such training, unlike formal apprenticeships, did not bring women the status of skilled workers. Nevertheless, elsewhere there were some industries, such as calico printing or pottery manufacture, where women could perform skilled work for a comparatively good wage.[18]

Despite this regional diversity, nationally, women's work was increasingly clustered in the clothing and textile industries.[19] Spinning had always been a vital economic resource for plebeian women, but lace-making, silk-weaving and cotton manufacture now also rose in importance. Indeed, women's labour in the textile and metal sectors was a key factor in the country's rapid industrialisation.[20] However, as the production of textile goods mushroomed from the late eighteenth century, women, in common with other social subordinates such as Irish immigrants, children and the elderly, tended to be associated with the least skilled and most poorly paid branches of the sector, such as the weaving of coarse cotton cloth. The ability to use this cheap labour (whose work was not restricted by guild regulations) could be more important than the impact of new technologies in the massive expansion of production during the late eighteenth and early nineteenth centuries.[21] Working in their own homes (or sometimes in small workshops) on a piece-rate basis, domestic manufacture – or protoindustrialisation – has been argued to have had profound and often empowering personal implications for women (see Chapter 3). But women's wages were pitifully low;

the work could be irregular; and workers lacked any bargaining power.[22] Occasionally, individuals did combine to negotiate for better pay, as in Loughborough in 1811,[23] but such initiatives remained sporadic and usually unsuccessful. Nevertheless, the capacity to contribute to the family economy could have an important impact upon women's well-being. When such work dried up, women could be left in a parlous situation, both socially and economically. In County Tipperary, for example, the decline in hand-spinning forced women to turn to begging to maintain their family contribution.[24] The Irish spinning industry was to be further devastated by the famine in the 1840s, leading to massive emigration in an attempt to find alternative economic opportunities.[25]

The threat to women's spinning was repeated across Britain. Advances in industrial technology had begun to make a serious impact upon women's labour from the late eighteenth century. Sophisticated spinning jennies and spinning mules had to be housed in large workshops and the heavy mules were thought to be more appropriate for male labour. The consequent boom in production wrought by the new technology created a huge demand for handloom weavers which did absorb some of the displaced female spinners; many other inventions were designed specifically for cheap female labour; and in some industries, female labour was used to introduce deskilled work practices.[26] However, the concentration of industry under the factory system meant that in numerous regions, unemployed domestic spinners were thrown into a desperate situation. Indeed, many historians agree that these years saw a steady, if uneven, deterioration in women's economic participation.[27] Across Britain, the result was considerable migration from rural to urban areas in an attempt to find work. Single women and widows in rural Essex, for example, prompted by the lack of spinning, moved to Colchester to take advantage of the opportunities in silk-weaving.[28]

It has been suggested that the lack of employment for young females in rural areas meant that they sometimes benefited from slightly higher school attendance than boys. The consequences of such a phenomenon were highly variable, however. For a tiny minority of the brightest village girls, participation on a pupil-teacher scheme enabled careers as primary school teachers. In this capacity, they might enjoy a limited degree of social mobility which few others could hope to attain. As a female teacher, women would soon discover that gender was closely imbricated into their professional role. Unlike their male peers, female teachers were expected to carry out ancillary and domestic work within the school. None the less, it is apparent that (much to the frustration of school inspectors), many such women refused to conform to establishment expectations of demure feminine behaviour – perhaps by slighting the importance of domestic education, dressing fashionably, or enjoying friendships with male pupils and teachers.[29]

However, for the majority of working-class girls, higher school attendance would rarely widen their opportunities, as the curriculum (except in Scotland) focused heavily upon needlework, or the rudiments of rural industries such as gloving, straw-plaiting and lace-making.[30] These trades were actively promoted by philanthropists and parish guardians in the early years of the century, particularly in Bedfordshire, Hertfordshire and Buckinghamshire, to ease the suffering caused by the demise of the domestic spinning industry.[31] For older women, who were less likely (or willing) to find employment in the factories, such trades could be vital. Most elderly women would have few other options. The more enterprising might set themselves up as a teacher in a village dame school – which required minimal academic attainment. Others might eke out a living as a village nurse, using traditional herbal remedies and assisting at childbirth.[32] The economic fate of older working-class women still awaits in-depth research. However, it was surely at this stage in the life-cycle, when many women had to return to the labour market, perhaps as widows, that suffering would have been particularly acute.

Women in Factories and Mines

By the 1830s, the mechanisation of cotton, woollen, worsted and some aspects of lace production led to growing numbers of women working in factories – initially as spinners and on preparatory processes, but increasingly as weavers. By 1847, approximately 300 000 women were employed in factories;[33] and in some areas, they formed a substantial proportion of the factory workforce. In 1838 women comprised nearly 70 per cent of the workforce in the Irish spinning mills, for example.[34] In the factory environment, the relationship between gender and technology continued to be highly complex. The plentiful supply of low-cost female labour could initially act as a disincentive for manufacturers to introduce expensive new technologies.[35] On the other hand, in a typical move, when the Dutch engine loom was introduced in Coventry, the ribbon weavers were divided into a 'skilled' male section which worked on the new looms, and an 'unskilled' female section which continued to use the single handloom.[36] In the Halstead silk mills, male operatives could expect to progress fairly automatically up the job ladder, while most women could only shift horizontally between weaving or winding.[37]

Although female factory work was comparatively well-paid to other women's work, a government report in 1833 revealed that the average woman's factory wage was less than 41 per cent that of men.[38] In many sectors, men were constructed as the 'primary' workers, eligible for perquisites such as coal allowances, while women were perceived as a subordinate workforce performing the more basic tasks at inferior wages.

However, in powerloom weaving, men and women were entitled to the same basic piece rates. Their take-home pay was still highly differentiated, as men were generally allocated the larger, more lucrative looms, as well as the task of tuning them.[39] Nevertheless, female powerloom weavers, a minority of whom worked on the prestigious four-loom weavers, enjoyed enhanced social status, higher wages and derived considerable pride in their skill.[40] Social reformers tended to obliterate these distinctions in their portrayal of a universally oppressed and exploited female factory workforce. Lord Ashley dwelt on manufacturers' proclivity to employ vulnerable female workers who could be induced to work harder for less pay.[41] Yet such an image is at striking variance with the passion and violence with which factory women engaged in industrial protest and associative activities. Indeed, in a contradictory move, Ashley revealed his repulsion that, 'Fifty or sixty females, married and single, form themselves into clubs, ostensibly for protection; but, in fact, they meet together to drink, sing, and smoke; they use, it is stated, the lowest, most brutal, and most disgusting language imaginable.'[42]

The robust nature of women's associative life has since been corroborated by several historians, although the story is a chequered one, closely imbricated in social conflicts within the factory communities. In the early years of the factory system, women were vigorous in industrial protest. During the first major strike of Lancashire cotton spinners in 1808, women were described as being 'more turbulent and mischievous than the men'.[43] However, a heightened gender antagonism is discernible from the 1820s, as male spinners became resentful at the employment of (low-paid) women, whom they perceived as a threat to their craft status. The decision of some employers to hire female spinners during strikes of male workers exacerbated tensions, resulting in several incidents of serious physical assault upon female blackleg labour. By the mid-1820s, as unionists began to project a more respectable public image, they shifted from physical to rhetorical strategies. Domesticity was now projected as central to the remaking of working-class aspirations and, consequently, the prohibition of female waged labour began to creep up the trade union agenda. When, in 1829 the Grand General Union of Operative Spinners was established, women were expressly excluded from the organisation.[44]

The antagonism of working-class men towards female factory labour was deepened by new labour practices which curtailed their patriarchal control. There was a decline in the practice of allowing male spinners to employ their own piecers (often family members) and an increasing tendency on the part of employers to pay wages individually, rather than to the male head of the household.[45] Many men evidently felt threatened by the authority which factory overlookers had over their wives' labour – sensitivities which must have been heightened by the high prevalence of sexual harassment to which women were often subjected by their supervisors.[46] By the 1840s committees of male factory workers campaigning for shorter hours (notably in West Riding) had gone so far as to call for the gradual withdrawal of all female labour from factories.[47]

However, other threads must be woven into this narrative. The increasing adoption of powerloom weaving from the 1820s, with its gender-neutral piece rates, allowed for a more co-operative ethos to develop in the weaving sectors and apparently encouraged women's confidence to engage in industrial activity. Female and male powerloom weavers acted together during the seven-week Manchester strike of 1842, for example. Women were equally prominent in the Preston lockout of 1853–4, when female delegates toured the local area, speaking at public meetings. Women's capacity for analysing the conditions of their employment, and their willingness to confront both employers and the establishment to effect improvements, was seen also in their contribution to the Ten Hours Movement (to restrict the length of their working day).[48]

This engagement with the politics of the workplace did not necessarily indicate women's accommodation to the factory system. Women frequently utilised their industrial activity to state broader social and personal objectives. A typical aspiration was voiced by 'sister operatives' in Macclesfield – that their husbands should be paid a sufficient wage so that they themselves would no longer have to work in the factories.[49]

Despite the clarity and self-assurance with which female workers often articulated their views, the ensuing factory acts classified women as 'protected' persons. To the frustration of utilitarian reformers, the 1844 Factory Act limited female labour to 12 hours a day and also prohibited the night-work of women. In 1847 further legislation established a maximum of 10 hours a day for women and young people labouring in the factories. The pioneer women's historian, Ivy Pinchbeck, celebrated the 1844 Factory Act as a major landmark to secure women's industrial interests,[50] yet the consequent reduction in wages must have hit single women and widows particularly hard. Modern historians have also focused upon factory legislation's conflation of women and children. The very questionnaires used by the commissioners in their investigations in 1833 posed the same (highly inappropriate) questions to women as to children. Moreover, the safety clauses of the 1844 Act reinforced male control over machine maintenance and adjustment, thus further limiting women's promotion prospects.[51] Factory legislation also sought to safeguard the education of juvenile workers by the introduction of the half-time system. Nevertheless, the heavy emphasis upon female morality in the curriculum, combined with widespread truancy, meant that such provision failed to solve the high levels of female illiteracy in factory communities such as Lancashire.[52]

It was not only the labour of women in factories which convulsed reforming sensibilities during these years. The revelations of the Royal Commission into the Employment of Children in Mines (1842), with its stark illustrations of the harsh and degrading labour performed by women and children, caused a furore. Although female pit work had already disappeared in many areas by this period, it still persisted in West Lancashire, parts of Yorkshire, East Scotland and South Wales. In these regions, women, as drawers or bearers, performed much of the haulage work, harnessing the tubs of coal with belts or ropes which often passed between their legs. This, plus the semi-nudity of some of the workers involved, revolted investigating commissioners.[53]

Not surprisingly, female mineworkers frequently asserted to the commissioners that were alternative work available, they would immediately leave the mines.[54] Yet despite the dreadful nature of their work, female miners do not appear to have perceived themselves to be a universally subjected and browbeaten workforce. Certainly, the environment of the pit and its community were considerably misrepresented in the commissioners' report. Assurances from female witnesses concerning the tact and rectitude of their male colleagues, especially when they were in a state of comparative undress, were omitted in the final report; as was evidence indicating women's pride in their ability to maintain good domestic arrangements. The commission dwelt instead upon lurid details as to the moral dangers they believed female labour in the mines to pose.[55] Moreover, despite female mineworkers' appalling exploitation, the fact that they often performed the most arduous tasks was interpreted by some women as proof of their superior resilience. As one female worker told a commissioner, 'lads are no fit to stand the work like women'.[56] There is also evidence to indicate that these women had a fierce sense of pride and personal confidence. One miner observed that, 'If a man was to offer any insult to a girl in a pit she would take her fist and give him a blow in his face.'[57]

The result of the commission was that females were banned from working underground in 1842, thus establishing the precedent of 'protective legislation'. In South Wales there was considerable evasion of the Act, while in Scotland, many women were given alternative employment at the pit-face, thus displacing male labour. Individual mine owners and their wives did sometimes provide schemes to train young girls for alternative employment in domestic service, but at the legislative level, little thought had been given as to the devastating impact the Act would have upon women's economic position in pit communities.[58]

Women and Urban Employment

Despite the rapid pace of industrialisation during these years, most women continued to work in traditional, non-mechanised industries. In York only 1.1 per cent of the city's female workers were involved in modern manufacture in 1851.[59] In the cities and environs of Leicester, Coventry, Nottingham and Northampton, women worked as homeworkers in the footwear, hosiery and silk lace industries.[60] In London, the massive expansion in production was largely achieved through a deskilling of the labour process. As Sally Alexander's pioneering essay demonstrated, immigrants flooded to the city hoping that the men would find employment on the docks or in the building industries, whilst their female relatives would contribute to the family economy by taking on 'slop work'. Atrociously paid, this 'sweated' work had first become widespread during the Napoleonic Wars when employers used cheap labour to profit from government contracts for military uniforms. Although the work was generally carried out within the workers' own homes, many were resident in dressmaking houses, which provided poor standards of food and accommodation and demanded excessive hours of work.[61]

The dreadful exploitation of these workers was such that, as the investigative journalist, Henry Mayhew, revealed to a shocked nation in 1849–50, many needlewomen – whose work was highly irregular due to the vagaries of the London season and the international markets – were forced to supplement their wages through prostitution. Indeed, as recent research has revealed, needlewomen became closely identified with prostitution in the public mind and the image of the pathetic needleworker, in need of protection and assistance, became commonplace.[62]

It was not only clothing that was subcontracted out in this way. Homework was plentiful, too, if equally badly paid, in the production of items such as matches, artificial flowers, brushes and boxes; and also in previously skilled trades, such as shoemaking and cabinet manufacture. However, as Alexander's work reminds us, we should not paint a picture of blanket exploitation across all female workers. The capital continued to see the survival of small, specialised crafts, such as engraving and watchmaking, in which a small number of women did retain their hold. Respectability and a (comparatively) reasonable income could also be found by women in some corners of the dressmaking and millinery trades, as well as in pearl-stringing, haberdashery, leather manufacture, hatting and bookbinding – all of which involved some element of apprenticeship (although female apprenticeships did not necessarily entail the same level of training as that of men's).[63]

For married women, in London as in other urban settings, work often meant assisting in their husbands' trades. This might involve taking responsibility for the retail of the goods, perhaps by selling items from a small shop at the front of the house. Selling, a customary female activity, was also resorted to by the poorest in hard times. Street-selling, hawking and peddling were common occupations of children and the aged alike; whilst nursing was seen as the lowest form of domestic service – cleaning and feeding the most vulnerable and contagious in society, and was often carried out by the elderly or alcoholic. More prosperous women could capitalise upon the growing service needs of expanding urban populations by acting as innkeepers, victuallers and lodging housekeepers; and washing, cooking, cleaning, laundry work, taking in lodgers, child-minding and even wet-nursing could provide vital sources of income to hard-pressed married women. Much of this work was self-evidently casual, intermittent and part-time, as such it went unrecorded in census statistics.[64] Yet such labour reveals women's resourcefulness and versatility, as well as their vital role in the economy of their local communities.

Domestic Work

In addition to paid employment, working-class women also performed the bulk of unpaid labour within the home. (Although domestic activities could often 'cross over' into paid work, as in the case of landladies and child-minders, for example.[65]) Some communities, such as Lancashire, had a 'Mary Anne' night in which all the family – including the menfolk – helped with the domestic chores. But this perhaps further underlined the assumption that on a day-to-day basis, the home was the woman's responsibility. As Davidoff acerbically comments, 'if he helped with heavy washing, or took the children out on a Sunday, it was much in the same tradition as the "kindly" squire and his lady who gave charitable extras to their retainers and villagers.'[66] Nevertheless, contrary to the critical assertions of factory reformers, women often took considerable pride in the maintenance of their homes. The reduction of working hours for factory employees under the Ten Hours Act (1847) was used by many women to perform additional household labour.[67]

For the poorest families, however, housework could indeed be minimal, as hostile critics noted. But attempts at cleanliness were futile in slums where raw sewage oozed into the very rooms. Furniture, utensils and ovens were found to be almost wholly lacking in the tenements of Glasgow, and a diet which revolved around bread and potatoes required little preparation. Still, women and children were generally responsible for seeing to basic household needs, most notably the arduous task of fetching water from communal taps.[68] (And women, of course, remained the primary carers of their children.) Greater domestic work would be prompted by a rise in living standards. Increased resources usually meant the preparation of more complex dishes; ornaments to polish; and more washing to launder. For the more prosperous, domestic cleanliness and order had already become implicated in a wider ideology of respectability.[69] For women, this could signal their family's independence from charitable or parochial assistance. It formed a counterpart to the desire of their husbands to keep the family from the workhouse, which was so central to working-class masculinities. As such, women's domestic labours might be seen not merely as a passive capitulation to middle-class domestic ideology, but as one of the femininities which comprised working-class culture.

Conclusion

The employment of working-class women during the first half of the nineteenth century was extremely chequered and highly diverse. Attempts at synthesis are in danger of failing to capture the enormous regional variations in both economic opportunities, local customs and even notions of gender capabilities. An important strata of women enjoyed reasonable pay and some status as upper servants, craft workers or teachers. Those in occupations with long-standing traditions, such as the bondagers of Scotland, also appear to have derived self-esteem from their work, despite poor pay and conditions. By contrast, women caught in the spiralling opportunism of the clothing trades had little means of resisting their exploitation or developing customs to regulate the sector. Elsewhere, growing numbers of women were faced with unemployment or chronic underemployment, and many single women left their communities to seek work in the emerging urban centres. This could be read as much as a sign of the crushing effects of industrialisation, as it can an indication of women's economic initiative; although women's determination to resist the worst excesses of capitalism was also evident in some sectors by dint of their trade union activity. Equally, whilst women displayed considerable resourcefulness in finding ways to earn money; the part-time, piecemeal and economically precarious nature of many of their activities mean that women's work might often be defined as varying survival strategies, rather than as 'occupations' or 'employment'. Meanwhile, the discursive meanings of women's work were beginning to shift, as the culture became increasingly reluctant to consider women as productive members of the economy. Discursively, a new, class-blind construction evolved of what it meant to be a 'woman', with femininity identified closely with domestic love and homely labours.[70] For the vast majority of working-class women, such images remained a chimera. Nevertheless, changes in agronomic practice, or cracks in the gender harmony of factory communities, could, as we have seen, encourage workingwomen to adopt new images of themselves, and of the work they aspired to perform.

2

POLITICS, COMMUNITY AND PROTEST

Introduction

Women and the female body were ubiquitous symbols within British political culture. As Britannia, they stood for patriotism and the union of the nation; dressed in white in electoral processions, women could symbolise the goddess of liberty.[1] In the protest movements of plebeian culture, male activists frequently dressed as women – an allusion to a 'world turned upside down' which articulated a sense of social grievance.[2] However, the extent to which women were significant political actors in their own right has been hotly debated. New studies have challenged the previous orthodoxy that women were unable to exert political agency during this period. It is now argued that plebeian women played a highly visible role in extra-parliamentary political culture from the eighteenth century. Their involvement in public celebrations, such as coronations or thanksgivings for peace, has also been noted.[3] Yet, the frequent tendency for political women to stress their familial obligations as the source of their actions has called into question women's ability to perceive themselves as independent political agents. Equally, the changing nature of popular protest with its moves towards formal organisation has been seen as jeopardising women's political involvement. However, it will be suggested that these arguments fail to capture the diversity and subtlety of women's political activity, or the richness of regional variations. Moreover, working-class women were acculturated to political activity from their childhood: whether it be through participation in food riots or the excitement of elections; enjoying the 'family culture' of Owenism and Chartism; being sent on errands to shops whose keepers shared

24

the family's politics. Politics was a central feature of working-class culture.

Community Protest

Working-class women played a critical role in fostering extra-familial networks within working-class communities. Occasionally, this became institutionalised into female friendly societies,[4] but of greater importance were women's informal networks of community support. During times of hardship, the exchange of resources such as food or medicine; or the lending of services, such as child-minding or nursing were vital survival strategies. Meeting together at bake-houses or markets, the swapping of local news was also central to the creation of community cohesion. This interaction fostered both social pressures and cultural mores (such as the condemnation of certain behaviours – domestic violence or promiscuity for example), and provided the opportunity to identify issues of grievance.[5]

Consequently women played a primary role in articulating and mobilising on issues of community discontent. In Wales, for example, women were active in anti-enclosure activity, and also in the 'Rebecca riots' which swept across much of the south-west, Glamorgan and mid-Wales between 1838 and 1843. Women were not usually implicated in the actual destruction of the hated toll-gates, which underlay much of the ferment (although they incited and plotted such activity). However, they were prominent in the broader community issues which preoccupied the movement. Women featured in attacks upon figures of authority, such as bailiffs and Poor Law officials, who were felt to be destroying the rights due to the poor. Equally, those believed to have betrayed community values – such as wife-beaters and fathers of illegitimate children – could find themselves faced by violent crowds of women, often summoned by the blowing of a horn.[6]

Women were also prominent during the vehement resistance launched against the Highland clearances in Scotland. These brutal tenant evictions were occasioned by landowners' desires to switch to large-scale sheep farming. As E. F. Richards has remarked, 'to a remarkable degree Highland riots were women's riots'. Women typically formed an advance party who repelled official land assessors with physical and verbal abuse. At Durness in 1840, for example, the officers were 'resisted by almost all the females of the district'.[7] In this context, women clearly perceived themselves to be integral to upholding the community's welfare.

Women's identification with threats to the community's well-being is further evidenced by their involvement in food riots, which were comparatively common at the beginning of this period. This has traditionally been explained by women's customary responsibility for the provision and purchase of food.[8] John Bohstedt vigorously denounces this, however, making the questionable assertion that women's role in protoindustrial manufacture gave them 'economic citizenship', 'enfranchising' them to act in politics.[9] It is perhaps more useful to consider women's involvement as signalling both their importance in maintaining the family's domestic needs and their significance as community actors. Food riots, as E. P. Thompson famously argued, registered a sense of community injustice. They were sparked by a rapid increase in grain prices, beyond that which the local community believed to be acceptable. Far from being acts of random violence, riots focused upon specific targets – warehouses and mills, or the carts or barges upon which food was being transported.[10]

John Bohstedt has also argued that there has been a tendency to exaggerate women's involvement in such activities.[11] Clearly women were not the sole constituent of food riots. For a start, they were often accompanied by their children; and often, women's actions could be secondary, as in Llandidloes in 1839 when women were credited with inciting the men to steal foodstuffs from local farmers. Women were also associated with perpetuating ancient rituals in these protests, such as covering loaves in black crepe to signify famine, or employing a bellman to indicate imminent action. Frequently, however, they were undeniably critical to the action themselves.[12] This was true of Hannah Smith in Manchester, whose actions led to her hanging as a highway robber.[13] Indeed, according to Nicholas Rogers, women were successful in effecting price reductions in the West Country, the North of England and the Midlands. In the growing industrial connurbations, female food rioters could be as violent as their male counterparts. The crowds who rampaged through Nottingham in September 1800 attacking granaries were predominantly female.[14] In smaller towns, the closer relationships between local inhabitants and figures of authority meant that specific individuals were often singled out for strenuous lobbying. It was local women who surrounded the house of their alarmed mayor at Blandford Forum in September 1800 to demand food at reasonable costs.[15]

In some English regions, women's determination to articulate and defend community values was vividly expressed not through popular protest, but by the passing phenomenon of female Methodist preachers, a practice condoned by the Bible Christians and the Primitive Methodists. These denominations flourished in areas of dislocation – for example those facing migration due to declining cottage industry, or in the emerging connurbations peopled by former rural labourers, as in Leeds. Female preachers discoursed, often with confrontational language, on the struggles of the poor and the devastating impact of the erosion of traditional common rights. Their creed appealed not to a sense of individual morality, but rather to the community values of sharing, and their ministry could help to recreate a sense of kinship among its adherents. Whilst female preachers were not accorded equality with their male peers within the organisation of the church, many individual women succeeded in establishing a significant following in their own right, as did Ann Carr's 'Female Revivalists' in Leeds. Others, such as Mary Porteus, earned themselves the title of 'Mother in Israel', which signified their importance as community leaders. By mid-century, though, as the churches shifted to more formalised, bureaucratised hierarchies, female preaching became seen as outdated and inappropriate.[16]

The squeezing out of women's participation is a pattern noted in other areas of plebeian discontent. By the 1820s and 1830s it has been assumed that the nature of women's involvement in popular protest had started to decline. Food riots became less common, with working-class discontent now focused on industrial protest or radical organisations. This is a process which, it is argued, eroded female political strength.[17] Such an analysis must be modified by the fact that in some areas, such as Ireland, women continued to act in food riots throughout the century. Also, 'traditional' forms of protest, such as the food riot, could persist alongside other activity, such as Luddism.[18] Moreover, women's protests did not invariably centre around 'bread and butter' issues, as those who argue for the decline in female political involvement assume. In Ireland, women were conspicuously active in the 'tithe-war' against payments to the Protestant clergy; whereas in Scotland, plebeian women were highly significant in patronage riots (whereby a congregation dissented from the minister assigned to them). Such riots, which could be extremely violent, demonstrated women's engagement with complex issues concerning local patronage structures and religious and political issues.[19]

Popular Radicalism

Women's interest in the wider arena of political issues is also evident in their contribution to electoral and radical politics. It has been suggested that the discourse of mutuality which female preachers expounded was symptomatic of women's alienation from the language of contemporary radicalism, with its stress upon rights and individualism.[20] However, important though the language of community was, women also responded to the issues arising from parliamentary politics. In addition to exclusive dealing to pressurise shopkeepers to vote for their preferred candidate, women might sport a candidate's colours and take part in public processions to register their support, as in the election of the radical Sir Francis Burdett in Middlesex in 1802.[21] Conversely, if a candidate was returned of whom they disapproved, women could react with violence. In Carmarthen, 1831, women and men pelted their new MP, John Jones (who had voted against a second reading of the Reform Bill) with stones.[22]

Furthermore, women were drawn to the emerging organisation of working-class political radicalism. Whilst the rhetoric and aims of reform may have been steeped in a masculinist language of rights, it presented itself as a movement 'of the people' and during 1819 a number of female radical reform societies were formed. These were mostly based in the north of England, where female factory labour, and traditions of female friendly societies and strike activity created favourable conditions for female radical organisation; but societies were also established in Scotland and the west of England. The societies were efficiently run, meeting every week to collect subscriptions, pass resolutions and to hear debates and lectures; they also published their own pamphlets and addresses.[23]

Radical organisers capitalised upon the presence of women at the great reform meetings to emphasise the movement's familial (and thus unthreatening) character. At the notorious Peterloo gathering, the President of the Manchester Female Reform Society, Mary Fildes, appeared on the platform with other women, alongside Henry Hunt. Women's involvement could also have considerable propaganda value, as in the aftermath of the Peterloo Massacre when the radical press exploited the women's suffering to the full.[24] Nevertheless, women frequently played a highly subversive role during the mass reform meetings. The Galston female reformers were typical in displaying an insurrectionary banner urging Britons to rise and assert their rights.[25]

During the summer of 1819, women began to present their hand-made caps of liberty – symbols of republicanism and revolution – to orators on the platform. These were moments of great drama, which threw down the gauntlet to the increasingly nervous authorities.[26]

It is the language employed by the female reformers which has attracted most attention, however. Occasionally, they exhibited a nascent feminism and argued that they sought the rights of men *and* women.[27] However, their primary intention was, in the words of the Blackburn Female Reform Society, 'to assist the male population of this country to obtain their rights and liberties'.[28] Their public addresses frequently apologised for their incursion into public politics; and they usually situated their involvement within the context of traditional female concerns. The Manchester Female Reform Society explained that they were campaigning for liberty 'as wives, mothers, daughters, in their social, domestic, moral capacities'.[29] To some degree female reformers had to display a regard for conventional understandings of women's role. At mass demonstrations they frequently dressed in white to symbolise their purity. Even then, as the Manchester female reformers complained, 'our intentions have been vilified, and our characters traduced'.[30] But their failure to develop a sustained discourse of feminist agency and their self-positioning as supportive kin have been interpreted as symptomatic of women's inability to develop their own political identity.[31] Yet in using the language of injured motherhood, the female reformers were developing their own discourse of protest which was to become increasingly influential. In claiming their right to engage in public politics as wives and mothers, they could challenge Evangelical proscriptions of women's domestic familial role, without compromising their engagement in highly radical politics.

During 1820, as the mass radical platform went into abeyance, working-class women became galvanised by the Queen Caroline affair. The decision of George IV to initiate divorce proceedings against his wife, Caroline of Brunswick, in an attempt to deprive her of the position of Royal Consort, scandalised public opinion. Caroline was popularly portrayed (somewhat inaccurately) as a virtuous woman whose rights as a wife and mother had been viciously denied by her 'natural protector' – her husband. In the tremendous public agitation which ensued women of all classes were highly prominent. They wrote pamphlets, poems, addresses and petitions, and organised mass demonstrations and processions. The extent of the female involvement was, notes Joan Perkin, 'an innovation in popular politics'.[32] Much of the agitation clearly drew on the organised radicalism of the 1810s – being particularly evident in such towns as Manchester, Blackburn, Bradford and Leeds, but the cause also succeeded in mobilising thousands of women elsewhere, notably in Bristol.[33]

For Anna Clark, the episode represents a turning point in the gendered development of working-class politics. The radical programme had previously been dominated by the languages of natural rights and constitutionalism, but the Queen Caroline affair foregrounded the subjects of women's right to protection within marriage and the iniquity of the sexual double standard. The emerging radical discourse recognised the importance of motherhood and emphasised a chivalric ideal of male support for the female sex. As such, Clark proposes, it accelerated the development of an 'inclusive political rhetoric of community, drawing upon people's experiences of family breakdown, unemployment, and hunger'.[34]

The Battle for Freedom of the Press

The battle for press freedom, which preoccupied a small but committed band of female followers during these years, did not adopt this new language of popular reform. Nevertheless, it illustrated the extent to which working women's concept of wifely duty or motherhood could be highly politicised. Here, it led them to act as independent political agents by taking over as booksellers, and publishers of radical and freethought material whilst their male kin were in prison for the cause. Richard Carlile, who dominated the movement, depended upon a network of female support to keep his business running during his time in jail. Susannah Wright, a Nottingham lace-maker who came to London to support Carlile, was, like Carlile's wife and sister, prosecuted for her efforts. In common with other defendants, she insisted on conducting her own defence.[35]

Wright's confident actions demonstrate that women should not be seen merely as auxiliaries. Far from being dependent upon a male-structured movement, women could draw upon alternative female networks of radical support across the country. The female reform societies of the north and south-west of England (and whose continued existence during the 1820s has been subject to little historical research) corresponded with female campaigners in London on precisely this issue and could be called upon to donate much-needed funds to the cause.[36]

Moreover, the rhetorical stance assumed by female reformers could lead to the arousal of protofeminist sentiments: 1832 saw the establishment of the all-female 'Friends of the Oppressed', to provide support to families whose breadwinners were imprisoned in the cause of press freedom. This society, composed chiefly of the wealthier artisan class, adhered to strict democratic procedures and organised debates, public meetings and lectures. Its secretary, Jane Hutson, was one of many members who believed that the society should engage in independent action of its own, suggesting, for example, a march on the House of Commons.[37] The society tackled specifically female issues, such as campaigning for the abolition of the 'absurd and superstitious practice of Churching women'. A minority of the women attached to the cause developed strong feminist tendencies and the society engaged Carlile's radical, feminist partner, Eliza Sharples, to lecture to them.[38]

Whilst the language of female support for their men was often predominant, this clearly did not preclude more trenchant, quasi-feminist discourses emerging from the campaign. In 1833, 150 Birmingham women published a bellicose letter supporting Richard Carlile. They disparaged the notion that men were naturally the best politicians claiming that, 'the men of England are the veriest asses on the face of God's earth!' The letter poured scorn upon the idea that men were the superior sex and argued firmly for women's right to participate in politics.[39]

Owenism

It was during the late 1820s that Owenism began to engage the sympathies of the more progressive constituency of working-class radicalism. Whilst arguing that gender traits were culturally conditioned, Owenism (which was strongly influenced both by Enlightenment environmentalism and French socialism) continued to argue that women's superior capacity to love would help to transform society. Among the artisanal classes there was a small, but dedicated female audience for the feminist and socialist ideals which lay at the heart of Owenism. This is demonstrated in their support for the co-operative trade unions and shops established by the movement during the late 1820s and early 1830s. Many of the women's Owenite associations also included educational activities and health insurance.[40]

Individual women, notably Margaret Chappellsmith and Frances Morrison, achieved a degree of prestige within Owenism in their capacity as salaried lecturers, and a number of Owenite journalists appear to have been female. However, despite occasional suggestions that branch committees should have an equal gender balance, only a minority of women were given positions of responsibility within their local associations.[41] Although women did play an important part in the family-centred culture which the movement was keen to promote, the Owenite press frequently lamented the failure to attract more women to the movement. Working-class women were no doubt alienated by the Owenite hostility to contemporary marriage. Its support for 'moral marriages', which might be ended by mutual consent, was a threat to women whose economic security and respectable reputation depended upon stable relationships.[42] Only a tiny minority of women were prepared to experiment with the sexual radicalism which lay at the fringes of the movement.[43] The movement was similarly unsuccessful in implementing feminism in its seven communities. Owenism promised the emancipation of women through the co-operative organisation of domestic responsibilities. In practice, a rota system did little to change the fact that it was still women who performed the community's domestic chores, often in addition to their work in the fields. At the Orbiston community in Scotland, the chaotic efforts to implement co-operative housework nearly occasioned a complete walk-out on the women's part. Despite the commitment of many individual women to the communitarian system, widespread female disillusionment was an instrumental factor in the failure of the Owenite project.[44]

However, on the fringes of Owenite culture, millenarian sects touched the working classes in far greater numbers. Fundamental to many of these sects was the identification of women with religion, to the extent that they prophesied the next messiah to be female. The most famous sect was founded by Joanna Southcott, a working-class woman from Devon, who claimed to have visions proclaiming her to be the new Saviour. Encouraged and sponsored by a small group of clergymen, Southcott began to attract a massive following, boosted by her lengthy tours of the country and the publication of her voluminous writings. By the time of her death in 1814, tens of thousands of people were members of the Southcottian church.[45] Scholars of the movement have been struck by the extent to which such sects appealed to a female audience. They note that Southcott's 'theological feminism' recast

Christian views of womankind by portraying Eve as a victim and sympathising with women's sexual victimisation.[46]

Chartism

It was in the Chartist movement that working-class women's political engagement reached its zenith. Chartist women were assiduous organisers, establishing hundreds of female Chartist associations across the country. A very small minority also succeeded in making their voices heard in the male structure of the moment – as Chartist lecturers, or very occasionally by chairing or speaking at mixed-sex meetings. Women were highly visible in the mass Chartist demonstrations and rallies, particularly during the early years of the movement. They also proved to be energetic petitioners, comprising approximately one-third of the signatories to the Chartist petitions of 1839 and 1841.[47] Although Anna Clark has suggested that the 'physical force' language employed by many Chartist women was largely a rhetorical stance, there is evidence that groups of Chartist women purchased arms in significant numbers. In Lancashire, it was reported in 1839 that 'women were now in a state of progress, and were purchasing pikes in large numbers'.[48]

Importantly, Chartist women also drew upon their own traditions of female political involvement. They organised highly efficient campaigns of 'exclusive dealing' – giving their patronage only to those shopkeepers who professed to support the Charter.[49] They also continued to develop the language of political wife and motherhood. According to Jutta Schwarzkopf, such self-positioning, 'effectively prevented them from establishing themselves as political agents in their own right with needs and aspirations specific to them as women'.[50]

Whether this emphasis upon their familial roles did limit the political agency of Chartist women so drastically is questionable. The Female Chartists of Manchester claimed it was primarily, 'A love for ourselves' which inspired them to act.[51] Also, Anna Clark notes that women's political identities could become more forceful as they gained in public confidence.[52] Equally, women's political preoccupation with their maternity arose from a perception of the active importance of motherhood. Indeed, great numbers of children were drawn into politics through their mothers. In a politicised move to undermine the influence of establishment schools, Chartist women set up educational institutes for their children, such as Chartist Sunday schools; and in many towns female Chartists organised their children into juvenile radical societies.[53] Political mothering also took place in the domestic site. As the Chartist leader, Henry Vincent, remarked, 'every kitchen is now a political *meeting-house*, the little children are members of the unions and the good mother is the political teacher.'[54] For Chartist women, political motherhood was both vital for the creation of a democratic society and a valid channel for the expression of their views.

It would be equally misguided to assume that Chartist women entered the movement only to fight for the political rights of their male kin. Their vision was far wider this. Much of women's early Chartist activity arose out of protests against the Poor Law Amendment Act of 1834. Women had already mobilised themselves in considerable force against this measure. In Elland, Yorkshire, women physically attacked Poor Law Commissioners and sent petitions opposing the act to parliament. Frustration at the Poor Law led to the establishment of many of the early female Chartist associations; and leading female Chartists argued that the injustice of the Poor Law was a central justification for the Charter.[55] The fact that female Chartist activity was so closely connected to anti-Poor Law agitation demonstrates that women were not merely acquiescing in a male-defined agenda, but fighting to protect themselves and their families from draconian legislation. Indeed, Chartist women did not necessarily define their aims in terms of a Paineite conception of 'rights'. Female Chartists had other priorities, as women in Warwick expressed when they held their banner defining the rights of women to be 'instruction, affection, protection'.[56]

The Chartist desire to return to 'traditional family values' forms a central focus of Jutta Schwarkzkopf's study. Although the existence of widespread radical debates on women throughout the Chartist movement has often been noted, Schwarzkopf depicts it as a reactionary movement, which was preoccupied with the moral and cultural implications of women's factory work.[57] Female Chartists did frequently share a desire to see an end to their factory labour and articulated a vision of a reformed social order in which the family would be respected and prioritised. But Chartist women also injected their own agendas into this debate. The tea parties, outings and family events for which they were responsible, and which were so important to the movement's cohesion, formed part of a wider objective to create a new, family-based culture.

Women's control over the social politics of the movement may be seen as an attempt to encourage their menfolk to eschew the public house. Male drinking was held to be responsible for widespread domestic violence and for exacerbating the financial problems of the poor. Significantly, women were particularly associated with temperance Chartism, allowing once again the space for women to address their own needs. Although the family and the community were never exclusive sources of working-women's political motivations (as their support for European nationalism and refugees testifies),[58] Chartist women's self-definition as wives and mothers evidently provided them with a rich cultural and political resource. They articulated a 'militant domesticity' which challenged prevailing, middle-class formulations of family life.[59]

Nevertheless, Dorothy Thompson has argued that by the late 1840s, women's participation in Chartism had declined dramatically. She maintains that gathering notions of female respectability made it difficult for women to participate in a movement whose meetings were increasingly located in pubs. She also suggests that by the middle of the century, working-class women may have internalised a view of themselves as domestic creatures who were ill-equipped to engage in politics.[60] However, David Jones observes that in the Midlands, London and major Scottish cities there was actually a florescence of female activity in the late 1840s. Jones notes the continued survival of female Chartist associations and female support for radical activities, particularly in towns such as Nottingham and Newcastle, well into the 1850s.[61] Indeed, it was in the early 1850s that a new strain of feminist Chartist activity briefly flowered with the formation of the Sheffield Women's Political Association, an association explicit in its desire to fight for women's rights. Sister organisations were founded in a number of other major cities, including Leeds, Edinburgh and Glasgow.[62]

Indeed, as Thompson herself noted, the apparent decline in reported female political activity may well reflect the wish of radical journals to underplay women's involvement in a bid to refashion the movement's public image.[63] But it is also possible that, far from dropping out of political activity, women began to engage or maintain other forms of political engagement. Schwarzkopf notes that during the late 1840s, women began increasingly to turn away from Chartist associations and to involve themselves in the Chartist Land Company.[64] It is also clear that radical women entertained an inclusive definition of politics. As female campaigners from Bath put it, 'What are politics but an important branch of morals relating to our duty to our neighbours and to the interest and well-being of all about us?'[65] Consequently, as Chapter 8 suggests, the home could continue to play a vital function in maintaining family traditions of radicalism. Moreover, the increasing formalisation of politics did not prevent women's participation in other modes of protest. Working-class women continued to involve themselves in electoral politics during these years, as recent research has demonstrated. This was often tied up with such activities as exclusive dealing; or with serious rioting as occurred in Belfast, Limerick and Cork during the 1850s.[66] Indeed, as Chapter 8 indicates, 'traditional' forms of women's protest persisted throughout nineteenth-century Britain, particularly in Scotland and Ireland.

Conclusion

Women's engagement in public and political affairs was highly diverse. The community remained a focal point for women's action throughout this period, particularly in Ireland, Scotland and Wales. Nevertheless, from the late 1810s women also began to develop a unique political vocabulary and to stake their own space within movements for radical reform. Although they never achieved prominence in the organisational structures of national reform movements, at a local and familial level their contributions were vital. If working-class women's identity was beginning to shift by the middle of the century, towards seeing themselves as more home-centred (and this has clearly been greatly exaggerated), this does not necessarily imply that they then designated politics as a purely male activity. Too rigid an application of the separate spheres analysis can submerge the complexities of contemporary women's lives and perceptions. Equally, a preoccupation with English developments can obscure continuities in women's political engagement in other parts of the British Isles.

3

FAMILIES, RELATIONSHIPS AND HOME LIFE

Introduction

The socio-economic dislocation caused by industrialisation had far-reaching consequences for the family lives of working-class people during this period. Social problems had been exacerbated by the long conflict with France and the privations of war were barely eased by the advent of peace in 1815. The passing of the Corn Laws and the onset of a deep agricultural depression marked the beginning of a period of considerable distress for the working classes. The most horrific conditions were to be found in Ireland, where hundreds of thousands died in the devastating famine of the mid-1840s.[1] No other region experienced such catastrophic suffering, but across rural Britain this was a time of severe economic and social problems with particular communities, such as those in rural Wales, undergoing dreadful deprivation.[2] Between 1830 and 1850, rural distress became acute when a sharp rise in population expansion combined with high unemployment, resulting in widespread incendiarism and rioting.[3] The environment of the emerging urban centres could be equally appalling. The nation's worst conditions were generally agreed to be found in Glasgow, where the tenements provided tiny one-room homes in a state of dreadful sanitation. Although F. M. L. Thompson reminds us that the vast majority of working people did not live in slum conditions, local governments remained extremely reluctant to establish proper drainage systems and water supplies throughout this period.[4]

The poverty, physical hardship and health problems faced by working people have led some historians to paint a bleak picture of the nature of the working-class family and marital relations. According to David Vincent, most marriages were based upon financial exigencies. Couples could hope only to battle together against the hardships they faced. Only for the more prosperous could love and affection flourish, for the majority, life was taken up with the 'struggle for existence'.[5] Many feminist scholars have provided equally bleak scenarios of gender relations within working-class families. The trade unions' demand for a family wage has been seen as an indication of the patriarchal assumptions inherent in contemporary marriages. By campaigning for the breadwinner's wage and emphasising the importance of domesticity, men, it is argued, revealed their desire to increase women's dependence upon them whilst continuing to benefit from women's performance of unwaged work, namely household duties and child care.[6] However, a growing body of work now suggests more subtle chronologies in the culture of working-class family life. Historians are increasingly interested, for example, in the impact of rural industries upon gender relations. Also, recent studies, such as that by Anna Clark, provide a more nuanced account of the comparative role of political rhetoric, ideology and female self-assertion in plebeian marriages across differing occupational groups.[7]

Adolescent Females and Courtship

According to Leonore Davidoff, most women experienced a 'lifetime of personal subordination', beginning with subjection to paternal control in their parents' home.[8] However, many contemporaries were worried about the extent to which paternal and hierarchical relationships within the working-class family were actually breaking down, often as a result of new employment practices. In particular, concern over the numbers of young female factory workers, led to a proliferation of images of confident, well-paid factory girls, stepping free of patriarchal dominance.[9] In Glasgow the financial independence of young female textile workers often induced them to leave home and to lodge in all-female households.[10] (Although it is worth noting that no research has yet been carried out into the possibilities of 'romantic friendship' or same-sex relationships amongst working-class women.) For Ivy Pinchbeck, it was young, single women who gained most from the factory system, receiving for the first time, a realistic wage and greater social freedom.[11] Neil McKendrick is similarly optimistic, arguing that factory work enabled women to act as consumers on a massive scale. Certainly, young factory girls were often castigated for their 'love of finery'.[12]

The important work of Tilly and Scott reminds us, however, that adolescents' independent earnings did not necessarily constitute an assault upon the workings of the plebeian family. The majority of working-class families continued to operate as a family economy, in which all members were expected to contribute their wages to a common family pool.[13] (Although the knowledge that they were contributing a good percentage of the family income may well have enhanced young women's confidence.) In some places, parental authority was further compounded by occupational control. This was true in a number of mining districts, where teenage girls frequently worked for their fathers.[14] Acquiescence in working-class familial mores did not, of course, preclude the development of independent attitudes and identities. When the young, single women employed by Courtauld in his Halstead silk mills were provided with a lodging house, the experiment was not a success. On one occasion the girls' resentment at the regime was symbolised by their burning of the rules. Despite this hostility towards the imposition of external forms of personal control, family ties continued to exert a powerful hold on these teenagers, with most sending their wages back to their families in the countryside.[15]

The courtship behaviour of plebeian women, who tended to have more freedom to choose than their middle- and upper-class contemporaries, demonstrated a similar blend of individual confidence with an acceptance of working-class cultural mores. In Middleton, the young women appropriated the Valentine Eve tradition by passing messages under the mens' doors. Elsewhere, communities threatened by change could breed new, strict codes of masculinity which challenged such female self-assurance. The rise in male immigration into some Welsh communities is a case in point. Girls found to be courting non-native males could be subject to the ritual of 'rhythus' whereby the local men would urinate on the girl.[16]

Working-class courtship traditions were strikingly different to those prevailing in other classes in more telling ways, however. Rural betrothal customs, for example, tended to encourage close physical intimacy. 'Bundling', whereby a young couple would spend the night together, often sharing a bed, was widely practised. In the 1840s a society was established in Dolgelly for its suppression, but it had to admit defeat when hardly anyone could be found to sign the pledge![17] Although a woman's sexual reputation was important in working-class communities, in many areas, to have sex with your boy/ girl-friend was seen as a symbolic gesture to commit yourself to marriage. One Pembrokeshire clergymen admitted that he and his colleagues rarely married a country girl who was not already pregnant. Pre-marital sex was a custom also supported by some religious institutions, such as the kirk in Scotland.[18] In addition, working-class people tended to have a fluid attitude towards marriage. The Hardwicke Act of 1753 had made legally recognised marriage expensive and so many, particularly at the start of this period, relied upon a simple folk ceremony – perhaps the public exchange of rings, or jumping over a broom. By the middle of the century, formal marriage was predominant; although local and occupational customs persisted. London costermongers, for example, were notorious for their relaxed approach to marriage, with young couples often setting up home together in their early teens. Many other women might be in semi-permanent relationships with soldiers, sailors or travelling agricultural labourers.[19]

However, from the end of the eighteenth century, cracks had started to appear in the functioning of working-class courtship and marriage practices. Anderson notes that by the early nineteenth century, nearly one in five of first births were illegitimate.[20] According to Hans Medick, this may be explained by the advent of protoindustry which he believes fostered greater sexual license among young people; (one of his suggestions is that the heat and proximity of busy households and workshops fostered an erotic environment!).[21] Given the economic vulnerability of young, single women (and the social censure against single motherhood in many communities, particularly in south and east England[22]), it is unlikely that many would have chosen to have children without the protection of a stable union. It seems more probable that the rise in illegitimacy was due both to a greater recourse to 'common law' unions, but also a growing threat to traditional courtship practices. Increasing levels of migration from the countryside to the growing towns meant that community pressure to enforce marriages, once pregnancy had occurred, was lacking. This left many women in a precarious state, particularly with the passing of the 1834 Poor Law Amendment Act, which until 1844 made women solely responsible for the maintenance of illegitimate children.[23] It was tensions such as these which became evident in the Welsh Rebecca Riots: one aspect of Rebecca's activity was to force men to marry their pregnant girlfriends.[24]

Nevertheless, it is also true that both the age and motives for marriage were shifting. For some scholars, the key lies again in the growth of protoindustrial communities. No longer expectant of inheriting small pieces of land, young people – now supposedly freer from parental pressure – sought partners for themselves at an earlier age, preferably someone with practical skills in weaving or spinning to assist the household's economic viability.[25] This has been questioned however, by those who note that the proletarianisation of farm labourers; the decline in lengthy apprenticeships; and a rise in rural poverty were probably just as influential as the decline in land inheritance in encouraging people to marry earlier.[26]

Despite the mounting stress upon rural courtship traditions, the custom of pre-marital sex as a precursor to marriage appears to have been transported to the emerging urban conurbations. This was a practice that was often interpreted by unsympathetic middle-class observers as promiscuity.[27] The precarious economic situation of young women in trades such as needlework could leave them vulnerable, however, to sexual partnerships in which the promise of marriage proved illusory.[28] For many first generation urban-dwellers, by contrast, the comparative freedom from village constraints (and perhaps from parental observation for young migrant workers) may have been very welcome. John Gillis notes that, 'Young women as well as men enjoyed great personal freedom and showed little awkwardness.'[29] Here, as elsewhere, although considerations such as practical skills, or savings might be important in the choice of a spouse, contemporaries still assigned great importance to an emotionally strong marriage – without this, the battle for survival would prove bleak indeed.[30]

Cohabitation and Marriage

Once in a common-law or formal marriage union, women's experiences varied widely. Those communities which remained the least touched by industrial advance appear to have harboured the most oppressive attitudes towards women. One middle-class contemporary noted of the Scottish Highlands in 1823 that, 'as in all semi-barbarous countries the woman seems to be regarded rather as the drudge than the companion of the man.'[31] In Ireland, the frequently observed practice of peasant women walking behind their husbands would seem to symbolise the strict gender hierarchy common to such societies.[32] Visiting Poor Law commissioners lamented that, 'She is made the drudge and the slave.' Nevertheless, such witnesses could not always capture the subtleties of local circumstances.[33] It is by no means clear that peasant women inevitably adopted abject and subordinate roles. As the previous chapter illustrated, women such as these were vociferous community actors. Whether this self-assertion and initiative enabled some women to negotiate more favourable relationships within the privacy of their own homes it is not possible to substantiate. Certainly many traditional communities did foster self-confident women. In the isolated, endogamous fishing community of Filey, women were renowned for their redoubtable strength of character: 'He would be a bold man,' it was said, 'who could stand for five minutes the fire of a Filey flither girl's tongue, even if not enforced by a sprinkling of empty shells from the collective forces of the sisterhood.'[34] Such assurance may have led to more combative marriages, within the structure of patriarchal hierarchy.

In protoindustrial situations, Hans Medick famously argued that there was a degree of role reversal between husband and wife, with men returning to the household to assist in the manufacture of goods and with domestic duties.[35] In Britain, some contemporaries were horrified that where women and children were engaged in domestic industry in the home, men sometimes abandoned their agricultural work.[36] It is not clear, however, that this would necessarily lead to new patterns of family chore allocation,[37] nor is it immediately apparent that women's earnings enhanced their status and position, as protoindustrial scholars presume.[38] Concrete evidence of women's improved consumption status is still wanting for the British experience, although women's social position in pre-famine Ireland was noted to decline drastically once the demise of the spinning industry meant they were no longer able to contribute to the family economy.[39] Yet, even when women could find outwork, they had no legal entitlement to their own earnings; and they might work to the point of physical exhaustion, only to have their meagre earnings immediately appropriated by their husbands. As one navvy confessed: 'When first I married I used to sit and look at my wife plaiting till the blood run out at the ends of her fingers; and when she'd done a good bit I'd say, "Now, old gal, go and sell that plait and get me a pint of beer".'[40] Admittedly, many local traditions granted greater financial independence to women. In some Irish communities, custom granted women the ownership and control of their earnings; and in the Welsh Ceirog, women passed their property down to their daughters rather than giving it up to their husbands.[41] However, women's earnings, especially in domestic manufacture, were so pitifully low and so vital to the family subsistence that for most, such customs probably had little practical benefit, although they may have been important for women's self-esteem and status.

In metropolitan marriages, men might be highly dependent upon their wives' financial or practical skills to assist with their trade, or to contribute to the family economy. This endowed women, believes John Gillis, with a 'real bargaining power'.[42] Such an image would accord with research into domestic violence in London during this period. Many magistrates tended to see working-class wives as tough, battling women, who often gave as good as they got.[43] Whilst this may have been true of many marriages, it was far from universally the case. Anna Clark paints a bleak picture of the endemic violence wrought against wives, particularly in certain occupational sectors, such as artisans and tailors, whose tough, male-dominated culture encouraged hard drinking and weakened the possibilities of successful companionate marriages. Working-class men, she notes, were often under the impression that they had a right to beat their wives, provided they used only their hands.[44] And, as noted above, women in the needlework trades were vulnerable to sexually exploitative relationships.

Elsewhere, despite growing cultural trends emphasising the importance of wifely submission, as in Evangelicalism and mainstream Methodism,[45] it is by no means clear that women necessarily adopted a subordinate role. In Cleveland and Lincolnshire, women retained their maiden names after marriage; in Yorkshire some women kept their thumbs free when they clasped hands with the groom during the marriage service to signal that they meant not to be dominated; others raced through their wedding vows, omitting the promise to 'obey' their husbands.[46] Furthermore both Anna Clark and Joan Perkin have pointed to the robust and defiant tone of early nineteenth-century women's songs:

> I'll be no submissive wife,
> No, not I – no, not I;
> I'll not be a slave for life,
> No, not I – no, not I.[47]

In the factory districts, the availability of comparatively well-paid work for women meant that it was less important to marry for economic motives. Indeed, Anna Clark has pointed to the co-operative nature of

gender relations in factory communities, noting that male textile workers tended to share consumption and leisure with their wives.[48] This
was a factor which enraged Evangelical campaigners, who abhorred the
proud, defiant female culture they believed factory work to breed.
Ashley noted with disgust the words of one pub-loving woman, 'If I
have the labour, I will also have the amusement.'[49]

Such attitudes did not apply in all areas of industry, however. Judy
Lown argues that women's subordinate position in the workplace was
replicated and strengthened by patriarchal family relationships.
Women might work in the mills whilst their hand-loom weaving husbands were at home minding the children, but this did not result in any
substantial alteration in power relations between the sexes. Men continued to assert their primary right to use their wives' wages to consume
beer; and it is evident, despite the concerns of social reformers as to
domestic neglect, that women continued to perform a double shift of
paid employment as well as functioning as the family's chief carer and
homemaker.[50]

Women's responsibility for running the home was reinforced by
many local customs. It was common in manufacturing areas for men
to publicly hand over their wages (minus the sum they kept back for
their own consumption) to their wives on the doorstep at the end of the
week. Some couples even drew up their own contracts to specify the
amount of housekeeping money the wife could expect to receive.[51]
Such sensitivities hint at the tensions which could erupt within the
home. Quarrels over money could often precipitate the sparks of violence. Interestingly, the Chartist William Lovett argued that marital
disharmony frequently stemmed from another source – the wife's
inability to share in her husband's political or literary pursuits.[52] However, the alacrity with which working-class women took advantage of
adult education facilities indicates a widespread desire to improve
intellectual attainments and a degree of self-respect and confidence.[53]

For those whose relationships did break broke down irretrievably, the
fluid and extra-legal nature of many working-class marriages, combined with a less restrictive moral code than that prevailing in other
classes, meant that separation was comparatively easy (but only if economic circumstances permitted). Those married by local custom might
obtain a community-sanctioned divorce by removing their marriage
ring, or jumping backwards over a broom.[54] Another form of unofficial
divorce was wife-selling, whereby a man would bring his wife to the
market place with a halter around her neck and sell her to the highest

bidder. In practice, it was often a surprisingly amicable affair – prearranged by all parties.[55] By the Victorian period, as legal marriage became the norm, these practices became increasingly uncommon, although bigamy still remained widespread as many people would simply marry a new partner, illegally, after leaving a relationship.[56] Meanwhile, the pitiful financial plight of women 'deserted' by their partners became a subject of mounting public concern. It was sympathy for their situation, rather than concurrence with feminist demands, which resulted in key clauses of the 1857 Divorce and Matrimonial Causes Act, allowing those abandoned by their husbands to apply for a magistrate's order to protect their own earnings.[57]

Family Relationships and Motherhood

The trend towards a lower age of marriage contributed to extremely large families. The country's population rose at a staggering rate during these years: England rising from 5.75 million in 1750 to 16.7 million in 1851, with the populations of Scotland and Wales also rising dramatically.[58] There has been very little research into the impact of the rise in family size for working-class women, or their experience of mothering during this period. It has been suggested, however, that the home-centred nature of early industrial manufacture allowed women to combine child care with labour in a particularly flexible way. However, as Maxine Berg notes tartly, 'the intensity of labour from a woman with young children even if she was working at home was not likely to be high.'[59] Moreover, it was at this stage of their life-cycle – as young parents with very small children – that labouring families could be pushed to the very edge of subsistence; not to mention the heartbreak and anxiety occasioned by frequent and serious illnesses and the tragically high levels of contemporary infant mortality.

The problems of combining paid employment with motherhood were brought sharply into focus by the furore surrounding factory working women in the 1830s and 1840s. Evangelical campaigners thundered that the employment of mothers in the factories was to blame for the high levels of infant mortality in many working-class districts. However, it would seem that only about 27 per cent of female factory workers were married and they tended to withdraw from factory labour once they had a number of young children.[60] Those who did continue to work appear to have made sensible arrangements for their offspring, often leaving them with a relative or a neighbourhood child-minder (although the use of opiates to tranquillise infants appears to have been widespread). Some were able to arrange to have their babies brought to them at the factory so that they might suckle them during breaks.[61]

As the debates on cottage industry and factory labour indicate, women undertook primary responsibility for the care of their children. As well as training them in practical skills, mothers also played a key function in instilling cultural values, such as respectability, and Chapter 2 has pointed to women's role in politicising their children. Yet, both contemporary observers and subsequent historians have been divided as to the degree of emotional commitment discernible in plebeian families. Lord Ashley believed the working-class family to be so dysfunctional as to be in imminent threat of extinction, a point also suggested by Friedrich Engels.[62] On the other hand, the contemporary writer, Elizabeth Gaskell, herself closely involved in Unitarian projects to visit the homes of the working classes, left a sensitive account of the centrality of loving family relationships, and especially the role of women, in novels such as *Mary Barton*.[63] Gaskell's interpretation was, of course, strongly imbued with prevalent discourses on the value of domesticity. Such rhetoric was, as we have seen, also increasingly central to the articulation of working-class politics. However, to what extent such emphases were implicated in deeper shifts in the culture of the working-class family is not easy to substantiate. (Although Anna Clark sensitively notes that failure to achieve the domestic ideal may have exacerbated tensions in those families where women had to go out to work.) [64]

Certainly, in a *laissez-faire* state, the family formed a central resource for the labouring poor. In his classic work on nineteenth-century Lancashire, the historical demographer, Michael Anderson, drew attention to the cohesive kinship networks and patterns of family support which bolstered working-class life, but he emphasised that this arose from calculative, rather than affective motives. Recent research by Shani D'Cruze similarly observes that the mother of the household frequently accepted a responsibility to care for extended family members such as nieces and nephews, who might move between homes to find better employment. In other households, the addition of grandparents could be highly beneficial in easing child-caring needs, thus also providing a role for older, particularly widowed women. Alternatively, a household might frequently contain newly married children, unable to yet set up house on their own. Such a situation might grant the now mature 'woman of the family' greater recognition as a senior family member. However, D'Cruze's work is also highly suggestive of the ways in which women 'quilted together' not only practical, but also personal needs within kinship groupings.[65]

Indeed, despite the enormous financial and functional pressures upon them, women appear to have invested tremendous emotional energy in the upbringing and support of their children, taking both the maternal role and wider family commitments extremely seriously.

Conclusion

Over the 60 years with which this chapter is concerned, there was a growing conformity to legal marriage and a discursive emphasis upon domesticity. Within these broad trends, however, women's experience of family life and the quality of their personal relationships depended significantly upon regional, economic and occupational variables. Despite a general pattern of patriarchal authority, and widespread evidence of domestic violence and abuse, the initiative and self-assertion which emerges in women's role as community actors; as economic agents determined to 'make shift'; and as managers of large and often extended families, indicates pride and confidence rather than personal subordination and passivity. Practical needs and support may have been strongly implicated in the ways in which women performed their roles as wives, mothers and kinship members, but emotional and affective commitment were closely woven into the fabric of these essential relationships.

PART II

MIDDLE-CLASS AND UPPER-CLASS WOMEN, 1800–1860

4

WORK

Introduction

Within the ubiquitous nineteenth-century discourse of separate spheres, women were portrayed as financially, intellectually and emotionally dependent upon their male kin. They were encouraged to perceive themselves as 'relative creatures', whose path in life was to nurture the family and to provide unstinting support for the head of the household. Furthermore, as the great exponent of domestic ideology, Sarah Ellis, proclaimed, if a woman did engage in paid work she, 'ceases to be a lady'.[1] However, as the following discussion will indicate, for countless middle-class families, such injunctions remained but an ideal. Much of the work performed by women – both in the upper and middle classes – such as social work, domestic labour, estate management and participation in family businesses was unpaid and non-contractual. As such, it has remained outside classic definitions of employment. Yet, women, even in the highest social classes, made a considerable contribution to the economic and domestic well-being of both their families and their communities.

Domestic Work

For the majority of women in these classes, work consisted of unpaid labour as child carers and household managers. Despite the popular image of the leisured and indulged aristocrat, from the beginning of the nineteenth century even upper-class women (save for the highest nobility) were increasingly assuming the responsibilities of household management, rather than delegating such duties to paid staff. This stemmed, in part, from the growing impetus for internal reform which characterised the aristocracy at this time. Indeed, as Jessica Gerard and others have pointed out, the performance of such labour could be an important source of women's self-validation. To be responsible for the accounts and financial management of an aristocratic household, as well as the entertainment of large numbers of upper-class guests, involved considerable work. In addition, landed women might have responsibilities for up to two dozen staff, necessitating considerable skills of management. The incessant turnover of servants served to heighten the central role of the female head of the household in ensuring domestic stability.[2]

Needless to say, middle-class women also made a massive input into the smooth running of their families through the performance of domestic chores and child-care duties. Patricia Branca's research demonstrated that over 40 per cent of the middle classes lived on an income of between £100 to £300. This meant that they would have had limited domestic help – perhaps one servant – to assist with an average of eight children, as well as running the home, shopping, cooking, fetching water, laundry and cleaning.[3] Lillian Faithful recalled that her mother made all the clothes for her eight children, as well as educating them, keeping complex household accounts and finding time for her own literary pursuits.[4]

In addition, the domestic work of women in this strata was becoming more complicated and onerous. The spate of household manuals produced during this period suggest high expectations of domestic performance. Growing consumerism meant extra ornaments to dust, carpets to beat, furnishings to wash and cutlery to polish. Additionally, new fashions in household management required more minute attention to detail, with the increasing use of timekeepers, weights and measures betraying a new concern with precise measurement and accuracy. This mentality also led to an emphasis upon the exact recording of household accords. The complication of household routines in this way drew the domestic manager into the need for ever tighter surveillance of her household. This process might, none the less, endow women with a sense of the importance of their labour.[5] Equally, such work formed a vital component of social entertaining, which could be essential for the consolidation of the family's business networks. Meanwhile, changing theories of child care, requiring greater attention to the individual child, raised the expectations of mothering practices; and most women also worked as teachers for their children (see Chapter 6).

Paid Positions

Not all women of these strata could take financial security for granted. Family bereavement or financial disasters ensured a continued pool of needy, genteel women.[6] For those with impeccable family credentials, personal respectability, excellent education and, above all, contacts, there were a handful of coveted, salaried positions in the royal household as ladies-in-waiting, women of the bedchamber or mistress of the robes.[7]

Lower down the social scale the options for impoverished young, single women from genteel backgrounds were extremely circumscribed. The lack of socialisation into the world of paid employment meant that those women who were forced to seek employment could face considerable problems of social identity and, at times, shame. The most likely option was to find employment as a paid companion or a governess – there were approximately 21 000 governesses in 1850.[8] Many governesses proved to be good teachers, forming affectionate bonds with their charges. The education they were expected to provide was generally the staple fare of basic literacy, history, geography and, abilities permitting, music, languages and painting: 'accomplishments' which, as historians have repeatedly pointed out, it was hoped would render privileged girls attractive to potential suitors.[9] It is also possible that such education was desired so as to produce culturally articulate young women who might promote and contribute to the culture and self-assurance of the British elite. Certainly, the superior class status of their charges could make a governess's life miserable. Governesses were generally thought too lowly to be welcomed as one of the family, but of too high a background to mix on easy terms with the servants. This was a theme which increasingly exercised the imagination of the reading public, as Anne Brontë's sensitive account, *Agnes Grey* (1847) testifies. The growing public recognition of the problems faced by governesses was signalled with the establishment of the Governesses' Benevolent Institution in 1841. In an attempt to remedy the frequently poor educational attainments of potential governesses, Queen's College was opened in 1848. This was followed in 1849 by the more radical, Unitarian-inspired, Bedford College for women.[10]

For those of lower social origin, other domestic posts were also a possibility – perhaps as a housekeeper, or lady's maid. For many, however, school teaching remained a likely option – albeit one constrained by the dictates of gender. Women's 'maternal nature' was thought to render them particularly suited to the teaching of infants of both sexes; but for reasons of propriety and received ideas of women's intellectual limits, women were not considered appropriate as tutors for boys. Furthermore, female schoolteachers often struggled to be taken seriously as professionals. As Mary Smith discovered, teaching in a small school in Carlisle, she was expected to undertake domestic duties as well as an arduous teaching timetable for little, and sometimes for no pay at all.[11] However, by the end of this period, pioneering girls' schools such as North London Collegiate School for Girls and Cheltenham Ladies' College were being established. These encouraged the public prominence of a new breed of teaching professionals, such as Frances Buss and Dorothea Beale, albeit only at the elite end of the market.[12]

Another emergent profession, nursing, was less successful at developing professional identities for its female practitioners. During this period nursing remained on the cusp between philanthropic and professional activities. From the 1830s, Anglican sisterhoods had fostered elite women's growing interest in nursing within the voluntary and religious sectors. St John's House, for example, inaugurated a training institute for nurses in 1848. It was, however, not until the Crimean War (1853–6) that female nursing obtruded on to public attention. Although many upper-class women served as nurses on a non-stipendiary basis under the leadership of Mary Stanley, it was Florence Nightingale's contribution which received the greatest recognition. Subsequent investigation has shown the impact of Nightingale upon the hospitals in the Crimea to have been greatly exaggerated.[13] Yet, the opening of the Nightingale School of Nursing at St Thomas's hospital in 1860 was to enshrine Nightingale's vision of the role of the lady within the nursing profession. The projection of the nursing lady as the dispenser of authority and moral grace was essential in drawing the upper classes into the profession.[14]

For those women of the middling ranks who required financial remuneration, but had little education or proclivity for teaching or nursing, the possibilities were increasingly limited. By the beginning of our period many of the trades previously considered as 'feminine' – such as bookbinding, brewing and hairdressing – were becoming identified as male pursuits. The most common path for those forced to seek employment was to take in needlework (this was a particularly useful resource for older women with children who would not be considered for live-in teaching posts) or to engage themselves to a dressmaking or millinery establishment. Apprenticeships in the most fashionable and high-class dressmaking houses were designed expressly for middle-class women, costing between £30 and £50 for a two to five-year apprentice.[15] Both living and working conditions during such apprenticeships could be extremely poor, however.

For a gifted few it was conceivable to derive an income from the arts. During the eighteenth century, writing became a popular recourse for impecunious middle-class and genteel women. By 1850, George Henry Lewes was satirising the fears of male writers that they were being usurped by an army of superior female novelists. Writers such as Elizabeth Gaskell, Charlotte Brontë, Elizabeth Barrett Browning, Anna Jameson and Charlotte Yonge thrived during this period. Some, such as Sarah Austin, derived an income from translations, whilst many preferred to take more conventional paths, such as writing for children. Yet even the most successful female writers had to pick their way through a complex maze of gendered assumptions. Social convention meant that women frequently felt obliged to insist that they did not write for money. Many female writers chose to adopt male pseudonyms because of the widespread bias as to the intellectual and artistic capabilities of women. Critical reviews of both *Jane Eyre* and *Adam Bede* altered significantly when it was discovered that they were authored by women.[16]

The response of Victorian culture to the phenomenon of female professionals was thus riddled with contradictions. On the one hand, support and capital were given to assist their efforts – as in the Governesses' Benevolent Institution; yet individual employers frequently failed to recognise female teachers as individual economic agents, treating them rather within the familial model, as dependent relatives. Female writers were immensely popular with the public, but found it difficult to project themselves as professional authors.

Some women found extraordinary ways to bypass these issues. Dr James Miranda Barry posed, undetected, as a highly successful male surgeon throughout her professional life.[17] A more plausible alternative was to emigrate to the new world. Commentators in Britain stressed the moral dimension to women's emigration. Caroline Chisholm, who campaigned on this issue, famously declared female emigrants in the colonies to be 'God's Police'.[18] However, in the colonies themselves, women forged a new concept of gentility which could incorporate the need for hard, physical work as pioneers, helping to run farms and to make homes habitable. Thus colonial discourses of womanhood could encompass characteristics such as strength, bravery and adaptability which, as the fiction produced by colonial women demonstrates, many embraced.[19]

Meanwhile, in Britain, from the late 1830s a group of young feminists attempted to challenge social contradictions by actively seeking financial independence through their work. Margaret Gillies, for example, established a considerable reputation as a professional portrait painter.[20] The need for women's economic independence was argued repeatedly in the feminist press of the day. The *Star in the East*, was typical in arguing that 'every woman should have her business or profession as well as every man'.[21] By 1859 a new generation of feminists, led by Jessie Boucherett and Adelaide Procter, had founded the first organised pressure group to campaign for the widening of women's employment opportunities: the Society for the Promotion of the Employment of Women (SPEW). SPEW ran classes in bookkeeping for women, as well as initiating a female law-copying office and an all-woman printing establishment, the Victoria Press. Philippa Levine has suggested that seeking only comparatively 'genteel' work for women (and only single women at that) 'dug them [SPEW] ever deeper into the trap of occupational suitability'.[22] However, one might argue that this was a reasonable strategy to follow, in a culture which was so deeply ambivalent about women and paid employment.

Women and the Family Enterprise

For many, perhaps most, women, active occupation was sought not out of feminist principles, or even the need for money, but was derived from the belief that part of their role as wives and mothers was to assist in the running of the family business. Indeed, Kim Reynolds talks of the 'dual nature of the management structure of many estates' in which aristocratic couples, such as the Duke and Duchess of Somerset, approached the running of their estates as a partnership. Some women, such as Lady Palmerston, assumed such responsibilities only on the death of their husbands, others not at all. Yet a number simply thrived in this capacity. The Duchess of Athole undertook most of the business of the family estate, merely keeping her husband informed of her decisions.[23]

If not all aristocratic women aspired to play a major role in organising the family estate, few considered themselves free from any responsibilities as to its smooth running. The landed estate played a central role in the rural community. As such, the aristocratic wife was expected to perform a wide range of social duties – from entertaining the local squierarchy, to organising feast-days for the tenantry. In particular, the pastoral care of an estate's tenants fell upon the aristocratic wife and her daughters. Although landed women could be as pitiless as many aristocratic men, some incorporated benevolent policies and duties into their wider management strategies. Mrs Arthbuthnot praised the Duchess of Rutland for managing her estate in ways which were 'essentially beneficial' 'to the poor and dependent around her'.[24] In addition to individual acts of charity, landed wives tended to involve themselves in projects for estate improvement, such as housing programmes and educational institutes.[25]

In the middle classes also (and particular in the middling and lower strata), married women expected to aid in the economic well-being of their families. This is a fact which has been greatly obscured by inconsistent and misleading census data. The census enumerators for 1841 were instructed that wives living at home and helping their husbands, but not receiving wages, need not be recorded. However, at the next census it was recognised that, 'Women … in certain branches of business at home render important services; such as the wives of farmers, of small shopkeepers, innkeepers, shoemakers, butchers', and should be so enumerated.[26]

None the less, the accepted historical wisdom is that by the early Victorian period, the cultural pressures of domestic ideology had rendered such work increasingly uncommon. In addition, as Catherine Hall maintains, by the 1830s and 1840s there was a growing tendency to separate the business or professional setting from the domestic environment. The greater specialisation and formalisation which was creeping into the business world required both more rigorous training and the utilisation of new male public spaces, such as chambers of commerce. This, combined with middle-class migration to pleasant urban dwellings, made women's informal contribution exceedingly difficult. They were no longer required to receive clients, cater for live-in assistants or to help with the books to the same extent.[27]

Theodore Koditschek has discovered that in 1851 only 6.6 per cent of middle-class households in Bradford contained live-in employees – indicating the separation of work from home.[28] Significantly, such developments were not necessarily regarded negatively by the women involved. Hall cites the case of the wife of a Birmingham chemist, who was immensely cheered once the family moved away from the site of the business, as it relieved her of a considerable amount of work.[29] Despite these broad trends, it is probable that many women, particularly in the lower middle class, continued to involve themselves in their husbands' work. Indeed, although the education of middle-class girls has been repeatedly criticised for its obvious lack of rigour and its attention to 'accomplishments' such as music and languages, it is possible that girls in this strata benefited from 'hands on' training in the family business. Through the participation of their mothers in the family enterprise, they learnt practical skills which could be put to great use. The female members of a grocer's family could make jam to be sold in the shop and serve customers at busy times; the wives and daughters of solicitors and estate agents might be expected to copy documents and correspondence; those whose husbands ran boarding schools would act as matrons; and the wives and daughters of clergymen would teach in local Sunday schools, organise fund-raising events and assist in their husbands' paper work.[30]

Women's contribution to the success of the family business could be particularly crucial if their husbands suffered from poor health, were heavy drinkers, or were simply incompetent. Joseph Farrar recalled that, 'My father made but little as a businessman and was greatly indebted to my mother for the position he occupied, she by her industry sustaining my father's failing fortunes at all times.'[31] Charlotte Bostock, whose assistance in her husband's chemist shop had always been important, assumed sole control over it in 1848 during his illness.[32] Such examples suggest that middle-class women were, like working-class women, perceived to be a part of the family economy and felt themselves to be implicated in their husbands' work. Occasionally, women could take their identification with their husbands' occupation to extreme lengths. During the Crimean War, Fanny Duberly rode with her husband at the head of the Eighth Hussars![33] Such examples have led one historian to claim that 'men's work *was* women's work'. Whilst this may be an exaggeration, it is none the less true that the language with which the wifely role was couched – as their husband's 'helpmeet' – may have been understood by contemporaries to have extended far beyond the rhetorical.[34]

Similar complexities underline the work of middle-class women in the countryside. An older historiographical tradition, led by Ivy Pinchbeck, pointed to the growing social aspirations of farmers' wives. It was argued that women were ever-more interested in the trappings of gentility and were reluctant to play their former role as business and dairy managers on their farms. Consequently, they were anxious to rid themselves of the burdens of catering to the needs of live-in farm workers.[35] It is perhaps not surprising that women should have expressed some relief at being spared the huge labour involved in feeding, washing and cleaning for large numbers of live-in farm servants.[36] However, Leonore Davidoff suggests that women's contribution to the farming enterprise was limited more by practical considerations than by notions of social climbing. Women's traditional role in marketing the farm produce was threatened with the rise of the more formal market halls and corn exchanges; and they were alienated from male pursuits such as hunting and farmers' clubs which facilitated farmers' business networks. Nevertheless, in 1851, 9.3 per cent of farm households in Essex and Suffolk were headed by women (most of them widows).[37] Examples from Wales also indicate that women maintained an active role in the business operations of their farms throughout this period, being particularly involved with the production and marketing of dairy and orchard goods.[38] Clearly, much greater local research is needed to ascertain a clearer picture of the economic role of farming women.

Mid-Victorian rhetoric, which lyrically espoused the virtues of angelic, domesticated women, has greatly contributed to the historical impression that in the manufacturing sectors also, women were withdrawing from active participation and instead structuring their lives around the home. However, individual case-studies point to the dangers of constructing such unproblematic narratives and illustrate the need for more subtle readings of these discursive tropes. In the late eighteenth and early nineteenth centuries, the Courtauld women, for example, supervised female workers in the family silk mills at Halstead. By the mid-nineteenth century such work was no longer considered appropriate. This development was seemingly reflected in a poem of 1846 written by employees as a company tribute to the 'ladies of the firm'. The Courtauld women were extolled as 'angels of the house', who ensured a sanctified and serene home whilst their husbands were engaged in business. Critically, such rhetoric masked the fact that the partners' wives had merely assumed a different role – that of catering to the pastoral and personnel needs of female workers. Ellen Courtauld was active in setting up a nursery for the children of married women workers at the mill and in organising educational provision. She also sought to expand the moral and practical horizons of the female employers, by taking groups of them with her when she made her regular visits to the local sick. Such activities should not be read simply as philanthropy, but were a strategy whereby women could contribute to industrial enterprise, often by articulating and implementing a business's progressive management ethos.[39] Hannah Greg, the wife of an industrialist in Styal, Cheshire, was similarly engaged in welfare and educational provision for the family's employees. In particular, Hannah encouraged her own daughters to take a particular interest in catering to the needs of the company's young apprentices.[40] In Bradford, it was the wives and daughters of local industrialists who organised education for the young female employees.[41] In Wales, it has been noted that workers at the Dowlais ironworks looked upon Lady Charlotte Guest, the wife of their employer, in a similar capacity to that of a personnel officer; taking their workplace complaints or requests to her.[42] It was clearly assumed that women's influence over their husbands extended far beyond domestic affairs, to the actual working of their businesses.

Substantial numbers of women clearly revelled in the opportunities afforded by their husbands' business concerns and became active business agents in their own right. A handful of aristocratic women were intimately involved in business ventures, thus illustrating the dangers of stereotyping the occupations of upper-class women. Frances Anne Londonderry, for example, assumed responsibility for her husband's large-scale colliery business in County Durham on his death in 1854 and was responsible for the introduction of blast-furnaces near Seaham Harbour. Disraeli, who visited her in 1861, found that 'she has a regular office, a fine stone building with her name and arms in front, and her flag flying above; and here she transacts with innumerable agents, immense business.' Sarah, Countess of Jersey was the owner and active senior partner of the London banking house, Child and Co.[43] Charlotte Guest became manager of the enormous iron works at Dowlais in Wales during her husband's illness and subsequent death. Despite the considerable obstacles facing a woman in this role, Charlotte Guest adored her work, where she always felt, 'in my proper sphere'. Significantly, Guest used the influence which her position wrought to implement a variety of educational projects, savings clubs and local civic improvements. As her historian points out, such work indicated the vital role played by industrialists' wives in 'ensuring social stability in the wake of social and political upheaval by adapting older paternalistic values to the new society'.[44] Certainly, well-to-do women who established their own business ventures were often motivated by social concerns. A number of genteel Scottish women set up spinning ventures in Glasgow and the Lowlands, in order to provide underemployed local women with jobs; during the Irish famine, Louisa Waterford established a clothing factory on her estate in Curraghmore to provide women with employment.[45]

Of course, not all women had the luxury of practising beneficent entrepreneurialism, many wished to run businesses for economic reasons. Contemporaries' often commented that such opportunities were on the wane. As the elderly Margaretta Grey complained to her diary in 1853: 'Men in want of employment have pressed their way into nearly all the shopping and retail businesses that in my early years were managed in whole, or in part, by women.'[46] Until recently, most historians propounded a similarly gloomy thesis. They note that whereas in previous centuries, women had participated in such businesses as property rental, money lending and catering, this was uncommon by the Victorian period. According to Davidoff and Hall, women's role in business became increasingly passive between 1750 and 1850. Daughters were likely to be bequeathed annuities, trust funds or life assurance: types of property which assumed their dependence. This was in contrast to the inheritances of their brothers who would be provided with capital intended for business enterprise and similar activities. Women's contribution to business generation, explain Davidoff and Hall, tended to be limited to contributing capital on marriage, and to lending money to male kin (although this could in itself enhance women's self-esteem and status).[47]

Nevertheless in certain localities and among specific occupational groups, recent research suggests that women's business ventures often thrived in the burgeoning capitalist economy. Far from reinforcing women's exclusion from business, as Davidoff and Hall suggest, inheritance practice could actually act as a spur to women's economic activity. In Hinckley, Leicestershire, it was common for framesmiths to leave their often sizeable businesses to women. Moreover, contra Davidoff and Hall, wills were often constructed to ensure that widows retained management for their life. Such findings have been corroborated for Bradford. Here, in 1850, there were 128 female-ran businesses which accounted for nearly all of the city's milliners and bonnet-makers, 45 per cent of the city's teachers, 13 per cent of its innkeepers and beersellers and 11 per cent of its grocers and shopkeepers.[48]

Although widows were likely to be the most prominent of economically active females; it is possible that the ventures of married women have been underestimated. Technically speaking, married women's businesses belonged to their husbands, making it highly probable that a number of businesses, listed as male, might in fact, be run by women. A number of these would have been short-term projects, prompted by a family crisis, such as a bereavement or financial loss. Charles Dickens's mother famously (and abortively) attempted to set up a girls' school when the family's finances reached crisis point in 1823.[49] However, there is evidence to suggest that in the country's burgeoning urban milieus, women could enjoy enhanced and sustained business opportunities. In cities such as Manchester and London, lower-middle-class women capitalised upon growing consumer markets to act as purveyors of fine and exotic foods. This could enable women to thrive as retailers and to sometimes preside at the heart of a series of overlapping business concerns, which might include retailing, money lending and the carriage and carrier business.[50]

It seems probable, especially given the emerging new evidence cited above, that women's withdrawal from economic activity, such as it may have been, was not a quick and linear phenomenon, but rather a piecemeal process effecting communities at different times and with varying impacts. Certainly, local traditions were important in defining the nature of women's economic contributions. For example, whereas in Manchester and London it was common for married businesswomen to advertise under their own names (and indeed in London wives were legally entitled to carry on their own businesses), such a practice was not condoned in Oxford.[51]

It was women of the lower middle class who seemed to have been most involved in business generation during these years; but this was not universally so. Women were often to be found at the head of high-class dressmaking establishments, where they might employ a number of young apprentices. Mrs Eliza Hakewell and her sister, of Grovesnor Square in London, ran such a business for over 20 years.[52] In Ireland there are examples of women founding large-scale lace manufactories. Emma Colston employed 80 children at her establishment in Kells, County Meath; in Coggeshall, Eliza and Sarah Johnson set up their own millinery and dressmaking business in 1839 and their sister, Hannah, had her own lace manufactory, at which she employed 100 workers.[53] More commonly, women proliferated as educational entrepreneurs. Many educational establishments were extremely small, catering for a handful of boarders and perhaps offering but minimal instruction. However, there were many highly successful and prestigious ventures. Sarah Bache established one such school in Birmingham with her half-sister, Phoebe Penn, where they sought to provide a 'useful' rather than a 'fashionable' education.[54]

Social Work

Philanthropy was a central component of the lives of women of this strata, drawing upon women's community, social, political, economic and religious affiliations (see Chapter 5). Many women developed their philanthropic activities to such a degree that we may regard them as having a quasi-professional (if unpaid) status. This was particularly evident in the field of education. For some, this might simply entail instructing at the local Sunday school; but for many others, it could amount to a full-time, (but non-remunerative) commitment. Catharine Spooner, for example, set up her own school for poor girls in Rugby where she worked nearly every day.[55] For missionary women abroad, teaching also formed a substantial part of their daily duties.[56]

Mary Carpenter, a Unitarian reformer, earned a national reputation for her work with delinquent children in Bristol. Carpenter herself had been able to profit from the superior education which denominations such as the Unitarians and Quakers, frequently gave to their girls.[57] Through her establishment of a 'ragged school' and reformatory institutions in Bristol, she developed a progressive philosophy of positive rehabilitation. Carpenter's extensive research and publications established her as an authority in this field. In 1852 she was invited to give evidence to the 1852 Parliamentary Committee into the problems of destitute and offending children, and she delivered many papers to the National Association for the Promotion of Social Science. In 1852 Carpenter organised, with Matthew Davenport Hill, the first national conference on juvenile delinquency.[58] Even so, as Seth Koven has pointed out, quasi-professionals such as Carpenter faced enormous obstacles from the male establishment, which was quick to wrest control from Carpenter once these institutions began to receive state funding.[59]

Louisa Twining was another example of a woman whose unpaid philanthropic work was pursued with a rigour and professional commitment that enabled her to develop extensive expertise in her chosen field – of workhouse reform. Twining both wrote and lectured on her subject for the National Association for the Promotion of Social Science and also became secretary of the Workhouse Visiting Society in 1858.[60] Women such as these illustrate the enormous potential in philanthropic-based occupations.

Conclusion

Women's involvement in social work highlights the inability of conventional definitions of work to capture the richness and significance of women's occupations. Historically, we are accustomed to think of 'work' as encompassing only that which is paid.[61] Many Victorian women of the middle and upper classes did fit this category, as we have seen. But others did not need to earn money, yet still wished (or were expected) to lead active, working lives and so make an important contribution either to their families or to social welfare. Equally, much activity that has been conventionally labelled simply as 'philanthropic' could, as we have seen, derive from a variety of impulses, including women's desire to contribute to the family enterprise. It could, on the one hand, be argued that in many ways this insight encapsulated the oppression of Victorian women – not only were they not permitted access to male professions, but they were expected to work for no financial gain to support male businesses, to create pleasurable homes and healthy children, and through philanthropy, to support the casualties of the social hierarchy. However, in marrying, the majority appear to have accepted that they would share the identity of their husbands, believing that they had an obligation to take on any work created by his occupation. Meanwhile, the growing importance of the middle-class home as a centre of consumption, rather than production, and the consequent focus upon women's domestic role, also appears to have been welcomed by most. Others, particularly those of the lower middle class, were active entrepreneurs in their own right. Those who sought leisured lives were not typical. Most women expected to contribute to the needs of their families and communities.

5

POLITICS, COMMUNITY AND PROTEST

Introduction

The involvement of middle-class and elite women in politics and community affairs is one of the newest areas of historiographical inquiry. Until recently, treatments of these topics tended to focus almost exclusively upon women's philanthropic contributions to the community. This activity was seen to reflect women's preoccupation with religion and their internalisation of ideologies concerning their supposedly caring, benevolent natures. Such work was simultaneously interpreted as a 'safety-valve': a means by which elite women, frustrated by the circumscribed nature of their lives, might find fulfilment beyond the domestic hearth.

However, in the last few years, historians have begun to unravel the myriad ways in which women interacted with community and current affairs. Contrary to the traditional assumption that politics lay beyond the reach of nineteenth-century women, historians are beginning to construct new and complex chronologies of their political involvement. During these years, the political influence of aristocratic women ebbed and shifted, whilst for middle-class women new avenues of public engagement were opening up and the first stirrings of the organised women's movement began to be felt.

Philanthropy

From the end of the eighteenth century, middle-class women began to organise themselves into charitable organisations on an unprecedented scale. This was traditionally understood in terms of the Evangelical revival, which emphasised female moral qualities and woman's duty to others.[1] As such, women's philanthropic work has often been constructed as the depoliticisation of female public activity. This interpretation fits neatly with the traditional historical argument concerning the contemporaneous cultural effects of the French Revolution. Society cleaved to the reassertion of gender differences, it has been argued, as it readjusted to the political and psychological shock of the French Revolution and the ensuing war with France.[2] However, the historical context of the post-Revolutionary years can be read very differently. Linda Colley has suggested that the deluge of prescriptive writing, urging upon women their role in the domestic sphere, should be seen as reactive propaganda, for women were 'becoming more involved in the public sphere than ever before'. Colley points to the prominent role women played in patriotic activity during the Napoleonic Wars: from the making of flags and banners for the regiments; presenting colours and making speeches to volunteer regiments; to collecting subscriptions for patriotic funds. As Colley notes, 'female patriots were staking out a civic role for themselves'.[3] Indeed, national emergencies such as the Napoleonic Wars, Frank Prochaska has observed, heightened female interest in public affairs.[4] Therefore, philanthropy emerged not merely out of the conservative vocabulary of Evangelicalism, but was vitally connected to the growing civic consciousness of British women at the turn of the century.

Female philanthropic work revealed a high degree of female consciousness, focusing as it did upon the plethora of societies which specialised in female misfortune, such as unwanted pregnancies. (Dealing with their 'less fortunate sisters' was also less problematic than forging relationships with lower-class men.) Middle-class women also began to embrace the aristocratic practice of home-visiting. They dispensed a judicious blend of practical assistance with religious and domestic advice, which stressed middle-class values such as cleanliness and thrift. In so doing, it has been argued, they sought to develop cross-class relationships at a time when middle-class men were becoming increasingly alienated from the lower orders.[5] (But more detailed research is required on the female working-class response to such initiatives.)

Female philanthropy, such as that propounded by the evangelical writer, Hannah More, has recently been re-evaluated as a radical 'woman-directed discourse' which sought social regeneration through the agency of women's actions and values.[6] Some conservative churchmen certainly viewed women's efforts to organise themselves into active and prosperous missionary, bible and relief societies as potentially subversive,[7] but to what extent the women involved saw themselves as cultural revolutionaries is open to question. Many women must evidently have perceived their activities to have a vital social and cultural significance, seeing it as part of their Christian duty to promote the welfare of their community. Evangelicalism placed a considerable stress upon women's capabilities as nurturers and educators. This enabled many to construct a positive and dynamic self-image, giving them the confidence to engage in difficult and sometimes dangerous social work.

Nevertheless, religious motivations remained highly diverse, frequently steeped in wider ideological agendas. For example, whereas Evangelicals discouraged teaching working-class children to read, Unitarians viewed Sunday schools as part of a larger liberal project to encourage the working classes to think and reason for themselves.[8] For many women, philanthropy, far from being a recourse for the frustrated and bored, formed part of an already rich and varied life. Elizabeth Heyrick fitted philanthropy into an active public life which included campaigning on humanitarian issues and writing political pamphlets.[9] Furthermore, whilst some women may have been content to confine their charity to a little home-visiting, or joining one of the plethora of new charitable societies, others were determined to make an impact upon the country's institutional life. Pioneers, like Elizabeth Fry, Catharine Cappe and Louisa Twining, sought access to prisons, workhouses and hospitals, often in the face of considerable management hostility. Female philanthropists typically worked to effect greater hygiene, access to religious education and humanitarian reforms in the regimes they visited.

It would be wrong to construct a straightforward narrative of women's growing influence in the public sector, however. From the 1830s the government increased their control over the nation's prisons and by the mid-century, women were still having to battle extremely hard to gain access to many workhouses. It was for this reason that Louisa Twining, as we have seen, established the Workhouse Visiting Society in 1858. The strategies and philosophy of this society revealed the gradual, but significant shifts occurring in the practice of female philanthropy. With its attempts to create specialist visitors focusing upon particular classes of inmates, the society revealed its debt to the new zeal for social investigation which characterised many reform movements of the day.[10] This desire to effect the greater professionalisation of philanthropy was a telling development and was to feed directly into the prominent role women were to play in local government in the coming years. The growing popularity of Anglican sisterhoods, which trained women in nursing and social work – such as that established by Lydia Sellon in Devonport in 1848 – were also an indication of the emerging possibilities for female occupation, which the philanthropic tradition encouraged.[11]

Involvement in philanthropy was equally significant in giving women experience in organisational and committee work. The administration required for the organisation of the large-scale charity bazaars which became popular from the 1820s, such as the massive bazaar held for the British Orphan Asylum at Kingsland in 1832, was formidable. Moreover, by the middle of the century, women were beginning to act on the councils of some mixed-sex executives and were not just confined to female auxiliary committees as had been the case at the turn of the century.[12]

By contrast, upper-class women performed philanthropy on an essentially personal basis.[13] Tending to the medical, material and pastoral needs of their tenants had long been accepted as one of the important roles played by the mistress of an estate. Landed women tended to view such work in terms of their social duty, and it formed an integral facet of the paternalist doctrine. Historians have recently noted that at the beginning of the period, inspired by the Evangelical message and a belief in the need to reform their class, there was renewed attention to the duty of providing succour to the poor. As such, women may be seen as at the vanguard of aristocratic reform, recognising that in order to retain political power, it was necessary for the landed classes to refashion their image and become accountable, responsible citizens.[14] Upper-class girls would be early socialised into such roles by accompanying their mothers on visits to tenants.[15]

For upper-class women, philanthropy could also form a means of exercising power within their community, as in the case of the Countess of Jersey who insisted that all children in Middleton Stoney should begin school at the age of two years. For other women charitable patronage could be linked to wider political or religious objectives within their neighbourhood. Lady Londonderry, for example, built a new church in New Seaham, enabling her to exert influence over the appointment of the minister.[16] At the school Lady Orford established in Callington, children were permitted to attend only if their parents had voted for her candidate during parliamentary elections.[17] The philanthropic activities of upper-class women clearly illustrates their wider involvement in the affairs of the nation and their own influence to effect change, both within their own community and in the larger polity.

Upper-Class Women and Politics

As a host of recent studies have clearly demonstrated, aristocratic women were closely involved in the politics of the day. Kim Reynolds, Elaine Chalus and Amanda Foreman have indicated that politics, far from being the preserve of men conducted in the masculine domain of committee rooms and clubs, was crucially connected to the dynastic and social world of the upper classes. These historians have elaborated upon what Chalus terms 'social politics' to demonstrate the vital importance of salons, dinners, electoral 'treating', garden parties, teas and visiting in the workings of contemporary politics. Upper-class women were at the centre of these activities, carefully orchestrating such social events to maximise their political advantage.[18] The political involvement of upper-class women was not confined to these traditionally 'female' activities, however, for women could also play a robust role in electioneering. Such activities were usually linked to supporting the political fortunes of male relatives, as was the case with Mary Anne Disraeli's enthusiastic canvassing during the general election of 1841.[19]

However, the political engagement of upper-class women was not uniquely defined by their loyalty to the political allegiance of their family and husbands. The eagerness with which upper-class women crowded themselves into the cramped 'ventilator' space in the House of Commons and behind the curtains in the House of Lords, to listen (often all night) to parliamentary debates, indicates a self-motivated thirst for political affairs.[20] And at times, women intervened in politics for their own ends. In Huntingdon, the redoubtable Lady Sandwich dominated local electoral affairs; whilst in Ripon in the West Riding, Ann Lister canvassed tirelessly, using her position as a landowner unashamedly to exert fierce pressure upon her tenants to vote Tory. Her neighbour, Elizabeth Lawrence, was also an extremely powerful political figure in the locality, having the power of veto over local election candidates.[21] This was a privilege shared by other aristocratic women, including, for example, Frances Anne Londonderry.[22] Consequently, Sarah Richardson has concluded that, 'As long as they had money, property, and political ambition women could succeed as well as any man.'[23]

The most prominent example of a woman who pursued an interest in politics independently of her husband was Georgiana, the Duchess of Devonshire. Georgiana's formidable political contacts and success in nurturing alliances behind the scenes enabled her, among other things, to play a major role in cementing the Fox-North coalition in 1804 and in keeping the 'Ministry of all the Talents' together in 1806.[24] Victorian upper-class women continued Georgiana's example in creating influential political salons. In a period of weak party organisation and communication, the salons established by women such as Lady Palmerston, Lady Holland, Lady Waldegrave and Lady Jersey provided a crucial space for party political discussion, consolidation and networking. They were particularly important during the fluid political situation of the 1840s, when they could also perform the function of party whips. As Leonore Davidoff noted of Lady Palmerston (the wife of the Prime Minister, and a potent political force in her own right): 'It was said that an invitation to her parties had determined many a wavering vote.'[25]

Accordingly, it has been asserted that the greater professionalisation of party politics, which followed in the wake of the 1832 Reform Act, diminished the role of female aristocratic political influence. Certainly, the earlier part of Victoria's reign witnessed a marked dip in such activity, a fact which Reynolds has attributed to the apparent triumph of domestic ideology during these years. Victoria's accession also brought to an end the political weight long enjoyed by royal mistresses (such as Lady Hertford and Lady Conyngham, mistresses of George IV) and consorts (namely Queen Charlotte, the wife of George III, and Queen Adelaide, the wife of William IV).[26] The extent to which Queen Victoria herself exercised significant political authority during the early years of her reign has yet to be fully analysed, although it is significant that in 1841 she had to back down from the position she assumed over the 'Bedchamber Crisis', in which she wished to keep Whig ladies-in-waiting in her court during a Tory administration.[27] It seems possible however, that the role of female networks in maintaining the crown's political authority has been underrated. For example, Victoria's correspondence with Charlotte Canning, the leading British woman in India, was vital in providing her with first-hand accounts of imperial affairs.[28]

Middle-Class Women and Politics

The involvement of middle-class women in politics has yet to be excavated in depth. Very little is known, for example, of the extent to which women of this class may have enjoyed a degree of formal political or community power. Traditionally, local offices were invested in property ownership, rather than the person. Therefore, some single women and widowed property-owners could exercise the right to act as vergers, sextons and parish clerks, thus enjoying a degree of community influence and prestige; and women were sometimes permitted to vote in meetings of Dissenting chapels.[29] It is also now apparent that women played an active role in the parliamentary electoral process. In some boroughs, the daughters of freemen were entitled to confer voting rights upon their husbands; and women were also active as negotiators or recipients of bribes during elections. What emerges from this new evidence is that the vote was often understood to be a piece of family property. Many women clearly felt that they had a stake in their husband's vote and believed themselves to enjoy a degree of political representation through it.[30]

By the turn of the nineteenth century a rich tradition of women's political writing had evolved which used not only the conventional political genres of the pamphlet and the political disquisition, but also poetry, novels and letters. Whilst research into the engagement of conservative women is still greatly needed, it is now clear that dissenting women, such as Mary Hays and Anna Laetitia Barbauld, readily exploited these opportunities. Through the use of correspondence networks and radical salons, as well as through the political education of their children, women were able to make a fruitful contribution to radical political culture.[31]

Equally, many radical middle-class women involved themselves in the political campaigns of the day. Although they tended to eschew collective action, many made an enormous impact on the cause of radical reform as individuals. This emerges clearly in women's involvement in the campaign for the freedom of the press. One of the most notorious incidents of female interception came in 1818 when Mary Ann Tocker, the sister of a Plymouth solicitor, was indicted for libel following a letter she wrote to the *West Briton and Cornwall Advertiser*, protesting against the corruption of a local lawyer, Richard Gurney. Tocker defended herself successfully in the ensuing, much-publicised court battle, to the jubilation of radical reformers.[32] Other women participated in the campaign for press freedom by lending their support to prominent male activists. Matilda Roalfe, a Sunday school teacher from Edinburgh, travelled to London to work with George Jacob Holyoake's Anti-Persecution Union. She then returned to Edinburgh to run the free-thought bookshop of Thomas Paterson during his imprisonment (for which she herself was put in prison). Eliza Sharples, the daughter of a Bolton manufacturer, moved to London to assist in the work of the radical campaigner, Richard Carlile (with whom she began an intimate relationship after visiting him frequently in prison). Sharples soon became a campaigner in her own right. In addition to taking control of Carlile's publishing concern, she began to give highly dramatic lectures at his Rotunda theatre and, in 1832, launched her feminist journal, *The Isis*. Sharples was exceptional in shaking off the mantle of female auxiliary to the cause. As she herself proclaimed to a mixed audience, 'which of you will not accept me for your general, your leader, your guide?'[33]

The majority of women demonstrated their commitment through assisting the activities of male radicals. This should not blind us to the intensity of political conviction and courage which such women displayed – a point which is well illustrated by the fact that women who were prosecuted for these activities frequently insisted on conducting their own defence. They thus demonstrated a highly evolved perception of their own political agency, as well as impressive confidence in the intellectual arguments surrounding their actions.[34]

Middle-class female involvement is also evident in the organised movements of early Victorian radicalism. Their contribution to the reform societies of the post-1815 period has yet to be investigated, although we occasionally catch glimpses of their inclusion.[35] We have more information on the affiliation of middle- and upper-class women to Owenism and Chartism. Some women succeeded in carving out their own niche within the radical culture of these movements. Anna Wheeler, for example, who hailed from the Irish gentry, was a pivotal figure in early socialism. Through her lectures and translations she disseminated the ideas of Charles Fourier and the Comte de Saint-Simon, as well as raising the priority of women's rights debates within British radicalism.[36] A small band of impoverished middle-class women, including Emma Martin and Eliza Macauley, attained fame and prestige within the Owenite movement for their lecturing activities. It is highly possible that a great number of rank and file Owenites may have been drawn from this social group, struggling on the brink of the lower middle class. Barbara Taylor notes that their precarious economic position and often unhappy marital experiences could help to propel them towards socialist and feminist philosophies.[37] Although women failed to make an impact upon the organisational structure of the Owenite movement, for the well-to-do there could be other ways of establishing authority within early socialism. The wealthy widow, Sophia C. Chichester, for example, achieved considerable respect among radical reformers by positioning herself as a patron to progressive causes.[38]

A similarly mixed pattern is discernible in the Chartist movement. Whilst middle-class women did not organise amongst themselves for the Charter, there are numerous examples of individual women – middle and lower middle class – campaigning for Chartism. They often did so through public lectures or periodical contributions; a tiny minority acted as delegates to regional conferences and assisted in the running of the National Charter Association. A handful, including Helen Macfarlane, Caroline Maria Williams and Susanna Inge, achieved national status within the Chartist movement.[39]

By contrast, middle-class women mobilised themselves *en masse* in the pressure-group politics of the day. In campaigns against the Corn Laws, women's organisation was extensive and resulted in ambitious fund-raising projects, women-only associations, door-to-door canvassing and consumerist politics.[40] This activity was fiercely denigrated by conservative commentators, *The Times* claiming it to be 'political prostitution'.[41] Such hostility reveals the comparative radicalism of the women's actions. In this context, the concept of 'women's mission', one that was utilised heavily by campaigners, emerges as a liberating concept – a 'social feminism' – which enabled women to claim the right to intervene in public affairs.[42]

This notion of women's duty to participate in current affairs is particularly evident in women's protests against slavery. Women privileged their position as defenders of morality to play a unique role in this campaign. Articulating what has been termed a 'moral radicalism', it was chiefly the women's societies which pushed for the immediate emancipation of slaves.[43] The women's contribution to the movement was strongly influenced by the philanthropic tradition. Women's anti-slavery societies, for example, gave a far higher proportion of their funds than did male societies to relief and education projects among black West Indians.[44] Yet, their work also extended far beyond such a perspective. By promoting a boycott of West Indian sugar, women succeeded in politicising consumer issues and drawing domestic culture into the campaign. This also had the advantage of delivering a very immediate political lesson to children, who were thus habituated to the practice of a 'moral politics' within the home.[45] As in the Anti-Corn Law movement, the anti-slavery movement drew women into wider public debates, not least the need to articulate arguments as to the validity of free-trade economic policies over protectionism.[46]

Women's actions in the anti-slavery campaign revealed the extent to which middle-class women desired to act as independent political agents. Significant numbers of women who supported the movement appear not to have had male kin similarly involved. Of the 73 female associations active during the years 1825–33, 31 appear to have been independent of male organisations. It was also thanks to a highly orchestrated and efficient campaign on the women's part that the first national anti-slavery petition was presented to parliament in May 1833, on the day the Emancipation Bill was introduced. This revealed, once again, the extent to which women were aware of the political dimension to their protest.[47]

Women's independent role in the anti-slavery campaign has led Clare Midgley to suggest that much of their work and attitude might be described as 'proto-feminist'. She maintains that their forthright disputes with both the movement's leadership and the male societies, 'involved a public questioning of male authority, an assertion of independence, and a recognition that their views were not adequately represented by men'.[48] When the World Anti-Slavery Convention was held in London in 1840, the issue of women's equality was brought forcibly to the movement's attention. The Garrisonian wing of the American campaign was staunchly feminist and included several females among its delegation. The British organisers caused uproar when they refused to allow the female delegates, who included such prestigious names as Lucretia Mott, to participate. Although the feminism of Mott and her associates did not succeed in appealing to the broad mass of anti-slavery campaigners, they forged strong links with a network of British activists, many of them Unitarians or Quakers, who had already begun to debate women's rights among themselves. These included prominent figures like Elizabeth Reid, Elizabeth Pease, Harriet Martineau and Anne Knight. During the 1850s the influence of Garrisonianism continued to be apparent among these coteries, as the foundation of the egalitarian Leeds Anti-Slavery Association in 1853 illustrated.[49] Such campaigners tended to view their anti-slavery work from a radical political perspective, often forming part of an anti-colonialist ideology.[50]

Anxieties concerning the abuse of British military power were also evident in other contemporary pressure groups. In the mid-1840s, Birmingham women attended public meetings to protest against the government's plans for raising a militia.[51] More striking was women's involvement in the contemporary peace movement. Founded in London in 1816, the, chiefly Quaker, London Peace Society could boast the existence of several female auxiliary societies by the 1820s. Despite the strong tradition of female preaching within the denomination, women were unable to find a voice within the national organisational structure of the movement; although Anne Knight occasioned much debate at the 1851 London Peace Congress when she asked (unsuccessfully) to be allowed to attend as a delegate. Yet the women's Olive Leaf Circles, which met together for discussion and to plan publications and correspondence activity, were particularly significant for the enduring contacts they developed with Continental peace campaigners.[52]

In the contemporaneous temperance movement, women successfully capitalised upon their ideological construction as preservers of domesticity to claim a public role. Arguing that alcoholism and the public house were the bane of family life, destroying domestic peace and brutalising its men folk, female temperance workers drew upon women's social expertise to arrange alternative family-friendly activities – such as tea parties and outings. Women formed numerous female auxiliary branches of temperance societies, as well as initiating their own projects – such as door-to-door collecting and the distribution of temperance literature. By 1853 a national Ladies Temperance Association was established to co-ordinate these activities. Additionally, the cause saw individual women developing national reputations. Clara Lucas Balfour (the wife of an MP) became famous for her nation-wide temperance lectures, whilst Ann Jane Carlile attracted widespread publicity through the juvenile 'Band of Hope' movement. As these examples suggest, female temperance workers developed a variety of strategies to fight their cause, making it unwise to classify them too readily in terms of stereotypical notions of fulfilling a 'supportive role', as one historian has suggested.[53]

Moreover, the temperance ideology was itself extremely broad and encompassed a wide variety of explicitly political motivations. At the most extreme end of the spectrum lay a group of transcendental reformers who propounded abstention not merely from alcohol, but from tobacco, all animal products and even sex. Within these reforming communities were women who were strongly influenced by the ideas of Charles Fourier. They consequently argued that a key to the social and moral regeneration of society was that women should be emancipated to enable them to assume the mantle of a new moral government. The president of the country's first vegetarian society was, significantly, a woman.[54] As this example indicates, Victorian pressure-group movements were often closely connected to the radical culture of the day. They provided women with a range of diverse outlets for the expression of their ideological and political viewpoints and succeeded in mobilising middle-class women on a substantial scale.

The Early Feminist Movement

It was during these years that the first stirrings of a feminist movement became discernible. As we have seen, contemporary left-wing philosophies had preached a powerful discourse of female emancipation. The traditional historiography of the women's rights movement has isolated these voices, arguing that they played no role in the organised feminist campaigns which began to coalesce in the 1850s.[55] However, recent research has illustrated the extent to which co-operative philosophies influenced the radical circles of artists, writers and reformers who began to publicise women's rights and wrongs from the 1830s. Of particular significance were the 'radical unitarians', a diverse intellectual community, strongly influenced by (but not necessarily affiliated to) the contemporary Unitarian movement. Their original inspiration was a Unitarian preacher, William Johnson Fox, whose ministry at South Place Chapel in Finsbury attracted considerable attention among the radical literati of the day. Fox encouraged dialogue with the Owenites and with the French socialist theories of Saint-Simon and Charles Fourier. The resulting philosophy was one which championed the Unitarian tradition of Enlightenment values, in particular, the rights of the individual and the importance of education; whilst incorporating what was identified as the Christ-like values of the co-operative movements. By the 1840s, radical unitarian circles enjoyed considerable publicity for their ideas through popular journals, such as those run by William and Mary Howitt and Eliza Cook. Their adherents campaigned for reform in the laws concerning prostitution, female adult education and reforms to married women's legal position. The ease with which radical unitarian feminists liaised with Evangelical reformers, and the fact that by the late 1840s they counted popular writers and up-and-coming solicitors among their numbers, suggests that attitudes towards female emancipation in early Victorian Britain were more tolerant than has traditionally been assumed.[56]

The radical unitarians laid many of the personnel networks which were to be so important in sustaining the organised women's rights movements of the coming decades. The two leading lights of the movement in the 1850s, Bessie Rayner Parkes and Barbara Smith Bodichon, had been strongly influenced by the radical unitarians in their youth.[57] The committee established in 1855 to co-ordinate a campaign to reform the laws concerning married women's property rights was spearheaded by Parkes, Bodichon, Anna Jameson (a writer closely connected with the radical unitarians), Elizabeth Reid (a former Unitarian who had earlier established Bedford College), Eliza Fox (the daughter of W. J. Fox) and boasted Mary Howitt as its secretary.[58] Yet the feminism of the 1850s was markedly different from that of the 1840s. During the 1840s feminism had formed but one part of a wider radical, humanitarian agenda amongst radical unitarian reformers (the most prominent of whom were men). In the early 1850s, feminism became detached from this wider reforming impulse (which had in any case frayed and weakened in the post-1848 disillusionment) and became a movement in its own right. Indeed, for Philippa Levine, mid-Victorian feminism was characterised by the strength of its female networks and the development of a powerful sense of sisterhood.[59] It is necessary to temper such judgements with the reminder that the movement continued to enjoy the support of male radicals and coteries, notably the Law Amendment Society and the National Association for the Promotion of Social Science, as well as many radicals associated with the Unitarian and Christian Socialist denominations. Nevertheless feminism was ostensibly now led by women. Primarily, the impetus came from the Langham Place circle, where Bodichon and Parkes were joined by other well-educated, middle-class feminists such as Jessie Boucherett, Adelaide Procter and Isa Craig. This coterie founded the country's first all-women feminist journal, the *English Woman's Journal*, in 1858, and a year later established the Society for the Promotion of the Employment of Women. However, as Sally Alexander perceptively argues, this emphasis upon practical objectives should not blind us to the 'transcendental aspiration' which underlay their aims, and whose theological radicalism led them to invoke the name of God to justify their demands.[60]

Conclusion

The first half of the nineteenth century was a critical period in the evolving public role of middle-class and elite women. The dominant historiography has seen these years as the triumph of domesticity, following in the wake of the cultural trauma of the French Revolution. There is clearly a need to apply more subtle analytical models if we are to capture the richness and diversity of women's contemporary public and political engagement. The home was not a depoliticised sphere – as the case of aristocratic women proves so well. Moreover, as the activities of middle-class women ably demonstrate, domestic ideology was not an overarching and monolithic discourse. It could be challenged, subverted and stretched to provide the rationale for intervention in public debates, particularly those associated with community welfare. Whilst we know far too little about the political activities of middle-class conservative women, research on women involved in radical politics and pressure-group movements, combined with the ever-expanding field of philanthropic endeavour, suggests that far from being years of political closure for women, this was a period of exciting developments in women's public and political expression. The rise of the early women's rights movement was but one sign of women's growing public confidence.

6

FAMILIES, RELATIONSHIPS AND HOME LIFE

Introduction

The two previous chapters concerning women's contribution to economic and political life have illustrated that middle-class and elite women enjoyed far richer experiences than traditional historical accounts often suggest. Nevertheless, the lives of most women (particularly those of the middle classes) remained structured primarily around domestic concerns. Historians have emphasised the extent to which, by the early Victorian period, such activities had become strongly influenced by the Evangelical project.[1] Yet, we must question how far most women would have cast themselves unproblematically in the wholly dependent and subordinate domestic roles exhorted of them in Evangelical discourses of domesticity. Women could attach very diverse meanings to the home and to their role within it.

Courtship

Lawrence Stone famously argued that this period witnessed a broad cultural shift amongst the landed classes, towards intimate, nuclear families and emotionally fulfilling marriages.[2] Yet recently, rather than portraying the period as a triumph of romantic and affective sensibilities, historians have pointed to the circumscribed nature of genteel society. Invitations to the balls and assemblies at which young aristocrats were expected to meet their marriage partners were strictly limited to those of a suitable class and income. The extensive use of chaperones for young, unmarried girls could also help to weed out unsuitable alliances. Although forced marriages were seen as increasingly unacceptable, the idea of a 'good match' continued to resonate powerfully throughout the upper-class world. While aristocratic society remained largely endogamous, the infusion of mercantile wealth into the aristocracy through marriage alliances brought a vitality and flexibility to the landed classes. Daughters were, explains F. M. L. Thompson, 'the instruments of family advance', with massive dowries being offered for an advantageous marriage.[3] Consequently, Judith Schneid Lewis suggests that the mounting discourse of romantic happiness had but a limited influence upon women's marriage choices.[4]

This does not mean to say that women were merely pawns within a patriarchal marriage system. Certainly some young women, out of a sense of religious or filial duty, might still feel constrained to marry men to whom they were not attracted. Nevertheless marriage held very different meanings for contemporary landed women, than it does for us today. It entailed the setting up of a costly establishment; extending their family's influence; and assuming philanthropic, social and often political obligations. Consequently, landed women appear to have welcomed marriages which were built upon a calculated mix of respect, mutual liking, social status and financial success.[5] As mothers, aunts or grandmothers, they actively promoted marriages based upon a combination of prudence and affection. Lord Monson reminded his son of the efforts made by his aunt to marry him to 'a nice girl with a good fortune'. Such cases prompted F. M. L. Thompson to write of the 'strong matriarchal undercurrent' in aristocratic life.[6]

Among the middle classes, potential marriage partners were likely to be met in the course of private social occasions. Historians of consumerism have pointed to the rising acquisition of dining-room furniture and pianos by the middle classes in the early nineteenth century, which signified the heightened role of the home as a site for social intercourse and courtship.[7] Private entertaining provided the ideal venue for facilitating interaction between business and family networks, both probable sources of possible marriage partners. Davidoff and Hall note the significant numbers of cousin-marriages among the middling classes, particularly in families united by business concerns. Marianne Kenrick, for example married her cousin, Samuel, in 1811, which served to consolidate his position as a new partner in her father's buckle business. Yet, Davidoff and Hall's examples also suggest a rather more subtle process in which women, far from passively cementing business and kinship associations, actively sought particular kinds of marriage alliances. They note that women could be as eager as men to confirm kinship and friendship ties through sibling marriage. Equally important as a venue for courtship were churches and chapels, which provided the middle classes with their own social calendars. For those of specific denominations, most notably the endogamous Quakers or Unitarians, religion provided access to a nation-wide network of contacts. The prevalence of marriages based upon religious affiliation at least suggests that women were able to choose from a cohort of men with similar values to themselves; and who were more likely to respect the enormously important private and public implications of women's religious identities.[8]

Childbirth and Motherhood

For the vast majority of women, marriage would of course, become synonymous with pregnancy. Birth control was held to be unnatural, immoral and irreligious by the majority of these classes well into the middle of the century. As such, until they reached the menopause, women might expect to spend most of their married lives either pregnant or caring for very young children. In Judith Lewis's study of aristocratic women, she found that those women in relationships of completed fertility had a median childbearing span of 18 years, with an average of eight children each. A later age of marriage in the middle-class strata resulted in a smaller childbearing span of 13 years in Davidoff and Hall's sample.[9]

Most women expected to enjoy life very much as normal during pregnancy. By the middle of the century the huge emphasis upon the importance of motherhood (rather than the physical act of producing children) reduced the cultural significance of the birth itself.[10] The application of chloroform to reduce labour pains also contributed towards the deritualisation of childbirth. Its employment was given greater respectability when Queen Victoria used it to assist in the birth of her eighth child in 1853.[11] Whilst there remained many for whom chloroform was ideologically unacceptable, the speed with which chloroform became an accepted part of delivery practice demonstrated that women felt themselves to be in control of their own bodies. As one contemporary physician remarked, 'obstetricians may oppose it, but I believe our patients themselves will force the use of it upon the profession.'[12]

Middle-class women tended to have less autonomy when it came to breast-feeding, as wet-nursing was probably usually resorted to only in cases of medical necessity. Among the elite, however, most women decided on the basis of their own preference and family traditions. Towards the end of their childbearing years, the contraceptive benefits of breast-feeding were particularly welcome. As the nineteenth century progressed, the practice of wet-nursing gradually began to fall out of favour as concerns about the welfare of the wet nurse's own infant began to alienate public opinion.[13]

From their offsprings' early infancy, the majority of mothers seem to have taken their role as educators seriously. Indeed, in this respect, the social importance of motherhood was rooted in practical demands. Particularly in the middle classes, mothers were typically responsible for their children's education (although where it was affordable, boys might be educated by a tutor or at a school once they reached primary school age). Doubtlessly, in many households the instruction given was limited, perhaps revolving around basic literacy and biblical teaching, and for their daughters, tuition in domestic skills, particularly sewing. However, a number employed the most up-to-date pedagogical theories – for motherhood was widely understood to be not the bland diffusion of tender love, but an active and challenging occupation which required study, innovation and application. Margaret Ruskin, the mother of the Victorian art critic, John Ruskin, adhered closely to the educational ideas of Maria and Richard Lovell Edgeworth. She followed their injunctions against training children to answer by rote and of allowing children only limited access to non-educational toys.[14]

In addition to their academic educative role, mothers were usually responsible for their children's spiritual and moral guidance. In practical terms this meant that women played a key role in socialising children into particular ideological or religious traditions.[15] The strength of this influence has led some historians to claim that maternal authority was a critical factor in the emergence of new masculinities during these years.[16] Whilst such a claim warrants much greater research and evaluation, there is no doubt that the veneration of motherhood became a ubiquitous facet of contemporary cultural life, and held many implications for early Victorian femininities. Nevertheless, we must not assume that women necessarily embraced this greater emphasis upon the maternal role. In particular, the extent to which women of the landed classes responded to the evolving philosophies of child-rearing, which placed a greater emphasis upon the role of mothers in infant development, is open to question. For Judith Lewis and Jessica Gerard, the new notions of motherhood could be critical in defining and shaping women's perceptions of their maternal role. Lady Ridley, for example, assiduously consulted child-rearing manuals and took professional advice regarding her children.[17] Other commentators are less convinced. Leonore Davidoff has claimed that in the aristocracy, child care was subordinated to the dynastic and social cares of upper-class mothers.[18] Yet aristocratic parents were observed to have affectionate relations with their children. The distancing of mothers from the daily, bodily care of their children may, it has been suggested, have contributed to children's idealisation of their mothers.[19]

Nevertheless, many women must have found the heavy emphasis upon their maternal role constricting. Women could feel overwhelmed and angry by the regularity with which new babies could appear in their lives. Lady Eddisbury believed her baby's fatal illness to be a punishment for her reluctance to have another child; and most women were understandably frightened at the prospect of childbirth and its inherent risks. Significantly, fertility declined markedly among the landed classes from the 1830s. Mrs Stanley, anxious to procure a miscarriage, wrote to her husband triumphantly that, 'A hot bath, a tremendous walk & a great dose have succeeded.'[20] Such misgivings about the maternal role could, of course, be found across the class spectrum. Lawrencina Potter, was an intensely intellectual women who, resenting the demands of motherhood, much preferred to study in her room than to interact with her daughters.[21] The middle classes, however, did not begin to limit their families sizes until well into the second half of the century.

Household Management and Domesticity

The new significance ascribed to motherhood was symptomatic of a broader cultural development in which the home was portrayed as a female-built haven of domestic peace and order. Indeed, even single women were generally expected to conform to this pattern. They typically acted as housekeepers and family companions within kinship settings and it was only at the very end of this period that public discussion came to focus seriously on the issue of 'redundant' women.[22]

Such images of the domesticated female were widely used in discussions of the 'separate spheres' in which women's mission was to preside over a loving home, whilst men were to brave the vicissitudes and demands of public and business life. This ideology has been seen as an imprisoning discourse which sealed women's banishment from productive lives, condemning them to a restrictive role within the home.[23] However, it has been noted that the writings of Sarah Ellis (the classic exponent of the 'woman's mission' discourse) contained an empowering message for their female audience. Given women's lack of legal rights and independence, the language of women's domestic authority was critical in fostering female self-respect and functioned to re-establish a balance of power between husband and wife.[24] Furthermore, women's domestic role could have far-reaching implications. Discussions on the nature of household management have already illustrated the weight of women's domestic demands (see Chapter 4). But the way in which women managed their households could also have far wider significance. Stana Nenadic credits women with responsibility for the emergence of 'affectionate consumption', in which the exchange of birthday, anniversary and christenings gifts helped to shape the acquisitive elements of domestic culture.[25] Conversely, among some strata, women were critical in establishing a family's 'underconsumption', a frugality which enabled the fulfilment of social aspirations.[26]

More broadly, women's predominance in the home enabled them to play a major role in the articulation of contemporary ideologies. Women appear to have been particularly exercised in upholding the social and sexual values of their class. This was often connected to the primary importance religion played in the lives of (particularly middle-class) women. Religion formed not only a major social resource for women, it could also bite hard into their consciences. (This could be vital in helping them to come to terms with family disasters, such as infant bereavement.[27]) It was such behaviour as attention to religious observances, the niceties of household duty and the maintenance of social proprieties which enabled the construction of a self-conscious belief among the middle and ruling classes that they were the highest exemplars of civilised behaviour. This conviction fuelled imperial assumptions concerning the superiority of the British.[28]

The sense shared by many women, that they were the architects of the domestic space defining its proprieties and values, is also evident in those women who went with their husbands to the colonies. In even the most isolated and minimalist abode, the colonial wife felt it her role to attempt British domestic standards of cleanliness and propriety. As Georgiana Molloy recorded when stationed in Augusta, Fremantle, in the 1840s: 'Although the dining room has a clay floor and opens into the dairy, the thatch appears overhead and there is not a single pane of glass on the premises... our entertainment, the style of manners of our host and hostess, their dress and conversation all conspired to show that genuine good breeding and gentlemanly deportment are not always lost sight of among English emigrants.'[29]

Such examples suggest that the ubiquitous language of 'woman's mission' was not merely feeding upon simple, bland constructions of women's domestic roles. Rather, it was fuelling and responding to the multifarious identities with which women could understand their domestic life – as mothers, employers, arbiters of social behaviour or colonial pioneers.

Nevertheless, it would be equally misleading to suggest that all women found meaning and a sense of purpose within the domestic site. In addition to the frustrations which motherhood could arouse, many women articulated clearly their intense dissatisfaction with the domestic-orientated nature of their lives, (although this was less common among upper-class women whose lives were less closely tied to the home.) As the intellectually brilliant Caroline Cornwallis lamented: 'It is provoking to have one's heart in a Greek Lexicon while the rest of the body is super-intending the making of a pudding or roasting a fowl'.[30] Even in liberal families, progressive ideas concerning women's education rarely extended to a challenge of the gendered hierarchy within their own families. The ensuing conflicts were to spur many educated women to join the feminist movement.[31]

Sexual Behaviour

Many historians have emphasised the extent to which elite women could enjoy a considerable degree of sexual freedom (provided they were discrete and that they had first provided their husbands with heirs). The Prince of Wales, for example, had a succession of married, aristocratic lovers who derived power and prestige from their position.[32] However, it must be remembered that sexual licence was condoned only in the highest aristocratic circles. Even then, women who did seek extra-marital satisfaction could face severe penalties if the marriage broke down. Divorce could lead to social ostracism and the loss of contact with one's children. Judith Lewis cites the pathetic case of divorcee, Lady Elizabeth Webster, who staged a mock funeral for her little girl, in a vain attempt to clandestinely keep the child. Yet Lewis, in common with Jessica Gerard, has been at pains to stress that on the whole, upper-class women appear to have enjoyed good sexual relationships within marriage. It was commonplace for example, to engage in sexual intercourse during pregnancy.[33]

In the middle-classes a permissive attitude towards sexuality was confined to specific ideologically motivated groups, such as those inspired by Owenism or Fourierism; and in the coteries of metropolitan radicalism, there was also considerable deviation from the ideal of conjugal fidelity.[34] For the great majority of the middle classes (and the lesser gentry), female sexual propriety was heralded as essential to the maintenance of respectability and family welfare. This emerged clearly in middle-class responses to the Queen Caroline affair (see Chapter 2) which, according to Davidoff and Hall, represents, 'one of the first *public* moments at which one view of marriage and of sexuality was decisively rejected in favour of another', as domestic duties and responsibilities were celebrated.[35]

The widespread refusal to condone the King's sexual exploits during the Queen Caroline furore further indicates that the much debated 'double standard' – that men should be allowed a sexual freedom prohibited to women – was a deeply contested notion. The double standard was to be enshrined in the Divorce and Matrimonial Causes Act (1857) which stipulated that although a husband could divorce his adulterous wife; for a wife to obtain a divorce, she had to prove her husband guilty not only of adultery, but also of incest, bigamy, or cruelty.[36] (The 'justification' was that adultery on the part of a wife might result in an illegitimate child inheriting the property of the husband.) Nevertheless, among the middle classes, and especially those influenced by Evangelicalism, there appears to have been an expectation (however widely transgressed) that men should control their behaviour. When, during the debate over the bill, Lord Cranworth remarked that 'it would be harsh' to bring the law to bear against a husband who was 'a little profligate' it caused indignation in the press.[37] Discussions on female sexuality were equally multivalent. Whilst contemporary literature placed an enormous emphasis upon the value of female chastity, the debates surrounding the Divorce Act evinced a palpable concern as to the 'disruptive potential of female sexuality'.[38] Recent reinterpretations of Victorian sexuality have also noticed the extent to which female sexuality was recognised and discussed, particularly in medical literature.[39] Yet, sexual intercourse must have been at least problematic for scores of nineteenth-century women who had been reared to regard sex and sex education as taboo; and for whom years of pregnancy rendered intercourse unwelcome.

Many women rejected heterosexuality altogether, although further research is much needed. Lesbianism had not yet been categorised as a social deviancy, as was to happen in the 1880s, and 'female marriages' were not uncommon. Some women, such as the Yorkshire landowner, Anne Lister, who had passionate relationships with female friends, attracted some attention for her masculine dress. The Quaker scholar, Anna Gurney, lived contentedly with her self-termed 'partner', Sarah Buxton, for many years, an arrangement happily accepted by their extended family. One such relationship, between Lady Eleanor Butler and Sarah Ponsonby, was feted by contemporary celebrities as an interesting curiosity rather than a moral outrage.[40]

Women's Experience of Marriage

As the discussion on courtship behaviour demonstrated, it was usually assumed that marriages would be formed on the basis of affection and trust, if not love. Such assumptions were beginning to have an impact upon behaviour, even in the highest aristocratic circles by 1860. In any case, the combination of mutual respect, prudence and realistic expectations which lay behind many an aristocratic marriage meant that they tended to work well. Throughout the period, warm marital relationships are frequently in evidence in this social strata. Lady Stanley lamented her 'cold bed', during her husband's absence, even after 20 years of marriage.[41] Of course, affectionate marriages might still consign women to a subordinate role and, needless to say, unhappy relationships were far from uncommon. Nevertheless, as noted in Chapter 4, Kim Reynolds has stressed the pervasive sense of partnership in landed marriages.[42] Furthermore, individual relationships with their infinite variations of personalities, backgrounds and ideological convictions could modify the impact of cultural pressures. Lady Shelley observed that Lady Jersey, 'tyrannised over her husband, who, adoring his commanding wife, almost trembled in her presence, and certainly never ventured to oppose her opinions'.[43] The redoubtable Bridget Widdowson, who terrified the Indian mutineers she was given to guard during the siege of Cawnpore, would probably never have fitted neatly into the mould of the acquiescent wife.[44] The existence of dominant wives was frequently acknowledged by contemporaries. Electoral canvassers noted that it was sometimes necessary to exert political pressure upon a wife, rather than her husband, as the 'wife wears the breeches'.[45]

Yet men reared to a notion of their own superiority could prove to be domineering and exacting husbands. Most historians are agreed that the majority of men accepted the prevailing understanding of marriage, in which the husband was to rule, albeit benignly, over his wife and children.[46] The Bradford manufacturer, Isaac Holden, was swift to upbraid his wife for her want of submission following a letter in which he felt she had addressed him in too peremptory a tone.[47] The authority assumed by husbands may have derived added weight from the fact that they tended to be older than their wives. In Davidoff and Hall's sample of middle-class families, 73 per cent of husbands were older than their wives by an average of 4.3 years.[48] Whilst there were obvious economic reasons for a man to delay marriage until he felt himself to be suitably financially placed, women's preference for older husbands may indicate a subtle internalisation of the idea that they should look up to their spouses. From infancy most girls were trained to put the interests of their brothers first. Except for the wealthy, girls' education was likely be home-based, whereas parents would aspire to send boys to school.[49] Girls' sheltered upbringing, it has been argued, may have inhibited sentiments of independence and made women more likely to perceive themselves as 'inferior' creatures, who had to depend upon the wisdom and experience of their husbands.[50] Yet the efforts of women to further their education, and create their own networks of intellectual support, indicates the self-respect and confidence frequently possessed by elite and middle-class women. They commonly established their own book clubs, attended public lectures and, as we have seen, instituted their own philanthropic societies. These avenues for female sociability, as well as visiting and tea and card parties, were important in creating alternative sources of personal support, leisure opportunities and space from the demands of domesticity. Women's private lives were not determined solely by their interaction with male relations.[51]

Women's Legal Position

Further insights into women's lives within marriage may be gained from an analysis of their legal position.[52] Under common law, once a woman married she became a 'feme covert'. All her personal property became her husband's and any freehold land passed into his possession; a married women was not even able to enter into contracts. (Although in Scotland, spouses held joint ownership in household goods.[53]) Until 1839, when, largely thanks to Caroline Norton's spirited campaign, the Infants' Custody Act gave women some limited rights to the access of young children, wives were denied custody of their children.[54] A husband could legally enforce his wife to live with him, even if this should necessitate her virtual imprisonment. The prevalence of informal separations is difficult to ascertain, but divorce, as we have seen, was extremely difficult to obtain if the marriage broke down, and, until 1857, separated women might still have their earnings and property taken by their husbands. In Ireland, custom permitted a 'country divorce', whereby a childless wife might be banished from the marital home and sent back to her family.[55]

Under the system of equity, however, women could enjoy much greater rights as property could be put under the direction of a male trustee for the woman's use. Women's financial freedom varied from case to case, however. Kim Reynolds has observed that upper-class women were often unable to raise ready cash and might be dependent upon a quarterly allowance from their husbands.[56]

In theory, then, particularly for those whose property was not protected by an equitable trust, marriage entailed a complete loss of women's legal identity. To what extent women felt themselves to be oppressed by these laws in practice, is of course, harder to ascertain. Patricia Branca is uncompromising on this point, declaring that 'Many of the legal rights of the husband were merely theoretical and never exercised in the great majority of middle-class homes.'[57] Given the enormous complexities of their legal situation, of which only a limited summary has been given above, it is possible that even the well-informed might not be fully aware of all the ramifications of the law. Two highly educated women, Harriet Grote and Millicent Garrett Fawcett, were astonished to find that when their purses were stolen, the items were described in court as being the property of their husbands.[58] Furthermore, James Hammerton has discovered that many business women displayed a blatant disregard (or ignorance) of the law in refusing to give up their property to their husbands.[59] Certainly, one of the early feminists' concerns was to raise women's awareness of their legal position.[60] Yet, it seems highly probable that in some sectors women had a reasonable working knowledge of the law. Maxine Berg's study of the wills of metalworkers in Sheffield and Birmingham in the eighteenth century revealed a widespread use of equitable trusts among small and middling manufacturing families. She reaches the important conclusion that, 'Women were not subordinated to their husband's control over property as the legal texts implied.' Women demonstrated a readiness to set up equitable trusts and both owned and bequeathed significant quantities of real property.[61]

Berg's research concentrates predominantly upon widows and spinsters in the pre-1800 period. As such, her findings do not wholly counteract the work of feminist scholars who have argued that over the 1780–1850 period, equitable trusts were increasingly used not to safeguard women's property, but to provide protected liquid capital for their husbands' business ventures. The common insertion of clauses to prevent women from selling their property has led to the depiction of women's financial status as passive carriers of property.[62] The considerable involvement of women in family businesses (see Chapter 4) may require us to qualify such pessimism, however.

In addition, recent research has highlighted another aspect of women's economic activity – their exploitation of the law of agency. The law of agency assumed a wife to be acting as her husband's agent and so could pledge his credit for the purchase of household 'necessaries'. It is evident from the litigation arising from such cases that contemporaries understood women to be acting as economic agents in their own right and therefore, 'at the level of much day-to-day life, the law of coverture is best described as existing in a state of suspended animation.'[63] As Amanda Vickery has lately demonstrated, women were active and lively consumers during this period, enjoying a range of shopping and leisure activities, particularly in the burgeoning urban culture of the day.[64]

For those who were widowed, such activities could be drastically curtailed. Again, this is an area where more research is greatly needed. However, widowhood could be a catastrophic event – financially, as well as personally. Pat Jalland has conveyed sensitively the profound shock of widowhood for nineteenth-century women. The cumbersome apparel of 'widow's weeds' was a visual signifier of the change in status wrought by widowhood.[65] The position of wives of professional men may have been particularly difficult as they were not able to continue their husbands' work. However, as Chapter 4 indicated, a considerable number, particularly in the lower middle or upper classes, would take over their husbands' business or the family estate. This may have been immensely stressful, but it is possible that some may have found that in the long term, it enhanced their self-esteem and confidence.

Conclusion

Domestic ideology was a predominant feature of early Victorian discourse. Yet, to present it as unassailable would be wholly inaccurate. It was never widely applicable to the lives of landed families; nor was it appropriate for lower-middle-class women who made a substantial contribution to the family's financial well-being. Even among the middle and upper middle classes, there were competing versions of the ideology. If, for some, such cultural pressures were stifling and restrictive, propelling them into the early women's rights movement; the majority appear to have invested their domestic-orientated lives with a plethora of political, religious, imperial and social meanings. Family life and marriage constituted not only the affective and bodily needs of women; they also formed the springboard for their contribution to early Victorian culture.

PART III
WORKING-CLASS WOMEN, 1860–1900

7

WORK

Introduction

In her study *Women in Industry* at the turn of the twentieth century the civil servant, Clara Collet, concluded that, 'In the past half century there has been no real invasion of industry generally by women, but rather a withdrawal from it.'[1] Census figures corroborate a pattern of steady decline in female economic participation. Thirty-one per cent of English and Welsh women were recorded as working in 1871 – a figure that went down to 27 per cent in 1891 and 26 per cent in 1911.[2] The expansion of heavy industries, particularly steel, iron and shipbuilding during the second half of the century, relied predominantly upon male labour and offered few opportunities to women.[3] Indeed, it has been argued that the brunt of the country's advancing industrialisation was born by women who suffered chronic underemployment in many regions.[4] While in Ireland, the economic position of women is thought to have declined dramatically as they lost their place in the labour market and became increasingly dependent upon male relatives.[5]

Cultural pressures were also militating against the employment of women. This period witnessed gathering restrictions on the hours and postnatal employment of women in many industries. The successive Factory and Workshops Acts of 1874 and 1878, for example, reduced women's work from 60 to 54 hours a week. The atmosphere was such that even the secretary of the Women's Trade Union League could argue for the 'gradual extension of labour protection to the point where mothers will be prohibited from working until their children have reached an age at which they can care for themselves'.[6] Yet this period also saw the rise of new job opportunities for working-class women in the fields of clerical work, teaching and retail. This chapter seeks to capture women's own reaction to these divergent discourses and trends, whilst also emphasising the extent to which paid employment remained central to the lives of women, and the formation of women's identities, in many sectors and regions.

Home-Based Work and Hand Manufacture

It has recently been suggested by Joanna Bourke that the trend for working women to eschew paid labour should be viewed as a rational choice, designed to optimise the comfort and resources of the working-class family. By staying at home, those above the poverty line could minimise the hidden costs of women's full-time work by baking their own bread, keeping clothes in good repair and caring for their children.[7] As one contemporary report into rural women observed: 'They seem to be arriving at the conviction that where a cottage is to be kept clean and tidy, and a family provided for, ... the money she can earn by going into the fields is insufficient to compensate her.'[8] The desire to give up paid employment is certainly understandable, for household work was in itself extremely onerous for women of this class. The difficulties of cleaning and washing for large families, when few working-class homes had even the luxury of running water and many had to cope with the most basic of cooking facilities, were considerable; and, as research into miners' wives in the Rhondda valley has revealed, could have a devastating impact upon women's health.[9]

Nevertheless, Bourke argues that women's full-time investment in domestic work both facilitated the rise in living standards among the higher strata of the British working class, and enabled women to construe the domestic space as their own arena of skilled work (see also Chapter 9). This thesis is an important corrective to those studies which imply that working-class women were a subordinate strata which capitulated to oppressive cultural mores during this period.[10]

It is necessary to point out two issues, however. Firstly, the census data, upon which this argument is based, is highly unreliable and exaggerates the trend towards domesticity. Eleanor Gordon, for example, has discovered that in some regions of Scotland, married women working in the woollen mills were listed simply as 'wives' in the census records. The census only recorded an individual's occupation for that night, thus occluding part-time, temporary, casual or seasonal work –

categories into which women's labour frequently fell.[11] Consequently, the census statistics also obscure the extent to which those who decided to remain at home were still expected to contribute to the family economy during times of hardship. Moreover, for those in the unskilled sectors of the working-class, full-time domesticity was rarely an option. One survey of working households in 1911 revealed that only about 5 per cent of unskilled workers' households could survive on the man's wages alone.[12] Despite the aspirations of the upper working classes, then, women's paid employment remained essential to the viability of the majority of working-class households. Staying at home may have begun to form a component of respectability for upper-working-class women in some regions, but even then women's paid labour formed an important reserve during times of financial difficulty.

For married women the family budget might be topped up by a range of sporadic and intermittent chores. These frequently revolved around either domestic skills – perhaps child-minding, taking in lodgers, sewing or washing; or retailing. The very poorest, usually elderly women, might resort to hawking wares in an attempt to earn just enough to keep them from the workhouse. Others could bake pies for busy local factory workers; whilst those with greater financial resources might set up a small shop (as did many Jewish immigrants in Manchester for example). Those with successful ventures might go on to act as informal money lenders to the neighbourhood.[13]

Such economic initiative served to underline the importance of women within local communities. Nevertheless, the range of money-making options was strongly influenced by local economic circumstances. For a majority of women their geographical location, combined with their child-care responsibilities; or the aspiration to stay at home; meant that home-working was the most likely option. Even in the second part of the nineteenth century, hand-based manufacture within the home remained of vital economic importance. Cottage trades (such as straw-plaiting in Buckinghamshire and Bedfordshire, embroidery in County Donegal or glove-making in many southern English counties) persisted throughout the period. More typically, however, northern English trades such as hosiery and footwear remained home-based until the 1870s and 1880s, when they, too, began to move into the factories. Yet as older cottage industries became displaced in this way, new trades could develop in their wake, soaking up the reservoir of cheap female labour. In High Wycombe, as the cottage lace-making industry was squeezed out by competition, women took up chair-caning, for example.

In London a whole variety of trades proliferated, from the making of umbrellas, tennis balls and artificial flowers to the unpleasant grind of sack-stitching and of course, clothing. Many trades such as matchbox-making involved simple, repetitive labour (in which children often assisted); but some of the domestic handicrafts involved a considerable degree of (unrecognised) skilled labour. A minority of women labouring in these industries might work in small workshops where they enjoyed the status and pay derived from making a product from start to finish. Most, however, were on piece rates, working in deskilled trades on a subcontracted basis. Wages for home-work were chronically depressed and fell continually in value between 1870 and 1890, a factor which led to its reputation as 'sweated' work. In the provinces remuneration was even worse than in the metropolis, with innovations such as the spread of the sewing machine from the 1850s failing to alter the status or pay of those engaged in clothing manufacture.[14]

It was not easy for workers to challenge the exploitative nature of this sporadic and casual work. Working within one's own home made it difficult to develop a sense of comradeship with fellow workers. This exasperated sectors of the unionised workforce, whose pay bargaining position was greatly weakened by the existence of cheap female out-workers. As an organisation of Scottish tailors dramatically pleaded to the Women's Trade Union League: 'Please send an organizer at once, for our Amalgamated Society has decided that if the women of this town cannot be organized, they must be exterminated.'[15] The trade union movement had been greatly strengthened since the 1870s with legisla-tion to protect funds and to legalise peaceful picketing and strikes. The following decade saw the rise of 'new unionism' – with the organisation of unskilled, low-pay workers. The most famous female illustration of this was the Matchmakers' Strike of 1888. Such success stories remained largely the exception, however. The Women's Protective and Provident League succeeded in encouraging the formation of several unions, for example, amongst the boot- and umbrella-makers; but these were invariably short-lived as they were too weak financially to survive dur-ing times of strikes or hardship. Despite a revived interest in the plight of home-workers following the Royal Commission on the Housing of the Working Classes (1884–5) and the Select Committee Report on the Sweating System (1888), home-working remained outside the remit of effective legislation until the twentieth century.[16]

Home-working also impacted negatively upon the lives of workers and their families, who might be obliged to work in the same room in which they also ate and perhaps slept. For those engaged in such tasks as fur-pulling, to home discomfort was added serious medical hazards. Feminist analysts argue that herein lies the irony of sweated work. Women accepted home-work because it enabled them to conform to a particular model of motherhood. The reality of home-working, however, was that women had to work chronically long hours, whilst jeopardising their health and that of their children.[17]

Similar problems beset those who turned to laundry work to make up the shortfall in the family budget. The second half of the nineteenth century witnessed a massive expansion in the demand for laundry services – a consequence of the enormous growth in the country's service industries and infrastructure. Restaurants and hotels, as well as the mushrooming of schools, colleges and universities, all fed the demand for laundry workers. The number of recorded laundry workers leapt from 167 607 in 1861 to 205 015 in 1901. Home-based laundry work could be a convenient option, requiring minimal outlay to set oneself up in business, but it was exhausting work with backbreaking hours. Labouring as the chief breadwinners (their husbands tended to be underemployed or seasonal workers), laundry women developed a reputation for hard-drinking and a tough persona. Yet such identities were fluid. Laundry work was largely seasonal, being triggered by the demands of the university term, or the holiday season, and taken up during times of personal hardship.[18]

Prostitution

In many cities and ports, impoverished women chose prostitution in order to make up the shortfall in their income. Prostitution held an enduring fascination in the Victorian public imagination, capturing as it did the very antithesis of cultural proscriptions of refined and pure womanhood. Feminists frequently conveyed prostitutes as victims, seeing them as the epitome of society's patriarchal sexual hierarchy; and rescue workers and campaigners tended to dwell upon the heartbreaking misery and sense of sin which wracked many they sought to help. Prostitutes could be more pragmatic about their situation, however, presenting the sex trade as a rational decision they had made in the context of their economic options. Nevertheless, successive legislation made the position of the prostitute increasingly difficult. As well as humiliating women and restricting their civil rights, the effect of the Contagious Diseases Acts (1864 and 1866) was to stigmatise prostitutes and to make it less likely that women might turn to prostitution as a short-term remedy. The gathering strength of the social purity movement (see Chapter 11) also resulted in considerable intolerance towards prostitutes. In particular, the crack down on brothels in the Criminal Law Amendment Act of 1885 forced many women to work under the cover of pimps, which could greatly increase their exploitation.[19]

Women such as prostitutes, home-workers and those making ends meet through various domestic-based activities were among the most exploited workers in the Victorian labour market. As workers meeting the sporadic, socio-economic, sexual, domestic and consumer demands of society they appear to have perceived their labour as a necessary, if often grim, strategy which would enable them to earn much-needed money whilst continuing to fulfil other domestic responsibilities.

Factory Work and Heavy Industry

By the end of the century more than half a million women were working in factories.[20] Factory workers in late Victorian Britain benefited from government legislation which established stricter controls over working hours and conditions. On the whole, this is a process which appears to have been welcomed by workers. Women in the larger, mechanised laundrettes mounted an impressive and ultimately successful campaign to be included in the 1891 Factory and Workshops Act.[21] However, women tended to profit comparatively little from increasing mechanisation. In the clothing trades, the introduction of machinery was, technically speaking, what differentiated a factory from a workshop. Yet the appallingly low wages meant that 'sweated labour' was just as much a problem in the factory environment.[22] Moreover, studies of women's employment in the fields of bookbinding and printing have concluded that mechanisation only brought opportunities for women's labour as unskilled or semi-skilled machine operators. As the contemporary manager of a periodicals firm asserted: 'If the machine is large and complicated, men will replace women, if it is small and simple, women will replace men.'[23]

Complex ideological factors construed what might be defined as 'skilled' work. In the chocolate factories of Bristol and Birmingham, female workers were confined to wrapping and packing goods. The mixing of the cocoa was deemed to be a skilled job which required male labour.[24] Broadly speaking, men tended to be identified with science, machines and progress; women with nature, instinct and tradition. Given these ideological barriers, it proved almost impossible for women to advance up the promotion ladders of industrial companies. In most industries, only men were given opportunities to train as machine tuners (and thus could rise to supervisory positions). This created, as Sonya Rose observes, a 'self-fulfilling prophecy' that women were less competent with machinery than men.[25]

However, unskilled work did not invariably equate with low levels of job-satisfaction (although this must have often been the case). The 'pit brow lasses', who were involved chiefly in preparing coal for transportation, stoked fierce controversy in the 1880s. Their labour was depicted, in both the daily press and union propaganda, as improper and 'unsexing'. Yet pit brow women hung fast to their individuality and femininity, adorning their heavy-duty work clothes with jewellery and brightly coloured shirts. And, in contrast to prevailing middle-class opinion (and rather in the face of the industry's health and safety record), colliery women themselves liked to argue that their outdoor, strenuous labour was healthy and invigorating.[26]

Equally, it would be wrong to cast too crude an impression of the invariably unskilled nature of female work. In many industrial sectors, women valued their technical skill and the consequent social and economic status it brought. If female ring spinners and cardroom workers comprised a subordinate and exploited part of the textile workforce, the same cannot be said for weavers. Weaving was considered as skilled work – a fact of fundamental importance to the construction of weavers' personal identities. In Dundee, the female weavers signalled their sense of superiority over spinners by wearing hats and gloves to work – a sign of their respectability.[27] If a weaver's skill was called into question, it could have devastating personal and emotional consequences, as the analysis of inquests into suicides among this strata has suggested.[28]

In many sectors women evidently enjoyed the comparative independence their employment entailed. Interviews with elderly cotton workers in Lancashire in 1913 revealed that they chose to continue working in the factory because of their liking for the job, its sociability and for the financial awards it brought – *not* because their families were financially dependent upon it.[29] A female subculture often developed in the mills and factories, with women learning lip-reading and developing sign language to overcome the noise of the machinery. Similar evidence of female occupational identification has been found for women engaged in chain-making in the Black Country. The physical stamina required, combined with the evident importance of women's economic contribution to the local community, endowed the women with a positive self-image and liking for their work.[30] In the Potteries, the skilled work performed by large numbers of female employees became woven into local cultural expectations of women's roles, one factory inspector noting that a woman was 'looked upon as lazy unless she takes her share in contributing to the family income'.[31] Indeed, although a number of individual factories were beginning to impose a marriage bar, this was far from universal. In the Macclesfield silk industry and the Dundee jute industry, for example, married women accounted for approximately one-third of the female workforce by the end of the century.[32]

Nevertheless, working mothers with young children faced a renewed barrage of criticism from the medical and political establishment during the last quarter of the century. An Act of 1891 made it illegal for employers knowingly to employ any woman within four weeks of having a baby – a law which was evaded, in large numbers, by the women themselves.[33]

Another striking aspect of factory work, and in particular textile factory work, was that this, more than any other form of employment, was successful in unionising women. Five-sixths of the considerable increase in female union membership which occurred during this period (rising from 37 000 in 1886 to 118 000 in 1906) was drawn from the textile industries.[34] In the Dundee jute industry, women fought strenuously for their own needs to be recognised by the local unions. With women's pay nationally averaging 42 per cent of that of men, wage increases were a top priority for many female workers. Dundee union officials were particularly angered that women's protests were usually unofficial and spontaneous. They frequently involved harassing employers, and tended to merge into local night life, with singing, dancing and drinking. The existence of this alternative female subculture of industrial and leisure activities may well have stemmed from the female camaraderie born in the local factories. With men profiting from alternative employment in heavy industry, there was little tradition of familial supervision in the factories.[35] By contrast, Lancashire men continued to play a significant role as spinners and overseers, and traditions of kinship supervision persisted. Here trade union activity was marked by far greater gender collaboration.

Trade union membership was not always an empowering experience for women. They could be pressured into membership by male kin, and might find their own needs and experiences ignored in male-dominated organisations.[36] At the national level women still battled against the fears and prejudices of the Trade Union Congress, where they rarely had a voice. Female representatives from the cotton textile unions had to fight hard to resist calls for the imposition of marriage bars.[37] Furthermore, many of the all-women unions established during this period owed a considerable debt to essentially middle-class organisations such as the Women's Trade Union League, which did not necessarily represent accurately the needs or views of working-class members.[38] However, within trade unionism there were significant localised successes (particularly among weavers), which enabled women to enjoy a sense of control over their labour experiences and also had important implications for their political engagement. Women formed two-thirds of the massive Northern Counties Amalgamated Association of Cotton Weavers; and in some localities, as in Oldham and Wigan, their predominance resulted in union management.[39]

Agriculture

According to the census, by the middle of the century, there were but 229 000 women engaged in agriculture, a figure which drops to an extraordinary low of 86 000 by 1901.[40] Whilst there does appear to have been a real decline in female agricultural labour in certain regions, this is but part of the story. Some census clerks were instructed that only men should be counted as *farm* servants. This confusion led to serious miscalculations in the census. Eleanor Gordon has calculated that 'it is possible that as late as 1891 as much as 20 per cent of the female labour force were employed in agriculture in Scotland, compared with the census figure of 5.1 per cent.'[41] Moreover considerable amounts of agricultural work, particularly during harvest time, was undertaken by cheap, casual labour, such as provided by Irish migrants, labour which tended to bypass the census forms.[42]

Whilst developments in agricultural practice, such as steam ploughing and the introduction of the reaper and binder, reduced the call for female and juvenile labour, it was not until the end of the century that machinery began to make a real impact on farming methods.[43] Agriculture therefore remained a labour-intensive process and women (especially farm labourers' wives) continued to be employed extensively, if sporadically, on farms throughout Scotland, Ireland, Wales and northern England. The nature of women's engagement still remained largely dictated by local custom. In Northumberland, the practice of employing female bondagers persisted well into the 1880s; although in Scotland the bondage system had evolved into a means of familial hire by this period. Despite the legislative restrictions placed on gang labour in 1867, the practice persisted in sparsely populated, corn-growing areas, such as the eastern English counties. In Cardigan, girls were trained in farm work and were given particular responsibility for cattle. Women's employment also remained vital to the rural economy of coastal areas, where they might repair fishing nets, or collect mussels and cockles, as in coastal Lancashire.[44]

Despite their evident utility, farming women faced considerable pressure to cease their work. Farm labour, like pit brow employment, was deemed to be dirty, hard work which fitted ill with contemporary stereotypes of femininity. The National Agricultural Labourers' Union, resenting the practice of hiring cheap female labour, made frequent calls for women to be prohibited from field work. Despite these pressures, it is evident that large sectors of the female population both relied upon farm work and derived some sense of collective identity from it. There are many cases of women uniting together in strike action in an attempt to raise their wage levels, as happened in Oxfordshire in 1867.[45]

Domestic Service

For the majority of middle-class observers, domestic service remained the most fitting employment for young working-class women. The desire to create dutiful servants, which emerges in the literature of countless philanthropic societies, illustrated a patent desire to control and tame plebeian women.[46] This was clearly understood by working-class women themselves, who manifested growing distaste for such employment. An impoverished needleworker was characteristically insulted when offered a position as a maid by a sympathetic American journalist: 'I go out to service! I wear caps and aprons, those badges of slavery! No, thank you. I prefer to keep my liberty and be independent.'[47] Such sentiments were particularly common among urban women, who had the most to gain from the mounting opportunities for leisure and mobility, brought about by buses, bicycles and trains. Despite this, domestic service remained the biggest employer of women, with numbers rising dramatically from 751 541 in 1851 to 1 386 167 in 1891 (although the figures included those performing domestic services for family members, and, as we have seen, many agricultural labourers also).[48]

As in the earlier period, the nature of domestic service varied tremendously from household to household; although, generally speaking, servants' right to time off became more established and accommodation more comfortable. Those employed by the landed or upper middle classes, might benefit from better living quarters and food, but employers of this strata were likely to expect a higher degree of subordination. The lower servants, performing the more menial tasks, might be permitted little contact with the higher-paid 'upper servants' who tended to their employers' personal needs. The upper servants were often career servants, who expected to spend most of their working life in domestic service, spending considerable time with each employer. In these situations, employees, who had clearly defined responsibilities, might take a considerable pride in their work. William Lanceley recalled the head housemaid in his place of employment, who had been with the family for 30 years and 'would allow nobody to handle the plates and dishes, but washed and wiped them herself and she alone would carry them to the dining-room door.'[49]

It is such identification with the needs and values of their employers which has led some historians to portray servants as an inherently conservative force. They are accredited, for example, with transmitting middle- and upper-class values to their own families.[50] However, the majority of servants, working in less exclusive establishments, tended to view service very differently. For these women, service was a stop-gap, which would usually end with marriage (although married 'daily' servants were increasingly common by the end of the century). Servants in these situations were not necessarily confined to domestic labour, but would, where appropriate, be expected to assist with the productive labour of the household.[51] Rather than developing enduring ties of loyalty towards their employers, the majority of servants moved frequently from one household to another to find the best situation. An official survey in 1899 revealed that a third of all servants in England and Wales had been in their post for less than a year.[52] In the absence of unionisation, mobility enabled servants to register dissatisfaction with an employer. Domestic servants might be in a subordinate position, but this does not mean to say that they were passive conduits for alien values and ideologies. As the diaries of Hannah Cullwick suggest, servants could prove to be both stubborn and recalcitrant towards their employers, and derive satisfaction from their manual work. Indeed, Cullwick appears to have perceived her situation as liberating when compared to the constraints of middle-class femininity.[53]

'White-Collar' Work

The expansion of state education during the second half of the nineteenth century enabled many working-class girls to move into new areas of employment. In 1876 school attendance until the age of 10 years old was made obligatory, rising to 11 years in 1893 and then to 14 years in 1899. The mores of both parents and establishment educationists frequently worked to circumscribe the effect of this legislation, however. Mothers commonly expected their daughters to miss school to lend domestic assistance. Such experiences might discourage girls from valuing their education and reinforce the cultural identification of women as home-makers. As Mrs Layton recalled: 'My fourth sister and I always stayed away from school on washing day to mind the babies.'[54] In many families, girls were pressured to leave school as early as possible so that they might contribute to the family economy (although many evidently felt pride in their new position as wage-earners) and local exemptions in some industrial areas permitted the half-day release of children from school in order to work. Furthermore, the nature of the school curriculum, which focused increasingly upon the acquisition of domestic skills for girls, militated against the provision of a more rigorous academic education. In 1876 domestic economy was made a compulsory girls' subject in schools receiving a state grant.[55]

Nevertheless, for those with supportive, or more prosperous backgrounds, there were growing avenues for educated working-class girls. The growth in retail services provided just such an opportunity. The number of shops increased by 56 per cent between 1875 and 1907[56] – a phenomenon particularly evident in the major cities, where the high street and the large department store were becoming an established part of urban topography. This created a massive demand for female shop assistants, usually drawn from the upper working or lower middle classes. Many young women (they were usually expected to resign their position on marriage) found such work greatly preferable to the monotony and isolation of domestic service. None the less, a considerable degree of formality was expected in the large city stores, and their lives were compared unfavourably with those of factory workers by contemporary investigators.[57] Levels of pay were low, and women earned only 60–65 per cent of their male peers' wages. The larger shops often insisted that their junior staff live in lodgings provided by the firm. These were run on a profit-making basis and severely hampered the personal lives and freedom of the workforce.[58]

The retailing industry also developed gender-specific employment practices which served to restrict and stereotype female employees. In the grocery outlets, customary female chores such as preserving and serving food, became defined as skilled work, to be undertaken by men after a lengthy apprenticeship. As a group of male colleagues complained to Linda McCullough, on her first day at a co-operative store, 'Grocering is a man's job. It's a skilled job.' Employment in the luxury shops selling jewellery, wines or fine books similarly remained male preserves. No such anxieties were raised about women working in the lower-status outlets such as tobacconists, bakeries and stationers.[59] Yet, at a time when respectability was an important component of working-class femininities, to work in a shop, notwithstanding these detractions, might still enhance women's self-esteem and their status within the community. Despite the egalitarian framework of the National Union of Shop Assistants, female shopworkers do not appear to have taken an active role in trade unionism during this period. However, women could find their own ways to subvert authority. Elizabeth Roberts notes that some employees developed their own strategies of covert workplace resistance, by making personal use of the firm's goods, for example.[60]

For those with greater educational skills, it was increasingly possible to find employment in clerical work. The proliferation of business interests required more clerks to process their activities; and the burgeoning functions of government necessitated a large, efficient civil service. The Post Office also mushroomed during this period, spurred on by the adoption of new inventions such as the telegraph and the telephone. All these innovations were to require an army of administrative staff and the development of complicated bureaucratic structures. The introduction of female office staff was mediated through highly gendered management strategies, however. Both for reasons of propriety and the need to placate threatened male clerical workers, job segregation was the norm in most of the larger establishments. The containment of women in routine functions, such as filing and typing, enabled employers to justify wide discrepancies in salaries between the sexes. Even when women and men were working in the same department, men would typically be allocated the more challenging tasks. Hence male telegraphists would be required to deal with long-distance calls and to operate the busiest circuits.[61] Most employers operated a marriage bar, requiring women to resign (albeit with a dowry) upon marriage. This effectively removed the incentive for employers to invest in training for young female clerks, and laid the way for a vast, readily renewable pool of cheap, young workers. (In 1911, two-thirds of all women clerks were under 25 years old.[62])

However, Meta Zimmeck argues that clerical work was enormously popular amongst women because it was well-paid, respectable and comfortable. Female clerical work may have been a means of deskilling the once prestigious post of clerk or secretary, but Meta Zimmeck sees female clerks as an active, assertive group of employees, keen to push forward their own rights and demands. They were adept at assessing the merits of different positions and would change jobs to find the conditions of service which best suited them, enjoying the comfort and respectability of clerical work.[63]

The other major 'white-collar' job open to working-class women was teaching. The number of female teachers rose dramatically during this period, from around 80 000 in 1861 to 172 000 in 1901.[64] Only a third of women teachers had formal teacher training in 1914 (although the majority had passed a qualifying examination), indicating that it was not a prohibitively difficult profession to enter.[65] Most came into the profession by training as a pupil teacher. This entailed a five-year apprenticeship, requiring considerable dedication, starting when the girl was 12 or 13. For the daughters of skilled workers it was sometimes possible to attend one of the new teacher training colleges, but this would have been beyond the means of labouring families. Oral evidence suggests that mothers were often responsible for encouraging their daughters to teach, for this was perceived as a secure – and most importantly, a respectable – profession which would ensure personal independence and a pension.[66] However, the introduction of a payment-by-results scheme in 1862 did much to lower staff morale; added to which teachers with working-class backgrounds could experience problems of social identity. One school inspector reported that the working-class teacher was 'separated...from the class to which she had originally belonged, while it did not bring her socially into contact with a different class'.[67] Teaching, none the less, remained one of the best employment options for bright and confident young working-class women.

Nursing was also increasingly seen as a respectable possibility for women of this class. The growing professionalisation of the medical body; advances in the understanding of disease; and improved diagnostic and curative skills all contributed to a desperate need for higher nursing standards. By the turn of the century there were around 64 000 nurses and midwives.[68] However, Florence Nightingale was not alone in asserting the importance of *ladies* in the profession, not least for their moral influence. (An exception was Ellen Ranyard's bible-nurses, who were employed both for religious and therapeutic reasons in the East End of London.[69]) Consequently, both in civilian and military hospitals, working-class nurses were treated as subordinates, with little hope of advancement. As in the earlier period, many women earned a living as midwives (often doubling as abortionists) for their local communities. By the end of the century there was increasing legislative pressure for trained and qualified nurses to replace the pool of self-taught midwives. Particularly motivated working-class women did seek to conform to the new standards, but in many working-class districts, traditional midwives, with their sensitivities to working-class needs, were still preferred.[70]

Conclusion

The employment of working-class women during the second half of the nineteenth century is testament to the continuing traditionalism of vast sectors of the British economy. As Ann Oakley has observed, 'In 1851, 1881 and 1891, the majority of wage-earning women were still in the same occupations as 1841', with female labour clustering in the domestic-related work of service, laundry, needlework and cleaning.[71] The tendency of women to perceive work as a temporary measure – either before marriage or during times of family hardship, and their consequent reluctance to join trade unions has been commonly assumed to have militated against women's identification as workers. Yet, as this chapter has shown, such an analysis does not hold true across all industrial sectors and geographical regions. In some situations, women's employment encouraged greater self-confidence, and at times enhanced their social status within their own communities. For many, their economic activities served to underline the crucial input of women into the fabric of neighbourhood life – as carers, nurses and retailers. Undoubtedly, employment opportunities were circumscribed – even the new avenues in white-collar work served to further entrench narrow definitions of gender capabilities; and the exploitation of scores of 'sweated labourers' should not be forgotten. Nevertheless, employment experiences and the construction of gender were not static and monolithic. Local circumstances and traditions fostered a proliferation of alternative practices and perceptions regarding women's work. The personal and social consequences of employment varied enormously, and a significant minority seem to have viewed their work positively.

8

POLITICS, COMMUNITY AND PROTEST

Introduction

It has been assumed that women's apparent acquiescence in new patterns of gender relations had, by mid-century, effectively silenced working women's potential for political activism.[1] Brian Harrison has suggested that women's housekeeping role moulded their political outlook, rendering them almost unconsciously right wing and politically apathetic.[2] Women's mass participation in politics is usually considered to have re-emerged towards the end of the century, when socialism and suffragism enticed women into political activity once more. However, as Chapter 2 indicated, it is highly questionable whether women's political involvement had ground to a halt by the mid-century. Recent studies have been at pains to stress the continuities of working-class politics during these years.[3] This chapter adopts a similar approach to women's political engagement, noting also the new perspectives which emerge by paying greater attention to the experience of Irish, Scottish and Welsh women. It also considers the degree to which familial, and even leisure pursuits, should not be divorced from political analyses, but could be closely implicated in women's political consciousness.

Community and Continuities

Women's involvement in community affairs was central to their public and private identities. Without wishing to romanticise a simple model of community goodwill, women's role in fostering relationships with neighbours and family members enabled them to construct networks

111

of reciprocal assistance and sharing. Working-class communities could also structure plebeian values and contest the distribution or abuse of power within the neighbourhood. For example, men who beat their wives could face fierce community condemnation.[4] Such community pressures were often linked with 'traditional' forms of protest. This was the case in Wales, where the *ceffyl pren* (a wooden horse or pole used in demonstrations of 'rough music') conveyed hostility towards the transgression of community norms, such as wife-beating or adultery. The practice was also resorted to during strikes, or tithe disputes. Women's participation in the *ceffyl pren* did decline significantly during the second half of the century, but it remained a form of protest used by both sexes into the twentieth century.[5]

This example illustrates the extent to which women's involvement in protest could be linked to community issues of perceived justice. This was particularly so in Ireland, where food riots continued to occur during times of dearth.[6] English colliery women also mobilised over the issue of food prices, although, interestingly, their actions demonstrate a blend of 'traditional' actions with evolved methods of political activity. In the early 1870s their protests against the price of beef drew upon a range of political forms, involving women-only meetings, letters to parliament, the composition and publication of campaign songs, and, again, the resort to rough music.[7]

Women continued to play a role in community disputes in other regions also. In Scotland, the fierce disputes over the Highland clearances resurfaced in the 1880s. The crofters' agitation was now directed towards the restoration of customary grazing riots and tenures. The initial strategy was to refuse to pay rent. As women were traditionally responsible for the household budget, including rent payment, this suggests considerable female initiative in the disputes. Women also maintained a high profile (and repeatedly violent) role in resisting the consequent eviction orders.[8] Similarly, in the bitter Irish land confrontations, women were prominent in clashes with the local authorities and in boycotting those shopkeepers who served 'land grabbers'. Irish peasant women joined the Ladies' Land League in large numbers during the Land War of the early 1880s, a handful of whom, such as Mrs Murphy of Roundwood, achieved positions of authority in the movement. Women's involvement was fuelled by incisive political convictions, for in Ireland the 'community' could also signify the wider concept of national identity.[9] British rule was bitterly resented, as was the social predominance of the landed class, a fact which was to lead to widespread female participation in the 1916 Easter Rising.[10] In Scotland, too, nationalist sentiments informed women's political engagement – as the working-class lecturer, Jessie Craigen, clearly appreciated when addressing a massive women's suffrage demonstration in Glasgow in 1882. Her declaration that 'England never conquered Scotland but we gave them a King', caused the meeting to explode with excitement.[11]

Women's public political participation also continued to encompass electoral involvement. In Rothesay, western Scotland, in 1868, local female mill workers attended the nomination procedure and held up their hands for the Liberal candidate; whilst in Carmarthen, a group of women assaulted a fisherman who had voted for the Conservatives.[12] Working women in Colchester and Pontefract used by-elections to vent their hostility towards the Contagious Diseases Acts.[13] Indeed, that working-class women continued to see themselves as part of the political process is evident from the testimony of electoral canvassers. As Jennie Churchill admitted when out canvassing for her husband during the 1885 general election: 'The wives of the Radicals were also admirably informed, and on more than one occasion routed me completely.' Women were perceived to have clear political allegiances and considerable influence which, to Churchill's exasperation, could threaten the voting behaviour of their husbands, so many of whom had been enfranchised in 1884.[14] Therefore, in the key areas of family dynamics, the electoral process, nationalist movements and community protest, women's political activity might be characterised as much by continuity as by change.

Labour Politics

Nevertheless, from the mid-1880s the revival of labour politics was breathing new political life into substantial sections of the working class. The nature of women's involvement in socialism was complex and highly varied. As Michael Savage has described in some detail, it was frequently dependent upon local social and economic circumstances.[15] In many areas this was made manifest in a commitment to trade unionism. Although the vast majority of women remained outside the trade union movement, for those engaged in textile manufacture, this was one obvious channel for political sentiments. In some disputes women attained considerable prominence. Women led the 1875 Heavy Woollen strike, for example, with Hannah Wood and Ann Ellis forming an all-female executive.[16] However, not all members of Yorkshire trade unions were politically active. Male relatives were instrumental in inducing teenage girls to join the union and their subscriptions were paid for them on a family basis. One worker recalled that her uncle refused to teach her to weave until she joined the union. In this situation, Bornat argues, women tended not to perceive any personal benefits from union membership.[17] The ambivalence of Yorkshire unions on the question of working mothers appears to have further undermined female confidence in political and union organisation.[18] Indeed, according to Elizabeth Roberts, only the 'most militant, most politically conscious women' were likely to be committed unionists in any area.[19] Indeed, it is highly significant as an indicator of the continuing role of the family in political socialisation that a number of the leading female campaigners came from families with active political traditions, often stretching back to Chartism. This was true of both Amie Hicks, (founder of the East London Ropemakers' Union) and Julia Varley.[20]

In some regions, trade union activity profited from older traditions of community and female mobilisation. Rough music formed part of the strike culture in agricultural Norfolk; whereas in the potteries, women utilised their role in community networks to prompt membership activity and respond to workers' needs.[21] In the Pendlebury miners strike of 1893, miners' wives drew upon their role as household managers to refuse to give in to the employers. Women emerged as the most militant in the strike, arguing that any pay cuts would make their families' economic position untenable.[22]

On the other hand, in Lancashire, women's union and workplace experiences were directly linked to the emergence of working-class feminism. Even here problems of union recruitment persisted, but, nevertheless, female textile workers made a major contribution to the late Victorian feminist movement. As Mrs Bury from Darwen explained: 'there are industries composed largely or wholly of women, and they ought to have a vote in making the laws and regulations of these industries.'[23] This perception explains the tremendous success met by middle-class feminists, Esther Roper and Eva Gore-Booth, in extending their suffrage campaign to female textile workers in Lancashire and Cheshire from 1893. Using paid working-class organisers, they launched their ambitious 'Special Appeal' to mobilise female workers on the issue. By 1900, a number of distinguished working-class campaigners had emerged from the mills, including Sarah Reddish and Sarah Dickenson. In 1901 a women's suffrage petition, signed exclusively by female Lancashire mill workers had secured 29 359 signatures.[24] This provided unequivocal evidence of the large audience for feminist ideas among working-class women, a phenomena which Leah Leneman also unearthed in Scotland.[25]

However, as the history of the Independent Labour Party (ILP) testifies, women's involvement in the labour movement did not necessarily move them to campaign for their rights. The ILP, formed in 1893, was the only political party to open its membership to women on equal terms with men, (although women frequently operated within women-only branches). The research of June Hannam has done much to reorientate the previous perception that the visibility of women within the movement was due to the prominence of a handful of exceptional journalists and lecturers. Just as an earlier generation of women were fundamental to the making of Owenite or Chartist culture, so did the women of the ILP widen the cultural base of the movement, through their organisation of Sunday schools, outings and concerts. And, as in the earlier period, such family-based activities formed a source of political socialisation for working-class girls. Women's fund-raising efforts were also essential to the financial viability of ILP branches,[26] while in Glasgow a Scottish Women's Labour Party was in existence during 1894-8.[27]

Nevertheless, the position of women within the ILP, and the discursive construction of women within its rhetoric, were potentially problematic. The movement had a theoretical sympathy for the cause of women's rights and it actively encouraged female participation. Yet an essentialist view of women's familial and caring role was a persistent feature of ILP discourse. The ILP commitment to prioritising wider social reformation and working-class needs often made the articulation of feminist demands difficult, and only a handful of working women suffrage campaigners (such as Ada Nield Chew and Selina Cooper) emerged from the ILP.[28] However, these factors did not necessarily alienate the majority of the female membership. The movement's profile clustered in the upper working and lower middle classes – precisely that strata in which women were increasingly choosing not to work outside of the home. Many of this constituency decried the employment of women with young children. The ILP's commitment to the family wage, and its insistence on the need to protect the working-class family from the assaults of capitalism, were therefore particularly in tune with the aspirations of both men and women of this strata. Many socialist women clearly perceived their political agency to derive from the familial and potential social benefits of motherhood. In addition, as Eleanor

Gordon has noted, the ILP, with its emphasis upon social and political, rather than industrial issues, restored attention to community needs – such as education, housing conditions and rent increases – a factor which greatly strengthened its popularity.[29]

Women could also become involved in socialist politics and culture through more informal means. The Clarion Cycling Clubs (named after the popular socialist journal, *The Clarion*) provided young working people with opportunities for leisure and sociability, whilst acting as a propaganda machine in bringing socialist lectures and meetings to more remote districts of northern England. In 1896 the Clarion Van undertook further ambitious tours of the northern English countryside. This provided valuable experience in public speaking for working women (who outnumbered men on the project). The van could also be of considerable significance to the communities it visited. Hannah Mitchell recalled that the van's arrival in her small Derbyshire mining village created considerable excitement, and many local people would follow the van for several days.[30]

The close associations between religion and socialism were very fruitful for women's political engagement, who were observed to be more prominent in religious observance than men. In Lancashire, the Nonconformist tradition was a vital factor in the development of late nineteenth-century socialism. Denominations such as the Primitive Methodists, with its emphasis on temperance and self-government, and the Independent Methodists fostered the culture from which the ILP was to grow.[31] The period also saw the brief florescence of John Trevor's Labour Churches, which provided a palatable blend of religion, socialism and sociability, including opportunities for adult education. Alice Collinge explained that 'social proclivities which had been lying dormant wakened' on becoming involved with the church in Bolton. For the young suffragist Cissy Foley and her family, the Labour Church (which encouraged women to play an equal role in its proceedings) provided a liberating opportunity to debate socialist and feminist ideas.[32]

The socialist Sunday school movement was similarly indebted to the activities of working-class women. It was Mary Gray, a working-class member of the Social Democratic Federation, who pioneered such initiatives in Battersea; in Glasgow, Lizzie Glasier (the sister of Bruce Glasier) insisted upon the necessity of providing Sunday schools at all local ILP branches.[33] Upper working-class women, were also prominent in the running of secular Sunday schools, where family Owenite or Chartist traditions were, once again, frequently in evidence.[34]

Therefore, by the mid-1890s, working-class women had the opportunity to engage with labour politics on a number of different levels, and many must have attained a considerable degree of political sophistication. The suffragette Annie Kenney later reminisced that 'Many, many are the happy evenings I have spent in some lonely cottage on the edge of the moors...The fire would have been lit...the lamp would be burning, and we would talk about politics, Labour questions, Emerson, Ruskin, Edward Carpenter, right into the night.'[35]

Those of more forthright Marxist convictions might be inclined to join the Social Democratic Federation (SDF), which drew upon a more extreme tradition of metropolitan radicalism.[36] As in the ILP, the position of women within the organisation, both ideologically and practically, remained unresolved. Some of the organisation's leading figures, notably Belfort Bax, entertained highly reactionary views on women. The SDF did have some prominent working-class women on its executive, namely Mary Gray and Amie Hicks, but these were not reflective of wider female leadership within the society. As one female member complained in 1912: 'women are not voted into many responsible positions unless they force themselves to the front. But they are allowed to hand round and sell cakes and coffee at dances and to wash up afterwards.'[37]

Nevertheless, it is evident that some women's branches were experimenting with their own forms of democratic organisation. The North Salford women's branch diverted from the practice of having a president, and instead each member took it in turns to act as chairwoman. Also, women may have felt themselves to be acting politically, whilst not following the path of organisational involvement. As Clara Zetkin claimed, 'many a mother and many a wife who imbues husband and children with class consciousness accomplishes just as much as the woman comrades whom we see at our meetings.'[38] Whilst such comments may be argued to typify the limitations of feminist argument within socialist movements, it may also be true that the celebration of women's domestic roles was embraced by women as an opportunity to exercise their political convictions.

Women's Co-operative Guild

The politicising potential of women's domestic role was made manifest in 1883 with the establishment of the Women's Co-operative Guild

(WCG). It sought to capitalise upon the capacity of women as consumers to further the cause of co-operation. The WCG focused upon women's role as domestic managers, offering advice on budgeting and classes in domestic economy. The guild tended to be opposed to married women working outside their home (and most of its members were married to skilled workers), but this did not prohibit them from arguing that women should be empowered to act as citizens. The Guild grew only slowly in the 1880s, but during the 1890s it began to truly flourish, offering meetings and lectures on a wide variety of contemporary issues. Although it incorporated women of diverse political views, under the (middle-class) leadership of Margaret Llewelyn Davies it was increasingly identified with socialist and feminist perspectives.[39]

In order to provide women with greater time for educational and political activities, guildswomen promoted co-operative laundries and bakeries. They sought to improve working-class housing in order to raise standards of health, and to facilitate house care.[40] Indeed, the WCG drew upon the traditions of communitarianism within working-class radicalism – a number of leading WCG members having parents who had been actively involved in Owenite politics.[41] It explicitly evoked the arguments of Robert Owen; and its lectures on 'Associated Homes' echoed strongly the ideas of radical feminists of the 1840s.[42] From the late 1880s the Guild began to make a significant impact upon the working-class women's suffrage movement. In 1893 the Scottish Co-operative Women's Guild sent their own women's suffrage petition to government.[43] Elsewhere, guildswoman were closely involved in local suffrage societies and in 1899 the Guild's Central Committee mobilised its members to protest against the abolition of parish vestries, which removed women's right to stand.[44]

Membership of the Guild had a profound personal impact upon its members. Many husbands felt uncomfortable about their wives' participation in public meetings, whilst others were threatened by the political lessons their wives subsequently learned. As one member recalled: 'The education I got in the Guildroom made me understand more about the laws of the country. So when I was ready to buy my house I had put the mortgage in my name. This caused a little friction between my husband and myself.'[45]

Another aspect of WCG activity was to encourage women to stand for election in local government, following the abolition of the property qualification in local government in 1894: in common with the ILP, the WCG made much of the social potential for women's caring role. One of the first to be elected to the board of guardians was Ada Nield (later Chew) in Crewe, but she was soon followed by a small, but steady stream of others, many of them well-known labour activists, such as Selina Cooper in Burnley and Hannah Mitchell in Ashton. In Battersea, Mary Gray was elected on the SDF ticket to the Board of Guardians in 1895. As Mary Clifford discovered when lecturing to local branches of the WCG, working women formed a responsive and enthusiastic audience on the subject of local government; yet women's organisations had to campaign hard in order to persuade working women to stand. Women played an important role in political canvassing during the elections of others, but a lack of confidence, combined with family pressures made it enormously difficult for working women to stand themselves.[46]

Despite the small numbers of working-class women who were elected to local government positions, historians have delivered very positive assessments of their contributions. According to Patricia Hollis, their personal experience of poverty and unemployment made them particularly well-equipped to make decisions in this field.[47] For Pat Thane, the work of such women had a more profound significance: by assessing women's political activity at the local, rather than the national level, it is possible to discern their contribution to notions of state responsibility, which would lead to the formation of the welfare state in the early twentieth century.[48]

Conservatism

Whilst women's involvement in the labour movement has attracted considerable attention, much less interest has been shown in women's allegiances to conservative politics. Working-class conservatism is best understood, for Leonore Davidoff, as a result of the high numbers engaged in domestic service who, as 'culture carriers', transposed the values of employers to their own class.[49] Yet, as Frank Prochaska and Brian Harrison have demonstrated, many aspects of the philanthropic movement provided a source of conservative political education for young working-class women. The Girls' Friendly Society, (GFS) was one such project. Phenomenally successful (by 1911 it had 1707 branches) it promoted Anglican religion, the importance of the family, loyalty to the monarchy and British imperialism. It attempted to diffuse social tensions by practising a form of class paternalism, offering assistance to particular occupational groups and organising emigration schemes.[50] The spread of mothers' meetings from the late 1850s played a similar role in attempting to inculcate the conservative message to working-class mothers. These meetings typically dispensed Christianity, domestic and child-rearing advice, and facilitated savings schemes, whilst members sewed clothes for their families. The movement was formalised with the establishment of the Mothers' Union in 1885, another spectacularly successful endeavour. In addition to the broader conservative message of thrift, family, religion and monarchy, many branches encouraged discussions on current affairs, including explicitly political and feminist issues.[51]

Of course, working women were far from being passive recipients of middle-class initiatives to tame and improve them. One woman recalled that she, 'had attended Mother's Meetings, where ladies came and lectured on the domestic affairs in the workers' homes ... I have boiled over many times at some of the things I have been obliged to listen to, without the chance of asking a question.'[52] For this woman, it was the WCG which offered her the opportunity for independent political initiative and organisation. Nevertheless, that many working-class women may have approved of the political sentiments fostered in these movements (even if disliking the condescension) is underlined by their involvement in the Primrose League.[53] The League was set up by the Conservative Party in 1883. In view of the expanding electorate and Gladstone's massive popularity, it was an attempt to broaden the party's appeal across the social spectrum. It promoted the broad Tory values of monarchy, imperialism and Anglicanism, whilst appealing to British medievalism to reinforce its message of the importance of paternalism and tradition. The League came into its own, however, in its provision of popular entertainment. The ventriloquists, dances, magic lanterns and garden parties it arranged attracted enormous attendances. Doubtless many came only for the social opportunities and did not feel particular allegiance to the values promoted by the League. Nevertheless, it is clear that substantial numbers of the working classes were subscribing to this version of 'popular toryism', which was also discernible in music hall culture. For many it formed a palatable alternative to the sombre temperance reputation of Liberalism and socialism. In areas such as Lancashire, where well-paid factory workers could enjoy its leisure provision, the League was able to draw upon older traditions of working-class toryism, as in the early Victorian support for the Tory reformer, Michael Oastler.[54] By 1900 the League had over 1.5 million members, of which up to half appear to have been women, many of them drawn from the upper working classes. In a handful of branches women predominated and in some habitations (in Newcastle and Wokingham for example) working women were more numerous than men as branch wardens.[55]

Conclusion

It is clear that working-class women's political engagement continued to be as rich and varied in this as in the earlier period. If the textile workers of Lancashire derived their political insights and motivations from their workplace experiences, then the WCG provides a fascinating example of the ways in which women's political mobilisation might equally emanate from the female channels of domesticity. It was the family which often kept political traditions alive, a factor which complicates any simple elision between domesticity and political withdrawal. Strong veins of popular political tradition continued to inform women's public political engagement as well. The working-class political lecturer, Jessie Craigen, used a bell-ringer – an old symbol of women's action – to announce her meetings. She also evoked the power of working-class political memory when, in speaking at a massive feminist rally in Manchester's Free Trade Hall in 1880, she dramatically observed that they were gathered together on the very site of Peterloo, where, 'On this ground sixty years ago, the blood of women was spilt for freedom.'[56] Craigen illustrates one of the many pitfalls in constructing narratives of political closure for working-class women. Working-class women's political activism remained a vibrant force throughout this period and was often empowered by the self-conscious knowledge of a political tradition.

9

FAMILIES, RELATIONSHIPS AND HOME LIFE

Introduction

The second half of the nineteenth century has been portrayed as a time when the working classes, now benefiting from a rise in real wages, became assimilated and reconciled to the society of industrial capitalism. Gareth Stedman Jones has argued that working-class culture became increasingly conservative and 'respectable'. The majority of working-class marriages were now legal unions; and, as traditions of artisan radicalism began to decline, so too did the heavy drinking which had characterised earlier plebeian life. Such pastimes as cockfighting and bearbaiting began to die out as working-class leisure interests centred upon sports like football, and upon institutions such as the music hall. A new consumerism began to seep into the lives of the working-class, as they began to enjoy fish and chips, seaside excursions and cheap, imported foodstuffs from the colonies. According to Stedman Jones, the focus of working-class culture switched from the workplace to the home, a process which was facilitated by the advent of shorter working days (typically nine-hour days, and a half day's holiday on Saturday).[1]

In many historical accounts, women tend to emerge as the apotheosis of this newly passive, more conservative, working class. Women's apparent embrace of domesticity and housewifery is often stressed. David Levine, for example, argues that the widespread acceptance of the idea of the male breadwinner wage led to the demise of the family wage economy. As a consequence, he suggests that gender roles within working-class life became increasingly compartmentalised. Thus, he claims that the second phase of industrialisation 'dramatically' 'reordered' the private lives of working people.[2] Such views were shared by the first generation of feminist historians. Nancy Tomes argued that the comparative decline in working-class domestic violence was partially explicable by the fact that once feisty, belligerent working-class women began to assume middle-class, acquiescent feminine roles.[3] Similarly, for Ann Oakley, the acceptance of new concepts of childhood (which stressed juvenile dependence) was one of the many factors which 'heralded the dependence of women in marriage and their restriction to the home'.[4] Advances in the field of women's history have, however, uncovered the complexities inherent in these cultural shifts. They also challenge the prevailing orthodoxy that women's characters became submissive and dependent, revealing that women found new ways to express their individuality and establish authority.

Young Women, Sexual Relations and Courtship

Working-class marriages tended to be perfunctory affairs, conducted with brief ceremony and little fuss. For, whilst personal affection and sentiment were normally vital factors in the choice of a partner, marriage was still contracted for important economic and social reasons. It was in this spirit that Lucy Luck, a straw-plaiter, married her husband, on the recommendation of her employer: 'My girl, you have poor Will; he will make you a good husband, and he will never hit you.'[5] Women would usually endeavour to save as much as they could for their marriage, as their financial contribution – or practical abilities – could be essential to the new household. Young Welsh women practised their dairying skills to make them more attractive as potential wives to local farmers.[6]

Middle-class observers were very hostile to the sexual behaviour of working-class women. Women with more than one lover, or who exhibited certain behaviours (such as drinking or engaging in sexual behaviour in public), might be classified as prostitutes.[7] However, in many urban areas, parents continued to exert considerable control over the movements and courtship of their daughters, although those who emigrated to the towns from the countryside or from Ireland might enjoy greater freedom from their parents.[8] In rural Ireland, however, patriarchal models of marital arrangement actually increased over these years. Here, arranged marriages were the norm and the practice of bridal dowries grew – largely due to the Irish Land Acts of 1885 and

1903 which encouraged peasant property holdings.[9] For many Irish women, however, the severe socio-economic dislocation occasioned by the famine, and the difficulties in saving for a dowry, meant that over a quarter of all women were remaining single.[10]

However, despite a general trend towards legal marriage across Britain, working-class definitions of 'respectability' and traditions of marriage and cohabitation could vary significantly between communities. In the East End of London it was frequently observed that the poor resided in stable – but unmarried – unions. In the Midlands, working people believed that marriage to a first partner gave social sanction and respectability to any future, 'common law' liaisons; whereas in Middlesborough, social workers discovered that women often refused to marry their partners for fear that it would worsen their position within the relationship.[11] Elsewhere, particularly in rural districts, older customs of bridal pregnancy and pre-marital sex continued to be accepted. As one disapproving observer noted in Cumbria in the late 1860s: 'No disgrace, scarcely any discredit, attaches to a girl who has had one illegitimate child'.[12] Meanwhile, in the metropolis, there was a little-discussed alternative sexual culture, often flowing into prostitution, in which upper-working-class girls might form transient partnerships with young middle-class bachelors who were seeking temporary domesticity and sex during an age of elite marriage delay.[13] These wide-ranging attitudes towards marriage and sexual relationships indicate the extent to which working-class women remained impervious to middle-class formulations of marriage. By examining women's role within the household, sources of marital tension and attitudes towards sexuality and birth control, the remainder of the chapter seeks to provide further insights into the complex dynamics of working- class families and relationships.

Domestic Management and Community Roles

The private lives of working-class families were dominated by their women folk. Working-class wives exercised responsibilities far beyond the performance of housework, food preparation and child care to encompass management over most aspects of the family's welfare. The working-class wife was the 'head and chancellor of the exchequer', as one contemporary woman put it.[14] The exigencies of such labour varied dramatically. The families of well-paid factory workers in

Blackburn, for example, were beginning to enjoy a higher standard of living, with more comfortable homes (from the 1890s this included council houses) and occasional holiday excursions.[15] Nevertheless, great swathes of the working class remained in appalling housing, with incomes barely reaching the poverty line. As we have seen (Chapter 7), many homes were dependent upon women's earnings. Consequently, for hundreds of thousands of women, the management of the household was a cheerless and heart-breakingly difficult responsibility.

At the same time, management of the household finances entailed considerable authority for women. They made all the major decisions in the family – when they should move to a different house; when the children should give up school to earn a living; and when the family situation required themselves to take in work. Women's supervision of the family expenditure had the potential for significant influence over their husbands' actions. Mrs Layton recalled that 'Soon after my husband joined his Trade Union, a Co-operative Store was formed at Child's Hill. I gave my husband the necessary 1/6 to join.'[16] Significantly, then, women's role as financial managers was at striking variance with their position (until 1882) under common law, which technically denied married women an economic role.[17]

Women's role in supervising the household budget also made them central to the petty cash economy of working-class neighbourhoods. The rhythms of working-class life led to a reliance upon pawning, particularly towards the end of the week. Women tended to pledge their own possessions first, and to redeem them last. Their husbands colluded in this silent sacrifice – in many families there was an unspoken agreement that husbands remained (or pretended to remain) in ignorance of their wives' pawning.[18]

In the eyes of middle-class reformers, women performed their role as household managers irrationally. They despaired of overcrowded families keeping one room of the house as a 'parlour' for occasional use; they also disapproved of the weekly cycle upon which many working-class families ran: with the wage packet coming in on Friday, the custom of Saturday drinking and a fulsome Sunday dinner were widespread, even though by Thursday, many households might be surviving on bread and treacle. Middle-class sceptics failed to perceive that for those living on the breadline, in cramped and insanitary accommodation, the thought of the Sunday dinner ahead could help to keep spirits up during the week; or that the parlour, often seen as a badge of respectability, was a means of creating one area of space and gave working-class families a sense of pride and comfort.[19]

More fundamentally, social workers were alarmed by women's adherence to a family hierarchy of consumption rights. Most men assumed that they had a right to money of their own to spend on drink, tobacco and the like. Moreover, as primary wage earners, men were far better fed than other family members. They ate meat regularly, even if the rest of the family (in particular, the wives) were going without. However, this practice should not be interpreted purely in terms of patriarchal gender relations. Amongst working-class women, such food allocation was rationalised as essential if the strength and health of the family's breadwinner was to be maintained: 'we must give our husbands sufficient food or we should have them home and not able to work', explained one woman.[20] Indeed, unemployed men could not continue to expect preferential nutrition and adolescent children of both sexes believed that they were entitled to better food rations once they went out to work.[21] Equally, in communities where women provided the family's main income, they insisted on enjoying the consumption rights of breadwinners. Female potters, for example, were known to form strong social and recreational networks of their own, enjoying the respect of their husbands, with whom they often shared equal consumption rights.[22]

Such examples should not overset the broader picture, however, in which wives' self-deprivation led to chronic health problems, exacerbated by their poor access to health care. Women were far less likely than men to belong to friendly societies which made some provision for medical care,[23] and their poor nutrition was particularly damaging when combined with the exigencies of repeated pregnancies and breast-feeding. Reproductive work was not accorded any benefits within the distribution of family resources. One woman recalled, 'I nearly lost my life through want of nourishment, and did after nine months of suffering lose my child.'[24] Many working-class girls were early habituated to the expectation that they should enjoy less access to family resources than their menfolk. Once in employment, working-class boys, for example, were typically given a greater proportion of their earnings for their own use than were their sisters.[25]

Clearly, women were greatly disadvantaged in the central areas of health, economic status and nutrition; and yet, within most working-class homes, they assumed a far greater control over their family's affairs than that enjoyed by women in higher social classes. As Helen Bosanquet wryly noted in 1906: 'Fathers are regarded by the children as plain inferior to mother in authority, in knowledge of right and wrong, and above all of 'manners'. Talk of the subjection of women, I doubt if the bare idea of father being equal to mother in rank and authority ever entered the mind of any child under sixteen.'[26] Clearly working-class girls were not without strong female role models as they grew up.

Bosanquet's comments also point to the fact that it was primarily the women of the family who were responsible for structuring its cultural and social world. Female kinship groups and women's community networks lay at the heart of working-class culture. This could be particularly important for disadvantaged groups such as Irish immigrants, who frequently faced hostility and violence from local people.[27] There is a danger, of course, in overemphasising the role of the community. The frequent moves undertaken by many working-class families, perhaps to seek work, evade rent, or to reflect a rise in status, could sever carefully nurtured neighbourhood networks.[28] However, for working-class women in this period, as earlier, the extended family was an important source of affective and practical support, with strong links being maintained with parents and siblings as well as more distant relatives. The family household was a fluid entity, with relatives (and perhaps lodgers, too) moving in and out of the home as personal needs dictated. Such ties were vital later in the life-cycle. Elderly widows could find themselves in an extremely precarious economic position. Although workhouse reforms rendered life in these institutions slightly more bearable, they remained loathed and feared; and family support could therefore prove a vital bulwark against misfortune.[29]

Women who were not assimilated into neighbourhood culture, perhaps because of differing domestic and child-rearing standards, or different socio-economic status, were noted by some middle-class observers to lead lonely lives. Seebohm Rowntree observed of artisans' wives in York that 'with advance in the social scale, family life becomes more private, and the women, left in the house all day while their husbands are at work, are largely thrown upon their own resources. These, as a rule, are sadly limited, and in the deadening monotony of their lives these women too often become mere hopeless drudges.'[30] Comparatively little research has been carried out into the lives of upper-working-class women such as these. However, women of this strata might develop other support links, such as membership of a church or chapel, or the Women's Co-operative Guild, which did not depend upon day-to-day contact with the immediate community.[31]

Rowntree's assumption that women's domestic labour rendered them 'drudges' further masks more subtle meanings which women themselves might attach to such work. For those whose labour was home-based, housework could form a means of establishing authority and self-respect. Although women's domestic responsibilities undoubtedly increased with the mounting pressure to send children to school (rather than keeping them at home to assist with younger children, washing and so on), housework was not merely a series of chores, but comprised part of the dynamics which structured family life. As one elderly woman exclaimed when asked if her father had helped in the home, 'My father? He wasn't allowed to!'[32] The performance of domestic chores was also imbued with wider symbolic and social significance. For Jewish immigrants, whose traditional religious habits were threatened by British customs such as Saturday working, women's domestic observances were critical in upholding Jewish identity.[33]

In those families where women contributed substantially to the family income, it is possible that some derived authority not from their domestic labour, but from their paid employment. Patricia Malcolmson notes that the husbands of laundry workers often assisted with child care and sometimes with cookery. In textile towns such as Burnley, where both spouses were weavers, it was common for a comparatively equitable division of labour to occur with husbands assisting with domestic chores.[34] These occupational variations are important in preventing the stereotyping of working-class families. Yet equally, it is true that many – perhaps most – factory women performed a 'double shift' of paid employment and domestic work. In Dundee, where male unemployment was high, men rarely looked after their children during the day, even if their wife was out at work.[35] Furthermore, women were socialised into taking responsibility for domestic chores from childhood. Oral interviews from urban Scotland have revealed that girls were often expected to perform services for their brothers and many were required to help with their mothers' domestic work even after they had left home. (The hostility displayed by many respondents to such practices, however, highlights the dangers in assuming that women passively accepted the social roles allotted to them.)[36]

For those living in homogenous working-class neighbourhoods, to scrub one's doorstep, or to ensure crisp white net curtains at the window could be a means of asserting your family's identity and respectability within the wider community.[37] Such rituals, whilst laborious and time-consuming, could contribute to a feeling of self-respect and domestic order, particularly in households where low budgets afforded few opportunities to create a sense of material well-being. Nevertheless, the very fact that the performance of such chores could be taken as a sign of respectability, necessarily means that there were others who could not or would not perform such labour. Social investigators were struck by the sheer diversity in the nature and cleanliness of working-class homes.[38] Within contemporary discourse, this distinction was often expressed as the 'respectables' and the 'roughs'. This is a dichotomy which Joan Perkin upholds, noting that respectables were those who valued independence and quiet living, who shunned debt and gambling; whilst the roughs, who might be known for their lax sexual relations, prioritised a good time – enjoying drinking, blood sports and entertainments over the desire to stay out of debt.[39] Yet, as Peter Bailey, among others have pointed out, the reality was far more fluid than this categorisation suggests. Respectability was a slippery concept which held different meanings across varying contexts. 'Almost no-one', notes Anna Davin, 'saw themselves as not respectable.'[40] And, of course, the behaviour and priority of individuals and families might fluctuate according to family fortunes, stages in the life-cycle and temperament.

The Dynamics of Marriage

Working-class marriages, as the previous discussion has indicated, tended to be based upon mutual expectations of economic advantage and broadly accepted (if regionally diverse) ideas of domains and responsibilities within marriage. Yet latent tensions could erupt if role assumptions were transgressed. Some women might initiate violence, particularly if their husbands stayed out too late at the pub, or questioned their fidelity.[41] Kathleen Dayus, brought up in a deprived part of Birmingham at the turn of the century, described her mother as a tyrant, who terrified her husband. Equally, women's command over the domestic space, might conflict with the patriarchal assumptions of authoritarian men, as Shani D'Cruze has recently suggested.[42] Wives who failed to provide expected domestic services (having a meal ready when their husband returned from work, for example) might be met with serious assaults. Nevertheless, male domestic violence does appear to have declined during this period. Increasing community disgust for men who beat their wives (sometimes expressed through traditional customs, such as 'Riding the Stang') suggests that such behaviour was neither universally condoned nor expected.[43] Yet it evidently remained woven into many strands of working-class culture. One young women tellingly testified that a man had 'knocked me down as if he was my husband.'[44] This was a problem which greatly troubled middle-class reformers, resulting in a number of legislative measures to protect working-class women. In 1878 magistrates were given the power to grant quick separation orders to women in the case of physical assault; a further act of 1882 gave police magistrates the power to flog violent husbands; and in 1895 wives could be granted cheap separation orders if their husbands were convicted to prison for at least two months.[45]

However, many of the matrimonial law reforms of this period were insensitive to the real needs of working-class women, and merely exacerbated their vulnerability. Time after time, separation orders proved but temporary, as destitute women felt compelled to return to abusive husbands for financial reasons. Many local authorities would not provide outdoor relief to deserted wives for the first 12 months – a policy which led to desperate poverty. Furthermore, the Central Divorce Court normally refused to make maintenance orders to wives who had been guilty of adultery. Some social researchers noted that working-class communities often had a very relaxed attitude towards marital break-up – simply setting up home with a new partner, but this was true only of particular cultures, (the East End of London, for example).[46] In fact, large numbers of working-class women fought hard for legislative assistance to end troubled marriages. Approximately one in five of divorces granted in Victorian England related to working-class couples and it was working women's organisations, such as the WCG, which campaigned for divorce reform in the 1900s.[47]

Yet, despite the physical and financial hardships against which so many working-class families had to battle, relationships could evidently be maintained with warmth and kindness. One woman, who suffered terribly with post-natal complications confided movingly that, 'my husband has always been husband, nurse, and mother. The pain was never quite so bad when he was near.'[48] Mrs Saunders remembered, 'I used to catch them [her parents] sometimes, kissing in the kitchen.'[49] Such testimony is rare as working-class families tended to be undemonstrative physically and particularly reticent about sexuality. Adolescents were rarely given any information on the facts of life and the condition of pregnancy was, in itself, regarded as embarrassing, particularly for older women. Indeed, it was common for mothers to say nothing of their pregnancy to the rest of the family. A Mrs Sharp reflected that, 'on the Sunday, Dorothy was born. Yet m' mother never talked to any of us, and said that she was having a baby. I was nineteen at the time.'[50] Such reserve may have stemmed from the need to preserve self-respect and propriety in crowded living conditions. In an atmosphere in which housing reformers muttered darkly about the prevalence of incest in overcrowded homes, working-class parents worked hard to inculcate sexual taboos. One woman, recalling her childhood in a cramped rural dwelling, explained that as soon as she and her sisters reached a certain age, their mother insisted on them sleeping in the parents' bedroom, rather than share a bed with their brothers.[51]

The perceived need for sexual repression, which formed part of the social education of so many working-class girls, was not likely to encourage an association between sexual activity and personal fulfilment. In any case, the potential for sexual pleasure was perhaps limited, given that sexual activity wrought repeated, draining, and often unsuccessful pregnancies. Little wonder, then, that oral evidence suggests that sex was viewed as a male, and not a female pleasure. Ellen Ross's research led her to conclude that, 'Intercourse was initiated by men, submitted to by women.'[52] However, the inculcation of repressive attitudes towards sexuality was one means whereby female culture might attempt to control the problems women experienced as a result of excessive child-bearing and rearing. It also married well with the mores of working-class respectability, with its emphasis upon self-restraint.

It is within this context that the major decline in fertility must be considered. Although working-class families were slower to limit their families than other strata, the phenomenon remains highly significant even among these social groups. McLaren notes that in the 1911 census, the ratio of births per 1000 married males were 119 for upper-and middle-class men; 153 for skilled workmen; and 213 for unskilled men.[53] It used to be implied that this indicated the working-classes' emulation of the culture of their social superiors,[54] but historians are now more sensitive of the need to appreciate the working class's own internal shifting dynamics and perceptions. Clearly, increasing affluence and rising aspirations were a critical factor. The poorest occupational groups, such as agricultural labourers and miners, were the last sectors to decrease the size of their families. Yet a lack of direct, testimonial evidence makes it enormously difficult to pinpoint with confidence the motivations of such private decisions as family size. A wide range of explanatory factors have been considered – including the demise of the church's authority; the growth of literacy (contributing to a greater self-awareness among women); a rise in standards of living (making child-labour less necessary and raising individual consumer aspirations); the impact of feminism and changes in the perception of childhood.[55] It is probable that all these issues played a role in creating a climate in which smaller families were seen as preferable; although detailed research at the local level may provide the most fruitful means of unearthing the rationale of family limitation within specific communities.[56] Nevertheless, it is clearly significant that regions of high employment opportunities for women were usually the first to experience a decrease in working-class family size, thus suggesting that female aspirations and confidence may have been a critical factor.[57]

The means by which working-class families reduced their family size also remains a vexed question. Michael Mason and Angus McLaren have pointed to the growing availability and commercial marketing from the 1860s of such devices as the douche, pessaries, diaphragms and condoms. Considerable publicity was additionally gained in 1877 when the free-thinkers, Annie Besant and Charles Bradlaugh, were prosecuted for promoting birth-control literature.[58] However, there is no simple corollary between awareness of birth-control material and its actual use. The oral evidence collected by Elizabeth Roberts shows not only widespread sexual ignorance, but hostility to 'artificial methods' of family limitation, which were associated with immorality and irreligion.[59] Although some of the contributors to the WCG's classic study, *Maternity*, hinted at the use of contraceptives, it is evident that many believed family limitation should be achieved through male self-control.[60] Indeed, most working-class couples appear to have recoursed to the traditional practices of coitus interruptus and abstinence. Diana Gittins has noted that working-class women sometimes praised husbands for 'being careful' (i.e. withdrawing before ejaculation) and Ellen Ross has drawn attention to the 'evasion' tactics women might employ to avoid sexual contact – sharing the marital bed with children, or even simply going to bed long after the husband.[61]

When these methods failed, women might turn to abortion. Women prepared to offer such services were resident in the majority of working-class neighbourhoods, although women also self-prescribed abortifacients. The psychological weight of taking such action was eased by the fact that abortion was commonly conceptualised not as the destruction of a foetus, but rather as restoring the menses.[62] Meanwhile, public opinion dwelt on the lurid phenomenon of 'baby farmers' – under whose 'care' a tiny minority of desperate mothers left their infants, with the tacit knowledge that they would die.[63] Therefore, whilst pressure groups, such as the WCG, were beginning to argue for the importance of birth control in improving women's health and social position, it would appear that traditional attitudes towards contraception began to change but slowly.

Motherhood

Motherhood continued to be the major structuring force within the lives of working-class women, and a vital component in the construction of contemporary plebeian femininities. Indeed, those unable to have children, particularly in Ireland, might often experience a loss in status and respect.[64] However, during the final decades of this period, the importance of motherhood began to acquire a new national and imperial significance. Fears concerning the persistently high level of infant mortality rates raised alarms over the health of the working-class population. At a time when national identity was becoming an increasingly sensitive issue, with imperial and European rivalries reaching a peak, public debate focused upon the need for a robust and vigorous population. Eugenicist ideas had already begun to work their influence, and now politicians, health workers and newspaper editors floated the spectre of a sickly and disintegrating nation before the public's eyes. Such discussions reached a climax during the Boer War (1899–1902), as revelations concerning the ill-health of potential working-class recruits fuelled anxieties as to the strength and status of imperial Britain. Although a number of initiatives were launched to improve child health (such as school meals and council house building programmes), attention focused above all upon the capabilities of working-class mothers. The result was a formidable infant welfare movement, encompassing both the voluntary sector and the state.[65]

Cultural alienation beset the project from the start (although interestingly, Jewish mothers with their particular practices of food preparation and low alcohol consumption were held up as examples of good parenting[66]). The widespread custom of insuring infants against their death was taken as evidence that working-class parents simply did not care sufficiently for their children. There was little understanding that a 'decent' funeral for a family member was a vital element of working-class respectability. Given the heart-breaking frequency with which working-class families had to bury infants, such customs had a rationale of their own. Between the 1870s and 1890s, the records of one maternity hospital in North Lambeth reveal that 62 per cent of its patients had lost two or more children, 40 per cent had lost more than three.[67] Grieving mothers were reluctant to share their feelings with middle-class observers. Shock and the desire for emotional privacy were often read as unconcern. Scottish care workers frequently expressed amazement that girls in reformatory and industrial schools were desperate to return to their homes, where to middle-class eyes, they had been sorely neglected.[68]

Equally, public debate over working mothers illustrated starkly the lack of understanding of working-class culture. Government officials assumed that infant mortality was often the direct result of the neglect and poor child care which supposedly ensued when a working-class mother went out to work. This concern lead to the 1891 Act to prevent women from working in factories for four weeks after the birth of a child. Although more sympathetic professionals, such as John Robertson, Birmingham's Medical Officer, noted that infants with working mothers fared better because of the family's higher income, others, such as Arthur Newsholme, the Medical Officer to the Local Government Board, continued to assert (in the face of his own statistics) into the twentieth century that working mothers were threatening the survival rates of their children.[69]

If labouring mothers were perceived as a threat to infant well-being, then maternal ignorance was presented as an even bigger problem. One prominent government official claimed that the infant death rate was 'more largely due to maternal ignorance, negligence and mismanagement than to any other single cause.'[70] Such ignorance was to be tackled both through the school curriculum, which increasingly focused upon domestic education for working-class girls; and through the establishment of infant welfare centres, particularly from the early 1900s, which encouraged middle-class ideals of baby-care.[71]

As Jane Lewis has demonstrated, in isolating mothers as the chief cause of juvenile ill-health, government officials side-stepped more critical environmental factors. Diarrhoea (the chief killer of infants) was blamed upon dirty homes and bottle-feeding, rather than insanitary sewage systems, or the problems poor women faced in feeding their babies in homes with no running water or fresh milk. Breast-feeding (which was probably practised by over three-quarters of working-class mothers for the first months of their babies' lives) was not the straightforward solution contemporary health workers often assumed it to be. Women were frequently too poorly nourished or too hard-pressed and exhausted to successfully suckle their children. Whilst middle-class homes were accustomed to separate nurseries, distinct nursery food and strict routines, working-class babies, particularly in the poorest sectors, tended to be absorbed into the family's activities, sharing their meals, outings and beds. Such practices, rather than chronically damp housing, were mistakenly blamed for infant bronchitis and pneumonia.[72]

Given such criticism it is perhaps not surprising that among the better off, the implementation of different child-care regimes, such as regular bedtimes and church attendance could contribute towards a woman's identity as a 'respectable' mother.[73] However, the desire to recreate working-class families in the middle-class image was usually also met with derision and resistance from those it most wished to reach. A Rochdale vicar lamented that, 'When he had endeavoured to tell the members of his mothers' meeting how to bring up their babies, those Lancashire women had told him to go and play at marbles!'[74] Female potters in Staffordshire were equally disdainful of the help proffered by philanthropists and health workers, preferring to utilise their own, community-based networks of support.[75] Likewise, legislative attempts to professionalise midwifery met with little support from working-class mothers, who continued to prefer the assistance of neighbourhood women, who would also help with house care and cooking.[76] Nevertheless, the infant welfare movement, combined with the contemporary eugenicist debate, put enormous pressure upon mothers to produce healthy, thriving children. The responsibilities of motherhood had probably never weighed so heavily.

Conclusion

Within the perimeters defined by their culture, it was possible for working-class wives to carve out a powerful role within family dynamics. Yet this could result in self-abnegatory behaviour which prioritised the needs of husbands and children, to the detriment of women's health. It would appear that those marriages in which both husband and wife were economically active outside the home appear to have earned women the most egalitarian relationships. Yet many women derived pride and self-esteem from the way in which they managed their households; and their domestic behaviour was strongly implicated in working-class constructions of respectability. Despite the problems of poverty, overcrowding and frequent ill-health, women were instrumental in creating families which were known for their resilience and affection, and in which they themselves held the central place.

PART IV

MIDDLE-CLASS AND UPPER-CLASS WOMEN, 1860–1900

10

WORK

Introduction

Between 1860 and 1900 many dramatic advances were seen in middle-class and elite women's employment. Improvements in educational provision facilitated access to a whole range of new occupations, notably in the medical, clerical, retailing and education sectors. One recent commentator has attributed these developments to the activities of the feminist movement, and in particular, the Society for the Promotion of the Employment of Women.[1] Feminist campaigns were undoubtedly vital in contributing to a climate in which women's paid employment was increasingly acceptable. However, structural changes in the economy and the continued adherence to notions of gender difference were often more influential in determining the nature of women's employment. Moreover, for the majority of women, this was period of a stasis, not change. Women continued to engage in 'traditional' activities – such as domestic management, child care and philanthropy. Most women entertained a broad definition of work which did not necessarily encompass the concept of paid employment.

Education Reform

It was during these years that major developments occurred in educational provision for middle-class girls, both at the secondary and tertiary levels. However, the story is a chequered one, as apparent advances were accommodated on to the cultural map only through adherence to certain gendered ideologies.

During the 1860s, the issue of girls' education moved swiftly up the public agenda, particularly in Ireland, England and Wales. Thanks largely to campaigning by feminists such as Emily Davies in England, the Taunton Commission (1864) included girls' secondary education in its report. This showed female secondary provision to be desultory. However, the opening of Cambridge local examinations to girls in 1863 (and later elsewhere) had provided an indicator of girls' academic potential. The following decades saw the establishment of a new generation of girls' schools. Thirty-eight were founded under the auspices of the feminist Girls' Public Day School Company; the Church School Company set up a further 33 Anglican schools; and over 90 girls' grammar schools, as well as a handful of elite boarding schools, such as Wycombe Abbey, were established.[2]

The new girls' schools were notable for their strict discipline, academic curricula and introduction of physical education. Newspapers and politics remained taboo, however, and the teaching of science, controversial. For, whilst the feminist agitation was clearly instrumental in achieving improvements to girls' secondary provision, the new institutions themselves were comparatively conservative. Most adhered to a 'double conformity': they felt obliged to achieve the educational standards reached in boys' schools, as well as conforming to prevailing notions of femininity (not least to assuage the anxieties of parents). The very iconography of Cheltenham Ladies' College was steeped in middle-class ideals of female chastity, the school badge being dominated by a Madonna lily. There were other limitations, too: at the institutional level, schools were usually managed by men, who allowed little female intervention. Furthermore, in many ways, the schools' ethos merely modernised an older tradition of educating women for their role as wives and mothers. The governing committee of Manchester High School for Girls sought to educate the girls, 'so that they may become intelligent companions and associates for their brothers, meet helps and counsellors for their husbands, and wise guides and trainers for the minds of their children.' In an age of imperial expansion, it was felt to be more important than ever that British culture should be upheld and diffused. Women, as 'natural guardians of the nation's culture' were seen as the ideal medium through which this might be achieved.[3]

Nevertheless, one of the most important consequences of the reformed girls' schools was that they became feeder institutions for the new opportunities in female higher education. By the 1860s a number of feminist-minded ladies' educational societies had been formed. These drew upon the long-standing tradition in urban culture of female attendance at public lectures.[4] The new societies encouraged sympathetic university lecturers, such as Henry Morley, to offer extension lectures to female audiences. In 1867, local initiatives in northern English cities were consolidated with the formation of the North of England Council for Promoting the Higher Education of Women. The professors connected to such schemes played a prominent role in securing women's admission to university. In 1878 the University of London became the first British university to admit women to degrees (with the exception of medical degrees); and many other institutions began to award women special higher certificates, as at St Andrews, without allowing them to graduate to full degrees.[5]

Clearly, these successes were not an unproblematic triumph for feminist activists. Emily Davies, who always had short shrift with any arguments concerning women's supposed 'difference' to men, was deeply concerned that giving women separate qualifications hindered women's university education from attaining an equal status. At Davies's Cambridge college, Girton (formerly Hitchin), and also at Somerville, Oxford, the students were placed under enormous pressure to complete courses within the same time-scale as men, despite the fact that they were seriously disadvantaged by their lack of classics tuition. This 'uncompromising' model owed much to Davies's feminism which eschewed gender differences. She was criticised by Professor Henry Sidgwick, who with Anne Jemima Clough, pioneered an alternative, 'separatist' model of female education at Newnham College, Cambridge (and practised also at Lady Margaret Hall, Oxford). These institutions drew upon broader debates concerning the need for curriculum reform throughout the educational establishment. In particular, they argued that the study of the classics should be superseded by subjects such as languages, science and mathematics. Consequently, Sidgwick accused Davies of loading 'a new institution ... with those very vices ... we deplore in an old one'.[6] Nevertheless, Davies's insight that to support separate female degrees could lead to the institutionalisation of reactionary views of women was prescient. In 1884 a Professor of Obstetrics, John Thorburn, argued that courses designed specifically for women were essential to circumvent the grievous effects which he believed the standard course of study would have upon the female constitution. Thorburn was not alone in insisting that unless women refrained from exertion during menstruation they could cause themselves severe mental and physical harm.[7] As women gained greater access to employment and education, the popularity of such theories, particularly among the scientific community, intensified.

By 1892 the four Scottish universities had admitted women to all classes and degrees; whilst the University of Wales accepted women as full members of the University in 1893. In Ireland, the Intermediary Act of 1878 made university grants available to both sexes and the following year the Royal University of Ireland was established which granted degrees to women. From the turn of the century the momentum gathered pace, with the numbers of female students rising dramatically, particularly in Scotland and Wales.[8] But to construct a narrative of linear progression towards the acceptance of female abilities would be misleading. As late as 1902, Owens College in Manchester required the parents of female students to provide a written statement that study would not endanger their daughters' health.[9]

Female students themselves faced considerable problems of assimilation into university life. The pioneers of women's university education believed it essential that female students should conform to upper-middle-class ideals of female behaviour. They were chaperoned constantly and the strictest of regulations surrounded their contact with male students. It was often difficult for women even to gain access to the requisite lectures. Male students exhibited considerable hostility towards the women, with medical students proving particularly abusive. In addition, female colleges remained extremely poorly resourced in comparison to established male institutions (and, in the early days, often badly managed). A high prevalence of wealthy students studying purely for motives of cultural development further exacerbated the problems of attracting funding.[10]

However, increasingly, save for those studying for expensive medical degrees, the majority of female students came from lower-middle-class families, the majority of whom were to become teachers. As Carol Dyhouse argues, the development of university education was intimately connected with the need for well-educated female teachers. This was reflected in the structure of government funding: from 1890, considerable grants were given to those universities with teacher training colleges attached.[11] Consequently, it has been argued the expansion in women's higher education did little to open up new opportunities for women, as over half of university-educated women continued to enter the old standby, teaching. In the words of Martha Vicinus, education was not an 'opening up of wider opportunities', but a 'narrow staircase'.[12]

However, the fact remains that for the vast majority of students, higher education was a liberating experience. To have a room of one's own was of particular importance. It provided women with privacy and immunity from household demands, the freedom to study, and a sense of independence. After all, when in 1868, Davies announced her plans for a female college, what most shocked her audience was that students would be living apart from their families.[13] The spectacular academic success of many female students were also important milestones in demonstrating the possible heights to which the female intellect could reach.

Teaching

As the previous discussion indicates, teaching was the predominant career for women of this strata. Between 1875 and 1914 the number of women teachers rose by 862.1 per cent (whereas that of men rose by 291.7 per cent).[14] At the 'top' end of the market, the tremendous spurt in the foundations of girls' schools created a demand for well-educated female teaching staff. These posts could be extremely demanding, often exacerbated by poor food and accommodation. The post of head teacher brought an increasing degree of social prestige, although some, fully conscious of this, tended to be authoritarian. They ruled over their institutions with intense commitment and expected the same of their staff. At North London Collegiate, Frances Buss disapproved of her teachers having interests outside of the school.[15] Nevertheless, according to Vicinus, these schools fostered a supportive, female community, which must have been especially welcome to those who had faced the sexual antagonism simmering in many of the universities. During the 1870s and 1880s growing numbers of middle-class women began to teach in elementary schools, where improved government funding had led to improvements in the standards of sanitation and building provision; a reduction in class sizes and somewhat healthier pupils. Such factors helped to dispel some of the middle-class prejudices about teaching in this sector, although women from the wealthy middle classes did not enter the field in significant numbers until the 1920s. The new day-colleges for teacher training, which began to spring up during the 1890s, were an acceptable option for lower-middle-class girls, although residential colleges, such as Whitelands Training College in Chelsea, were also beginning to witness an increasing intake from girls with such backgrounds by the turn of the century.[16]

Despite female teachers' education and financial independence, this was a period of transition, in which Evangelical notions of women's religious and moral vocation were reconciled uneasily with the notion of the female professional. Leading female figures in the profession projected themselves as following a religious vocation, particularly during the earlier part of the period. Alice Ottley, the head teacher at Worcester High School, helped to establish the Society of the Holy Name in 1872, to provide Christian fellowship for teachers; and J. S. Pedersen talks of the 'quasi-sacerdotal functions' which heads wove into the school day – with frequent prayers and bible lessons. This was curiously at odds with the growing secularisation of the male profession, although it may have helped to diffuse conservative anxieties over female professional authority.[17] However, increasingly, a new generation of teachers began to protest against the gendered inequalities in the profession. Concerns over their lack of promotion prospects and poor pay led to the formation of a number of separate female teaching unions in the 1880s and 1890s, such as the London Mistresses' Association.[18]

In oral histories, some working-class women recall that lady teachers abused their authority in the classroom; although the pressures on such teachers were no doubt heightened by the 'payment by results' scheme. But it is equally true that many women went into teaching out of genuine pedagogical and altruistic motives. They demonstrated sympathy for the extreme fatigue suffered by 'half-timers' (pupils who spent the first half of their day in a factory), allowing them to sleep during lessons, for example.[19] Similar motives might inspire those who taught outside formal educational structures. In addition to the plethora of Sunday schools and village schools established and often staffed by middle-class and elite female volunteers, these years saw an increase in adult educational institutes (where women might teach a variety of subjects to both sexes) and mothers' meetings. Elma Paget, published edited collections of articles, advice and sermons to be used by women teaching mothers in their parish. As M. J. Peterson notes, through such dedication, women made a significant, but unpaid, contribution to the development of mass education.[20]

Meanwhile, women's growing access to higher education meant a corresponding opportunity for careers in academia. It was extremely difficult for women to obtain appointments, though, and a separate, female career path emerged in numerous institutions. In teacher training departments, for example, female lecturers were given the inferior titles of 'Mistress of Method' or 'Normal Mistress'. Again, the academy often failed to contemplate women as independent professionals. When plans were drawn up for a female students' hostel in Cardiff in 1884, it was thought 'that some Lady interested in the work of Women's Education might be willing to undertake it...at any rate for the first year or two, without a salary.'[21] But equally, the professional identities of female academics themselves could be easily fractured by family demands. Helen Gladstone had to turn down an offer to become the first Principle of Royal Holloway College, as she was required to care for her elderly parents.[22] Eleanor Ormerod, one of the country's top agricultural entomologists, declined a salary for her post as consultant to the Royal Agricultural Society. For such wealthy women, occupation could be viewed not as the road to professionalism, but as an extension of elite women's customary recourse to amateur occupation.[23]

Despite initiatives to facilitate female networking, such as the University Club for Ladies (1887), academic women remained institutionally weak and were frequently denied access to research libraries, laboratories, common rooms and grants; and rarely permitted a voice in university government. Even by the 1930s women comprised only approximately 13 per cent of the profession (a figure which had changed little by the 1970s). None the less, academe remained an attractive option, with many female lecturers embracing the opportunity for fellowship in the women's colleges, which also offered good accommodation and maid service.[24]

Medicine

A small number of determined middle-class women gained entry to the medical profession during these years, but only after a protracted and bitter battle; and by 1894 there were still fewer than 180 female doctors.[25] Much of the ideological impulse behind the campaign for female doctors lay not in the liberal model of campaigning for rights, but rather in the philanthropic and evangelical tradition. This was epitomised by Elizabeth Garrett Anderson who opened a dispensary for the treatment of gynaecological, obstetric and paediatric disorders in a working-class area of Marylebone in 1866.[26] It was certainly never advanced that women should practice medicine on equal terms with men, but rather that they were particularly suited for treating (only) women and children. Such a strategy had a sharp feminist edge. Ideas concerning the sanctity of the female body (which most feminists fully endorsed) and notions of social propriety repelled many from enduring intimate examinations at the hands of a man. The campaign against the Contagious Diseases Acts had heightened awareness of these issues. Moreover, feminists such as Elizabeth Blackwell tended to stress a holistic approach to medicine, which emphasised the importance of a patient's emotional condition. Consequently, it was argued that women required female doctors in whom they could confide. Additionally, campaigners turned to the empire, claiming it their duty to liberate native women from 'barbarous' customs. They focused upon the need for female doctors in the zenanas of India, where it was believed that women were deprived of medical care because of their enforced seclusion from men. Many of the first female doctors set up practice in India, including Edith Pechey and Agnes McLaren.[27]

Philanthropic and imperial values also proved critical to the rise of military nursing. Women formed an official (if minute) part of the army nursing service from 1861, in which the energetic and independent-minded could enjoy superior pay and pension provision. In addition, thousands took advantage of the training provided by the St John's Ambulance Association to volunteer for the 1882–5 Egyptian campaign. For feminists, such as Ethel Fenwick of the British Nurses' Association, women's involvement in British military campaigns was a powerful argument for giving them the vote. In practice, however, as Ann Summers points out, the organisation of female efforts into separate, subordinate societies may have counteracted egalitarian outcomes. Nevertheless, independent female initiatives such as the Women's Volunteer Medical Staff Corps (1894), in which women also learned drilling and musketry, were an important indicator of women's subscription to the mounting militarism and patriotism of the pre-1914 years.[28]

Whilst high social class was not a requirement for school or workhouse nursing, which also expanded greatly during this period, both military and civilian nursing dwelt upon the importance of lady nursing sisters. The architects of the country's emerging medical infrastructure wished to transplant the social hierarchies of class into hospital wards to ensure that a regime of authority and propriety would be preserved. Under Nightingale's training schemes (instituted at the Nightingale School at St Thomas's Hospital and later copied in other major hospitals), lady probationers were exempt from many of the more arduous or dirty tasks. Reformers suggested that good nursing involved the 'uniquely female' activities of moral guidance as well as scrupulous hygiene – as such, nurses should be under the authority not of doctors, but of matrons.[29]

The practice of engaging upper-class women brought with it its own problems. Jane Shaw Steward, who presided over the training of female military nurses at Netley, acted as if the wards were her own domain, even beating the lower-class nurses on occasion. Certainly, many ladies intervened in nursing out of long-standing traditions of upper-class philanthropic authority. During the Egyptian campaign (1882–5), a group of upper-class women founded the Princess of Wales's Branch of the National Aid Society so that they might send nurses to the conflict under their own jurisdiction. However, as doctors began to insist upon the necessity of having their own authority over nurses and their training, the older model of upper-class female authority had to give way to standardised, hierarchical structures in which nursing sisters were answerable to the medical and military staff above them.[30] Meanwhile, a subcommittee's report into the state of metropolitan district nursing insisted that nurses desist from attempts at religious teaching. One 'Queen's Nurse' (a district nurse employed by the Queen Victoria's Jubilee Institute, 1889, which organised district nursing nationally) explained proudly: 'One went into those homes, not as 'my lady bountiful', but as a fellow human being.'[31]

By the end of the period a new generation of nurses had emerged which sought professionalisation and greater public recognition. Against fierce opposition from the establishment (Nightingale included), nurses articulated a growing demand for state registration. The British Nurses' Association (1891) won a major victory for the cause of professional women by winning a royal charter of incorporation in 1893. In 1894, the Matrons' Council was formed which, in 1900, established a National League of Certificated Nurses (although full state registration was not achieved until 1919).[32] A parallel process was underway in the field of midwifery. Growing numbers of middle-class women sought entry to the profession as new examinations, such as those introduced by the London Obstetrical Society in 1872, distanced it from the practices of untrained, lower-class women. Zepherina Veitch established the Midwives' Institute (formerly the Matrons' Aid Society) to push for the registration of properly qualified midwives.[33] Nursing was gradually beginning to detach itself from the philanthropic tradition from which it had emerged.

Clerical Work and Retailing

Clerical work was an increasingly attractive proposition for middle-class women. The numbers of female clerical workers simply rocketed during this period, with over 85 000 in such work in 1901, compared to but 6000 20 years previously.[34] Clerical work required a good standard of personal presentation and literacy, and drew upon supposed characteristics of the genteel female, one Post Office official praising the 'delicacy of touch' of female telegraphers.[35] Female propriety was ensured in many of the larger companies by arranging separate entrances and staggered lunch-hours for male and female staff. Distinctions were also made in the nature and remuneration of the work. Companies frequently created a dual labour market within their management structure: inexpensive 'lady' clerks could be hired to perform the routine clerical tasks, leaving more responsible positions for the male staff, who were thus assured the opportunity for promotion.[36]

Yet, Meta Zimmeck argues that the flood of female applicants which clerical posts attracted is a sign that despite the marriage bar, the low pay, the poor promotion respects and the frequently poor working conditions, 'the typewriter, the ledger, and the shorthandwriter's pad were instruments not of oppression but of liberation.' Middle-class women, still a minority in the sector, could find positions at the top of the clerical range. Private firms might offer between £2 and £4 a week to clerks with language skills and a superior education. Nevertheless, it was more senior women who suffered most from prohibitive practices such as the marriage bar. Women in the lower grades of the Civil Service appear to have welcomed the marriage bar, entitling them as it did to a substantial 'dowry'; but those in the upper grades fought a long battle for its abolition.[37] Women continued to be thought unfit to perform the top jobs in the Civil Service, although, at the very end of this period, a handful of women, including the feminist Clara Collet, succeeded in gaining appointments in the factory inspectorate. However, they were employed to protect the interests of women workers, and were not required to oversee technical issues.[38] By the 1890s, female clerical workers were becoming highly sensitive to their differentiated treatment. When the Post Office announced a cut in female salaries from £65 to £55 to place them on the same level as a new post of male assistant clerk, women were quick to mobilise in protest.[39]

Shop work, with its connotations of serving and money handling, was not looked upon as a high-status job and was unlikely to appeal to any but the lowest sectors of the class, for whom it could form a necessary stop gap before marriage. Nevertheless, according to Lee Holcombe, shop assistants were 'by far the largest single-group of middle-class women workers in the country'.[40] By the turn of the twentieth century there were approximately a quarter of a million female shop assistants.[41] At the top end of the market, the large up-market stores required a constant supply of young, single women of refined manners who could afford the fashionable dress and elegant coiffure deemed necessary to sell to high-class customers. This new emphasis upon standards of service and appearance, which effectively commercialised women's appearance, was vital if retail outlets were to capitalise upon the growing perception of shopping as a leisure activity.[42] It is probable that many women would have derived a pride from handling the fashionable merchandise in the elegant environment of which they were a part. However, pay was low and legislation to improve the poor working conditions proved inadequate; moreover, the majority actually laboured in medium-sized outlets of about ten assistants. A lack of research into shopworkers means that we remain largely ignorant as to the true nature of their experiences. Furthermore, although women were permitted membership of some clerical and shopworkers' unions from the 1890s, they did not became a major force in these organisations until the new century.[43] Yet, shop work, in common with clerical opportunities, now furnished single women with a respectable means of earning a living. This was a substantial advance from the pitiful position in which such women might have found themselves earlier in the century.

Continuities and Traditional Roles

Despite the innovations in educational reform and expanding job opportunities for many, for the majority of women in these classes, and especially for those in the upper middle or landed classes, this was a period of but gradual change. Even in 1911, women formed but 6 per cent of the higher professions.[44] The new girls' schools lay beyond the financial reach of most middle-class families. The majority remained in small traditional schools, many of which, as one observer pointed out, remained 'totally unaffected' by educational reforms, even in the 1890s.[45] For those in the upper middle and upper classes, education remained a sporadic and informal process, although girls in such families benefited from a high level of cultural exposure. As attitudes towards female abilities widened, such a background could provide individuals with avenues for stimulating occupations as artists, scientists and musicians. An amateur interest in science led Marianne North to become one of many female travellers. She traversed the world to research and paint rare flora, eventually giving her massive archive to Kew Gardens. Cecilia Stainer spent many years as an independent musical researcher, writing several entries for Grove's *Dictionary of Music and Musicians*.[46]

Such lives of useful occupation are at variance with the classic thesis of J. A. and Olive Banks. They argued that the period witnessed a shift from the perfect wife to the perfect lady, with the employment of greater numbers of servants allowing women to lead a more leisured existence.[47] This might have applied to a small proportion of upper-middle-class women, but it was not the norm. 'Home', as Barbara Caine discovered in her investigations into the sisters of Beatrice Webb, 'was their place of work'.[48] Running a household, caring for children, supervising servants, organising lavish entertainment and adhering to ritualised codes of female visiting (so important in maintaining a family's social status) provided most women with a full-time occupation. It is interesting to note that the female members of many comfortable middle-class families (including adult daughters and elderly mothers) were listed as servants in the census returns – a frank recognition of the domestic labour they performed within their families.[49] By the end of the period, feminists such as Mona Caird and Louisa Martindale were arguing for co-operative housework and greater paternal responsibility for child care.[50] Such schemes were not popular, however. For most women, management of the household appears to have been critical to their self-perception. Significantly, a complaint in many divorce suits was that husbands had attempted to wrest their wives' domestic authority from them.[51]

For the wealthiest, the work involved in taking on the management of a large establishment was felt to be a daunting prospect. The young Emily Jowett vacillated over becoming the wife of Dearman Birchall because of the skills required of a country house mistress. 'It is an awfully responsible position for me', she explained.[52] Certainly, many landed women continued to have a significant role in estate supervision. Shortly before her marriage to Lord Norton, Julia Leigh learnt that she should have 'the entire care and management of the villages – the schools and clubs and cottages'.[53] The leisure-filled lives of socialites such as Lady Sitwell were far from the norm.[54]

Equally, the wives of professionals expected to assist their husbands in their work. Academic wives, such as Netty Huxley (wife of T. H. Huxley) might fulfil many of the duties which would now be performed by a research student and, in common with other professional wives, act as their husbands' clerks or amanuenses. Catharine Tait, whose husband was the Archbishop of Canterbury, took on responsibility for much of the church's financial accounting; and bishops' wives made an important contribution to the cohesion of the diocese by organising Clergy Wives Days (they could also play the role of arbiter during heated Lambeth conferences!). Lady Roberts, as wife of the Commander-in-Chief for India, felt it her duty to contribute to the well-being of the imperial forces, introducing British female nurses into Indian military hospitals in 1887.[55] Much of women's work, precisely because it was performed for male kin, has sunk from the historical record. Just occasionally, we catch glimpses of their forgotten labours. Blanche Cripps illustrated her husband's books on cancer of the rectum and abdominal surgery; a Miss Henslow prepared the botanical illustrations for her brother's publications.[56]

Lower middle-class women, in particular widows or those whose families were facing financial difficulties, would often take in homework, perhaps sewing, to supplement the family income. Indeed, it has been claimed that, 'homework played a part in helping to bolster up the Victorian ideal of the family and women's natural domesticity' – a subject which warrants much greater investigation.[57] Equally, very little work has been carried out into the role of business women during these years. There is some evidence to suggest that at the lower end of the spectrum women did remain engaged in business. Pamela Horn found that women ran nearly one in five of the advertised businesses, including wheelwrights and beer retailers, in certain small Northamptonshire villages in 1877.[58] Even less is known of the economic life of rural women in the middling strata. Over 4 000 women were listed as farmers in their own right in England and Wales in the 1911 census. Many of these were presumably widows, although some women were actively seeking an agricultural career by the end of the period. (In 1899, for example, a Women's Agricultural and Horticultural International Union was established.)[59] It seems likely that other middle-class women would have put their domestic skills to commercial advantage during times of financial need. Widows and single women (or those prepared to live apart from their children) might find employment as a housekeeper or cook. Others established nursing homes to cater for the elderly, whilst a small number functioned as foster mothers for children whose parents were in India.[60] One new development was the incursion of upper-class women into business ventures. Retail outlets such as fashionable clothes shops and florists became a popular means of income production, sometimes for philanthropic ends.[61]

However, according to Lady Violet Greville, for the aristocratic spinster, professional occupations remained 'out of the question'; although a few of the very highest family background might still turn to a place at court. The financial position of Susan Baring was salvaged when the Queen invited her to became a maid-of-honour in 1897, following the death of her father.[62] For those of less exalted status, there was but a very narrow range of genteel options – especially if they lacked the educational sophistication of many of their middle-class peers. Impoverished gentlewomen might exploit their knowledge of luxury goods by offering their services as high-class freelance cooks, or perhaps cleaning jewellery or precious furniture.[63] Others might seek positions as paid companions. There were some (unsuccessful) attempts to formalise this form of elite domestic service. One of these, the 'Office of Lady Helps' was set up by the suffragist, Rose Mary Crawshay, in the 1870s.[64]

For those not in need of remuneration there were many fields in which women might find occupational fulfilment. Catharine Paget Thompson, for example, was typical in explicitly referring to her charity visiting as 'work'.[65] In 1893, it was estimated that half a million women were engaged 'continuously and semi-professionally in philanthropy'.[66] Those inspired by religion could enjoy an active life as missionaries, and by 1900 women predominated in a number of missionary societies.[67] While, in Ireland, the number of nuns rose dramatically during this period, many of whom worked in workhouses and hospitals.[68] By the second half of the nineteenth century women were performing, on a voluntary basis, many of the functions that later became the responsibility of social work professionals. Increasingly, women committed to working with the poor, criminal or ill, had a university education, and perhaps specialist training as well. Octavia Hill's Charity Organisation Society trained voluntary workers for house-to-house visiting, investigating the circumstances and characters of the needy poor. Hill had also instructed lady volunteers in her model-housing projects, where, in addition to collecting the rent, they were expected to befriend and 'improve' their tenants. Women with such a background were welcomed in the burgeoning settlement movement. These were charitable communities, where middle-class reformers lived and worked among the poorest members of society, providing health care and recreational facilities. The enthusiasm of female students for such ventures was demonstrated with the foundation of the Women's University Settlement (WUS) in 1887, which also sought to prepare its members for greater professionalisation. However, despite their pioneering work, as government bodies began to take over responsibility for disabled children, postnatal care and so on, the role of settlement workers became reduced to more mundane, subordinate positions at the hands of a male-dominated bureaucracy.[69] Even so, for thousands of women, social work – paid or unpaid – presented a fulfilling means of uniting the cultural pressures of Christian duty and female benevolence with individual desires for occupation and personal utility, while also forging an identity separate to that of their families.

Conclusion

Growing numbers of women benefited from major advances in educational and employment opportunities during this period – but neither represented a simple capitulation to feminist arguments. The demands of a modernising economy created a gap in the labour market, particularly in teaching, retailing and clerical work, with immense implications for the welfare of single women. However, the stability of nineteenth-century society and its gender relations were consolidated by the reiteration of gender differences which accompanied women's entry into these positions. By expanding the significance of such concepts of women's benevolence and gentility (as happened in the medical and nursing professions, for instance), women succeeded in laying claim to new territory. It was only right at the end of this period that women appear to have developed more egalitarian concepts of their professional identities. Meanwhile, this process was complicated by the fact that women's unpaid labour remained central to contemporary social welfare projects; while, for the vast majority of married women, the professional, affective and physical demands of their families continued to provide the central ambit of their work.

11

POLITICS, COMMUNITY AND PROTEST

Introduction

During the second half of the nineteenth century new opportunities emerged for female involvement in public and political affairs. In addition to the evolving philanthropic tradition, women gained access to local government office and direct involvement in party politics. The women's rights movement also burgeoned, bringing with it the growth of a feminist sensibility which embraced not just women's rights, but such issues as temperance, social morality and peace. In all these areas, women's confidence to engage with the 'public sphere' drew upon a complex mix of cultural influences. Evangelical, feminist, political, imperial and national discourses proliferated and diverged to produce enormous diversity in both women's activities and their ideological motivations. Meanwhile, the consolidation of a female consciousness encouraged many female activists to seek cross-class collaboration – ambitions which frequently foundered upon the particularity of their own political visions.

Philanthropy

Philanthropy continued to be a major occupation of middle- and upper-class women (see also Chapter 10). For many women this was an added burden in an already demanding life, but for countless others – particularly single women – philanthropy remained an important source of fulfilment. Most landed women continued to take some responsibility for the well-being of their tenants.[1] Such activities were part of the cultural fabric of rural life, underlining community ties of authority and deference. Lady Suffield and her daughter visited their local tenants in Norfolk in 1877 to persuade the women that they 'ought not to allow their husbands to strike'.[2] Nevertheless, this tradition was beginning to falter: public debate over 'dependant paupers', combined with aristocratic parsimony during the agricultural depression, encouraged a shift from personal to organised philanthropy. Many charitable societies had mixed-sex committees and by the end of the century it was assumed that those catering for women and children should be entrusted to the management of female volunteers.[3]

At the local level, landed women were active in setting up branches of the Mothers' Union, the Brabazon Society (for workhouse reform), Girls' Friendly Societies, and also in encouraging district nursing services in their locality.[4] Meanwhile, wider horizons for philanthropic work were emerging in the British empire, particularly in the field of education. Annette Ackroyd Beveridge, who opened her own girls' school in India, is one example of the articulation of a 'maternal imperialism', in which Indian women were constructed as 'helpless, voiceless, hopeless'. Less typical were the Irish educationist, Margaret Noble, and the feminist theosophist, Annie Besant, whose work in India eventually led them to support Indian nationalism.[5]

The philanthropic tradition was also evolving in other directions. A number of women were now seeking to assist working-class women by promoting trade unionism. The Women's Protective and Provident League (WPPL), established in 1874 by Emma Paterson, aimed to safeguard the industrial interests of working-class women and to encourage working women to mobilise themselves. Similar motives inspired the Glasgow Council for Women's Trades and the Women's Industrial Council (WIC, 1894) which also campaigned for improved educational provision. The feminist-inspired, middle-class organisers hoped that their actions would herald a new era of cross-class sisterhood. In practice, the philanthropic relationship failed to provide insights into the real needs of working women. Middle-class organisations were mostly opposed to protective legislation, seeing it as an unwarranted restriction upon women's right to work. They struggled to appreciate that most working-class women perceived such measures as a positive contribution to their employment welfare, often bringing a welcome reduction in hours. It was not until the end of the nineteenth century that some middle-class campaigners, in particular those influenced by socialism, such as Clementina Black, encouraged the WPPL (now renamed the Women's Trade Union League and led by Lady

Emilia Dilke) to forge closer ties with the trade union movement and to campaign in favour of employment regulation.[6]

Those with little sympathy for socialism, or the needs of women as workers, found in the Charity Organisation Society (1869) a means of modernising older traditions of philanthropic visiting and cross-class relationships. The COS, which attracted prominent reformers such as Octavia Hill, aimed to establish charity upon rational principles by giving relief only to those who they believed to be truly deserving. Despite the organisation's often harsh image, its individualist philosophy could be construed by its practitioners to promote 'feminine' values of caring and solicitude. However, the recipients of its services were probably more struck by the intrusion into their personal lives which the COS's interviewing techniques afforded.[7]

Elsewhere, women's activities were hindered by the greater professionalism of state activities. The creation of a uniform prison inspectorate, for example, made the work of individual female prison visitors increasingly untenable.[8] The proliferation of state responsibilities were not merely imposed upon British people, however. The demands of even unenfranchised citizens were playing an ever-greater role in fashioning expectations of government activity. In particular, social purity campaigners demanded that the state recognise the social and political importance of sexual restraint. During these years over 200 societies were formed (aided by the incessant activity of Ellice Hopkins) devoted to the cause of moral reform. The social purity movement reached its zenith with the formation of the National Vigilance Association (the NVA) in 1886. The NVA sought to act as a watchdog to the implementation of the Criminal Law Amendment Act of 1885, which tightened up laws concerning brothels and sexual assault; criminalised homosexual activity; and raised the age of consent. This legislation had been passed following public outcries over William T. Stead's lurid revelations of widespread, illicit and paedophiliac sexual activity, published in the *Pall Mall Gazette*. The NVA (in which women played a major role) also campaigned for the prohibition of certain literature (including Rabelais and Zola); the closure of music halls deemed immoral (the redoubtable Laura Ormiston Chant's fights against the Empire Music Hall became legendary); and the introduction of female magistrates and police officers. It was particularly concerned with the issue of prostitution – a mounting concern of philanthropic workers since the late 1850s, when intrepid rescue workers had begun to venture into brothels and slums in an attempt to reform prostitutes.[9]

Women's striking commitment to moral reform was also evident in the temperance movement. Greatly inspired by American evangelism (as was the passing phenomenon of female preachers in the early 1860s[10]) in 1876, the British Women's Temperance Association (BWTA) was founded, which benefited from committed local activists, particularly in Scotland and Ireland. Until the late 1880s, the organisation remained timid both ideologically and in terms of reforming strategies. However, by 1893, the redoubtable Lady Isabel Somerset had succeeded in fostering a progressive following within the association. Under Somerset's control, the renamed National British Women's Temperance Association became strongly involved in feminist activities. A breakaway group, led by the more conservative Mary Dowcra, established the Women's Total Abstinence Union.[11] Meanwhile, the temperance cause was boosted by the work of the Salvation Army. The dynamic figure-head of Catherine Booth ensured that the Salvation Army became the first British religious organisation to grant fully equal status to both male and female members.[12]

In positioning themselves as guardians of the nation's morals, women expanded upon evangelical concepts of their beneficent and loving natures. Many reformers eschewed the concept of women's rights, yet exhibited a powerful 'feminine consciousness', not least in their insistence that women's contribution was vital to the reformation of modern society.

Local Politics

During this period, local government was gradually absorbing many of the functions of traditional philanthropy, such as the care of neglected children, the sick and the elderly. Women became important conduits of this evolution – bringing experience they had gained in philanthropic endeavour. In 1869, the Municipal Franchise Act granted the municipal vote to female ratepayers in England and Wales (this was later narrowed to unmarried women ratepayers). This was followed by the creation of school boards in 1870, which permitted female candidates; by the election of the first female Poor Law guardian, Martha Merrington in 1875; and by female candidacy in Parish and District Councils in 1894.[13] In Scotland women were not granted the municipal franchise until 1882; and Irish women had to wait until the 1898 Local Government Act (which enfranchised 100 000 women as local government electors) for significant local political power. In Ireland, school boards were not established, although Irish women were permitted to act as Poor Law guardians in 1896.[14] Although female office-holders were numerically tiny (by the late 1890s about 1500 English women held elected local office), their privileged socio-economic position enabled them to produce effects which far outweighed their numbers.[15]

This was particularly noticeable in the workhouses, although despite the efforts of the Women Guardians' Society (1881), significant numbers of female guardians did not materialise until 1894 when the property qualification was dropped. Female guardians frequently faced hostility and obstruction from male board members, who were often of a lower social class and might prioritise low rates, rather than institutional improvements. Nevertheless, many women managed to extend many of the reforms they had introduced as workhouse visitors: improving meals, providing comfortable chairs for the elderly, as well as curtains, books and the like. They were also pioneering in their efforts to foster out workhouse children to neighbouring families. However, the philanthropic sensibility was not the only motivating factor for female guardians. Many, particularly in the 1890s, came from the co-operative movement, being patrons of the WCG. Equally, a number had cut their teeth in the COS. These women were known for their rigid refusal to grant outdoor relief and their condemnation for those whose poverty, was, they believed the result of intemperate living.[16]

Women who stood for office in the newly created school boards, by contrast, found themselves in high prestige positions which attracted a good deal of political interest. School board members tended to adopt a conciliatory approach towards the local community because all rate payers (save for married women) were entitled to vote for them. They soon became noted for their pioneering work in reforming the scandalously punitive 'industrial schools' for delinquent children; for establishing proper care regimes for the mentally and physically disabled; and for introducing kindergarten techniques for infants. In addition, they organised massive feeding programmes and regular medical inspections for deprived children. In carving out these areas of expertise, women might be seen as drawing upon their own experience as mothers and philanthropists; but, more pragmatically, keeping to 'female' concerns helped to gain their acceptance with antagonistic fellow board members.[17] From 1894, women were permitted to seek office on the London vestries, or on the Parish and District Councils. Such work, which required technical knowledge of drainage, sewage and roads, did not marry well with contemporary assumptions of female abilities. Only a handful of women, such as Jane Escombe in Penshurst, Kent, used these positions to push for community improvements.[18]

Despite the obvious parallels between women's charitable work and their activities in local government, many women stood for election not from philanthropic motives, but out of feminist principles. As members of the London School Board, Emily Davies and Elizabeth Garrett (later Anderson) focused upon such issues as the amount of domestic education taught to girls; and the pay and conditions of female teachers.[19] Towards the end of the period, as more female board members tended to have a university education and educational experience, professional motives also came into play. Margaret Pillow was elected to the Norwich board in 1893 where, as the first NUT representative, she fought to raise teachers' pay and autonomy.[20] 'By the 1880s a considerable number of women had begun to stand for local office out of explicitly political objectives, typically that of Liberalism. The Women's Local Government Society (1888) was dominated by a network of well-connected female Liberals, prominent among them Annie Leigh Browne.[21] Women tended to be marginalised within the Liberal party, but their own networks of temperance, social purity and philanthropic connections could provide alternative sources of support in their local government endeavours. The NVA's close alliance with the London County Council in its efforts to reform the nature of the capital's music halls, is testament to this powerful ideological brew.[22]

Women's local government involvement reached its zenith during this period as it was able to capitalise upon the leisure, wealth, connections and philanthropic experience of middle- and upper-middle class women who could easily merge voluntary with official contributions. Patricia Hollis has discovered that in Norfolk, 'more women held elected office at district level, and took a larger and more effective share in local government in 1900...than they were doing around 1980.'[23] In 1899 the vestries were abolished in favour of new London boroughs, for which women were not permitted to stand. Such developments were symptomatic of the chequered course of women's access to local government office (which conservatives had always feared would further campaigns for female suffrage). Women's intervention in the management of local affairs was to re-emerge during the First World War, with such bodies as the Women's Institute.[24] However, in local politics, as in the voluntary sector, as the machinery of state

became increasingly subject to uniformity, bureaucracy and meritocratic principles, women tended to lose access to formal power.[25]

Aristocratic Influence

The political position of both the Queen and the female aristocracy was
increasingly modified by the greater democratisation of the state. The
Reform Acts of 1867 and 1884 lessened the political role of the Crown;
and, as party structures became tighter and more disciplined, so the
informal processes of social politics declined in importance. Within this
general framework, however, there was still a considerable role for
women to play. Although the Queen's withdrawal from public life
following the death of Prince Albert in 1861 has often been noted,
Reynolds argues that the apparent domesticity of the Victorian court
may have concealed the queen's participation in affairs of state. Indeed,
Pugh notes that Victoria found covert ways to express her (increasingly
conservative) political opinions, For example she supported Conservative charities, such as the fund for distressed Irish ladies who had
suffered from the Liberal's Irish land policies.[26]

Despite the waning importance of social politics, contacts and entertaining still remained an essential component of the political elite.
Political hostesses (such as Lady Londonderry and Lady Landsdowne,
for the Conservatives; and Lady Spencer and Lady Tweedmouth, for
the Liberals) continued to wield influence.[27] As Justin McCarthy proclaimed in 1870: 'The drawing-room often settles the fate of the division in the House of Commons.'[28] The expectation of the splendid
court Lady Waldegrave would establish in Dublin – vital for creating
ties of loyalty to the British government – was a primary reason for her
husband's appointment as Chief Secretary to Ireland in 1870.[29]
Recently, Gerry Maguire has suggested that there is 'something rather
pathetic' about the political activities of such women, arguing that they
had no power in their own right, their influence being derived solely
from their relationships with men.[30] Pat Jalland also hazarded caution
in her study of political wives, noting that despite their social and
personal influence, they were not able to guide the political agenda
itself. Certainly, most women appear to have enjoyed political authority
but indirectly, as in the case of Mary Gladstone who acted as her father's
private secretary between 1880–5.[31] There were, however, important
exceptions. Martin Pugh has drawn attention to elite couples in which

the wife was as politically influential as her husband. This was the case with Frances, Duchess of Marlborough, who (as Maguire also notes) even chaired a departmental meeting during her husband's period of office at the Board of Education.[32]

Towards the end of the period, women were finding a new outlet for their political sympathies. The Corrupt Practices Act of 1883, which prohibited the payment of canvassers, necessitated a fresh reliance upon women's willingness to act as unpaid electoral workers. Exceptionally, Lady Jennie Churchill took over her husband's entire election campaign in 1885, even holding daily conferences.[33] Canvassing effectively exploited women's goodwill to assist in a political structure in which they played no official role. However, for most, their activities derived from deeply held political beliefs which were increasingly manifest in women's independent political organisations.

Women and Political Parties

The first local women's Liberal associations were formed in the 1870s. By 1887 there were over 40 women's Liberal associations across the country and they banded together as the Women's Liberal Federation (the WLF) under the leadership of Sophia Fry.[34] (A year later, dissension over the Irish question led to the formation of a break-away group, the Women's Liberal Unionist Association). The WLF encouraged each branch to decide its own policies, but a unifying theme of support for women's suffrage soon emerged. Members could exert considerable pressure by refusing to help those Liberal candidates hostile to women's suffrage. By 1893, when Lady Rosalind Carlisle became president, the WLF had become a major campaigning organisation for women's suffrage.[35] This was a position a minority of WLF members found unacceptable, leading to the formation of another splinter group in 1892 – the Women's National Liberal Association.

The ideology of Liberal women, many of whom tended to be Nonconformist, was strongly informed by a moral agenda. This was dramatically illustrated in 1889 by their fierce attack upon the candidacy of politician Charles Dilke, who had been implicated in a divorce scandal. In their articulation of these ideas, Liberal women drew upon Evangelical notions of women's role as guardian of the nation's morals. They focused upon such issues as public health, temperance, education and domestic violence, which they believed illustrated the need for a female political voice.[36] Conservative women, on the other hand, promoted a less radical interpretation of the Evangelical doctrine, arguing only for indirect political influence. As Lady Jersey explained: 'we don't wish to govern the country...we want to assist in placing men in government.'[37] The Primrose League (1883), devoted to widening the electoral appeal of the Conservatives, provided just such an opportunity. Women held a quarter of executive positions in the Welsh and English habitations (local mixed-sex branches) in the late 1880s.[38] However, the habitations possessed none of the local autonomy enjoyed by the WLF; and women's influence within the organisation at large was restricted to the aristocratic Ladies' Grand Council whose impact was largely limited to methods (for example introducing light entertainments in a bid to appeal to the lower classes) rather than policy. Although individual Conservative women might hold deep-seated feminist views (Lady Balfour resigned from the organisation when her local MP voted against a women's suffrage bill), the League refrained from making women's suffrage a policy issue.[39]

Despite the reluctance of Conservative women to promote their own political position, they were enormously important to local political organisation. Their superb organisational skills and detailed experience of the community, often gained during philanthropic activities, enabled them to distribute material, collate names for the electoral register and assiduously canvass the local electorate. As the Liberal Millicent Garrett Fawcett was forced to acknowledge, 'the Primrose League has done more to give women the position which has been so long and so rigidly withheld than any other organisation in this or in any period of the world's history.'[40]

Left-wing politics were similarly indebted to women's input. Middle-class women, as Chapter 5 discussed, had played a small but important part in the early socialist movement. When socialism revived in the 1880s, their involvement was again in evidence, only despite equal membership terms, women still played but a tiny role in the movement's organisational structures. The Social Democratic Federation (the SDF, 1884), the Fabian Society (1884) and the Independent Labour Party (ILP, 1893) were all theoretically in favour of female emancipation, yet believed this goal should be subordinate to the wider aim of socialist reform. Nevertheless, as in the earlier period, women's cultural contribution as lecturers, writers and fund-raisers was integral to the movement's vitality. This was particularly true of the ILP, in which well-educated women, such as Isabella Ford, Caroline Martyn and Enid

Stacy, emerged as popular speakers and organisers, creating an environment conducive to female involvement. Despite being a predominantly working-class organisation, by the turn of the century the ILP had attracted a committed band of middle-class (especially lower-middle-class) women, whose membership boosted the fortunes of local ILP branches.[41]

Socialist women, as we have seen, also acted as patrons to working-class causes. They were active, for example, in promoting trade unions. Notably, Isabella Ford founded the Leeds Tailoresses Union in 1889 which she later helped to amalgamate with the Amalgamated Union of Clothing Operatives.[42] In Manchester, middle-class activists such as Eva Gore–Booth and Esther Roper were instrumental in galvanising female textile workers in their campaign for the suffrage, although by the 1890s working women were demonstrating their own abilities for leadership in the cause.[43] Indeed, such relationships could prove thorny. The working-class lecturer Jessie Craigen discovered that her freedom of speech, and even her personal appearance, were compromised by the patronage of middle-class feminists.[44] Politicised philanthropy was also in evidence in the Women's Co-operative Guild, which under the influence of Margaret Llewelyn Davies (the niece of Emily Davies) became a campaigning force for female suffrage; although at times middle-class reforming zeal could overstep the day-to-day needs of the working-class members.[45] Women's involvement in party politics was, then, highly differentiated, revealing the complexity of contemporary ideologies concerning women's social and political roles. It also indicated the considerable cultural problems of forging cross-class collaboration amongst women.

Victorian Feminisms

Preceding discussions have highlighted the extensive feminist campaigns in education, employment, social purity and local government. (Chapter 12 will also point to feminist endeavours to challenge the basis of conventional families lives.) Clearly, however, these endeavours should be considered not only in isolation, but must be related to the broader feminist movement of the day. This was a movement which was increasingly self-confident about women's potential, and, as we have seen, which trumpeted the unique female qualities which women might bring to the 'public world' through their work and action. Although strongly influenced by Victorian liberalism, particularly in its arguments concerning the need to remove obstructions to women's access to employment and education, it moved beyond liberalism in its analysis of the sexual oppression of women.[46]

Despite the wide-ranging agenda of contemporary feminism, historians have noted that by the last decade of the century there were growing numbers of activists who were concentrating more exclusively upon the fight for women's suffrage. In part this was spurred, no doubt, by the importance which other radical constitutencies, such as the Labour movement, were now attaching to parliamentary representation.[47] However, this greater focus upon the vote did not imply that feminism was simply capitulating to liberal shibboleths as to the value of civic independence. Rather, as radical feminist and cultural historians have suggested, feminism cohered around far-reaching visions to challenge the nature of sexual relations. Feminists portrayed the campaign for the vote as imperative if women's sexual oppression was to be relieved. As Elizabeth Wolstenholme Elmy observed wryly in 1897: 'It is the fear of men that women will cease to be any longer their sexual slaves either in or out of marriage that is at the root of the whole opposition to our just claim. No doubt their fear is justified, for this is precisely what we do mean.'[48]

Such an assessment is derided by the most recent work on the suffrage campaign by Martin Pugh, who strips the movement of all its intricate and enriching cultural connections and portrays it as a repeatedly misguided parliamentary campaign.[49] By contrast, an influential study by Philippa Levine has emphasised the central role played by an emergent feminist culture during this period. Drawing upon kinship and friendship networks, and facilitated by growing numbers of female-only clubs (particularly in London), feminism, she argues, subverted traditional 'male' modes of political organisation. The result was a powerful and empowering movement, which attempted to restructure private relationships as well as public practices.[50]

Certainly, feminist sensibilities could also defy simple categorisation into the 'male' defined agendas of party politics. Ideological currents inspired by holistic humanitarianism, sometimes encompassing animal rights and vegetarianism, cut across party lines.[51] Moreover, as Levine argues, the emergent 'woman-centred' culture of Victorian feminism gave activists the confidence to tackle wider issues of moral authority.[52] Indeed, many middle-class women may have been inspired more by these issues than by the campaign for the vote itself. This emerged clearly during the campaign against the Contagious Diseases Acts. The Acts (passed in 1864 and 1866) gave magistrates in designated areas the powers to detain for compulsory medical inspection and treatment any woman deemed to be a prostitute. Feminists argued that the legislation was a clear illustration of the sexual double standard in which women were criminalised whilst men incurred no penalty. The use of the speculum upon suspected women was depicted as 'instrumental rape', exposing the sexual oppression of women at the hands of a male-dominated system in which police, magistrates, doctors and legislators could discriminate blatantly against them.[53]

In drawing upon melodramatic (if inaccurate) narratives of women's sexual exploitation by upper-class 'rakes', feminists were able to forge a brief alliance with working-class radicals – a coalition which helped to preserve women's own identity within the middle-class repeal movement. (Although they continued to benefit from the support of prominent middle-class male reformers, such as James Stansfeld.)[54] However, feminists also hoped that the campaign would foster a model of cross-class sisterhood. These hopes were rarely realised. They did provide useful legal advice to working-class prostitutes, but the campaign did not enjoy significant success among a wider female working-class audience, not least because the latter apparently felt restricted by conventions of social propriety. The campaign also split the women's suffrage movement, as activists such as Millicent Garrett Fawcett and John Stuart Mill believed it pragmatic to distance the campaign for the vote from the agitation against the Acts. Despite these set-backs, the movement for repeal politicised large numbers of middle-class women. The Ladies National Association (for the Repeal of the Contagious Diseases Acts), led by the charismatic, religiously inspired Josephine Butler, had 104 local branches by 1884.[55] When the Acts were rescinded in 1886, this energetic constituency began to fight for repeal in British India. They drew upon the imperial assumption that the moral influence of British womanhood was essential to the well-being of their 'oppressed sisters' across the world, for whom they presumed to speak.[56] Many of the repeal activists also went on to became involved in the campaigns for social purity. As 'feminist vigilantes', they supported the NVA by endorsing the removal of children from prostitute mothers and approved local government repression of streetwalkers. This was a development which alarmed feminists such as Josephine Butler and Emilie Venturi, who adhered to a *laissez-faire* view of state intervention. They had long been members of the Vigilance Association for the Defence of Personal

Rights (VA), formed in 1871.[57] The Vigilance Association (now renamed as the Personal Rights Association) was particularly concerned at the NVA's policy of brothel closures. Wolstenholme Elmy spoke of her disillusionment with 'those with whom for 17 years I have worked for the Repeal of the Contagious Diseases Acts', who, 'by a strange perversion, now sanction and command the means and the methods of a cruel repression'.[58]

As Elmy's comments perhaps indicate, feminism cannot be understood purely with reference to the emergence of a female consciousness. Whilst Levine's work is extremely suggestive, it is instructive to temper her analysis by emphasising the other ideological impulses (such as liberalism, socialism, religious motivations and so on) which intersected feminism. These influences highlight the many potential sources of ideological conflict within the movement, as well as indicating the role of mixed-sex networks and male assistance. Although the organised movement of this period dates back to the Kensington Ladies' Discussion Society (1865), founded by women such as Emily Davies, Sophia Jex-Blake, Elizabeth Wolstoneholme (later Elmy), Barbara Bodichon and Elizabeth Garrett; they inevitably had to rely upon sympathetic male support (in this case, the philosophical liberal, James Stuart Mill) to present their suffrage petition to parliament in 1866.[59] The following year, the Manchester Women's Suffrage Society was founded, whose leader, Lydia Becker, was to be a crucial figure in establishing the national movement. However, in Manchester as elsewhere, the early phases of the movement relied considerably upon male backing. In Bristol, prominent male reformers, such as Matthew Davenport Hill and Francis W. Newman, from progressive Unitarian and radical circles played an instrumental role in the foundation of a women's suffrage society. Equally, women were reliant upon lawyers, such as Richard Pankhurst (who was to be a founder of the ILP), to frame proposed women's rights bills for them.[60]

Movements such as Unitarianism and socialism articulated problematic and complex vocabularies on the 'woman question'. Nevertheless, their philosophical commitment to women's rights means that feminism cannot be seen as arising purely from female initiative and women's networks.[61] Indeed, the potential for female sisterhood was always jeopardised by women's loyalties to other political movements. In 1888 the suffrage movement became split because of a disagreement as to whether women's party political societies should be allowed to affiliate – a move which many feared would amount to a take-over by the WLF. It was not until 1897 that a unified suffrage organisation was formed: the National Union of Women's Suffrage Societies (NUWSS or National Union), under the leadership of Millicent Garrett Fawcett.[62]

Certainly, the great symbolic (and increasingly practical importance) which feminists attached to securing the vote masked the many conflicting theories and ideologies which drove individuals to support the campaign. In their public statements, feminists frequently stressed utilitarian arguments – such as the benefit which female enfranchisement would confer upon the whole community, by dint of women's peculiar qualities of beneficence and altruism. As Sandra Stanley Holton explains: 'The vote, then, became a tool with which women of all classes were to reconstruct society in accordance with female values and needs, to create a reformed and "feminised" democracy. That is to say, suffragists did not seek merely an entry to a male-defined sphere, but the opportunity to redefine that sphere.'[63] Nevertheless, even those, such as Frances Power Cobbe, who were firm believers in the differences between the sexes might highlight other arguments. Cobbe, noting that English political rights rested upon property ownership, argued that women should be permitted to vote as property owners and ratepayers.[64] At other times campaigners argued that as women had enjoyed political rights under Anglo-Saxon law, suffragists were merely campaigning for the restitution of women's rights, as in Charlotte Carmichael Stopes's 1894 work, *British Freewomen*. Such arguments drew upon the constitutionalist tradition within British radical and democratic discourse. However, the connotations of racial pride in an Anglo-Saxon heritage, which resonated through these narratives, succeeded in appealing to political conservatives such as Cobbe, as well as to the more overtly radical.[65]

Whilst these competing arguments for female suffrage were often the result of tactical strategies, other conflicting voices were the result of serious ideological differences within the movement. Two of the leading suffrage campaigners, Lydia Becker and Millicent Garrett Fawcett, both argued that the women's suffrage bills submitted to parliament should seek to enfranchise only unmarried or widowed women. This incensed more radical feminists such as Wolstenholme Elmy, who set up an alternative Women's Franchise League (WFL) in 1889 in protest. To the WFL, to refrain from demanding the vote for married women was to reinforce the doctrine of female subordination within marriage, against which they were fighting so fiercely in other areas, notably women's legal rights, domestic violence and marital rape.[66]

Towards the end of the period, another fundamental issue was beginning to emerge within suffrage circles. Many of the younger generation of activists, particularly those influenced by socialism, perceived the suffrage movement as part of a broader political project to secure a humanitarian and egalitarian society. As a consequence, they emphasised the importance of fighting for *adult* and not merely women's suffrage.[67] Whilst many suffrage leaders, such as Fawcett, were extremely wary of democracy, Dora Montefiore (who was to later become a founder member of the British Communist Party) was insisting from the late 1890s that it was working women who were most in need of the vote.[68] By contrast, by this period many Conservatives had also mobilised over the issue of women's suffrage (even the National Union of Conservative Associations had begun to approve resolutions on women's suffrage and a Church League for Women's Suffrage was formed[69]). For Conservatives, women's suffrage could be seen as a means of countering the working-class vote, and such campaigners were likely to have little in common with either Montefiore's socialism or the progressive impulses of the radical liberals within the suffragist camp.

Whilst the leaders of the suffrage movement may well have formed part of a larger and supportive network of feminist activists (and Levine's study was derived from a group biography), many rank and file members of the various suffrage societies may have felt that their political identities were rooted primarily with reference to party or religious allegiances (Jewish and Catholic women both had their own suffrage societies). Within these positions, however, most appeared to have felt that they had a unique contribution to make as women, and that their authority in moral affairs enabled them, at times, to transcend customary affiliations and to join hands with women across political and ideological divides.

Whilst this section has focused on the explicitly feminist, it is important to note that support for women's public activity or campaigns to secure women's higher education could be tangential to the women's rights movement. Indeed, the author Mary Humphrey Ward, herself a supporter of both women's local government activities and higher education, was one of many publicly active women who by the 1890s were channelling some of their energies into the *anti*-suffrage debate. Although a fully organised anti-suffrage movement did not emerge until the new century, none the less, initiatives such as Ward's 1889 "Appeal Against Female Suffrage" which was signed by 100 female sympathisers, highlighted some of the anxieties prevalent in the anti-suffrage camp. Anti-suffragists detached the concept of women's citizenship from enfranchisement, arguing that natural gender differences necessitated that women and men should perform their civic duties in different spheres. Needless to say, public opinion was not neatly divided into suffragist or anti-suffragist; individual positions were often fluid as circumstances, strategies or arguments modulated. Many prominent women, such as Beatrice Webb and Florence Nightingale, hovered in the 'anti' camp before finally plumping for the suffrage cause. Victorian feminism, then, was not a static, monolithic construct, but a shifting sea of many currents.[70]

National Identities

As the campaign against the Contagious Diseases Act testifies, the articulation of British feminism was often infused by a consciousness of women's potential to redeem the British Empire.[71] This was a pervasive, but not a universal position, however. Many found the militarism implicit in imperialism ideologically distasteful, and their consciousness of a 'moral citizenship' led them to protest against government policies. During the 1880s, when Britain was fighting the Afghans and the Zulus, the Quaker activist, Priscilla Peckover, launched the Women's Local Peace Association. Soon, thousands of local branch members were distributing literature; arranging fund-raising bazaars; and canvassing assiduously for the Peace Pledge. By the end of the century, such Quaker-inspired activism was being overtaken by socialist international theories, which, often influenced by feminism, advocated a more organisational approach to women's peace activities. The International Council of Women, for example, established a Standing Committee on Peace and International Arbitration in 1899.[72]

National identities were also central to women's political activism. In Ireland such issues were obviously critical. On the one hand, feminists in the Irish Unionist camp used their feminist networks to promote loyalist politics. The Irish feminist and Unionist, Isabella Tod, arranged a women's committee to protest against Gladstone's Home Rule Bill in 1886, resulting in a petition of over 100 000 signatures which was presented to the Queen in 1893. Irish Unionist women exploited contacts with the English Women's Liberal Unionist Association to organise protest meetings in England.[73] More dramatic was women's involvement in Irish nationalism. In 1881 when the members of the male Land League were facing imprisonment, the Ladies' Land League took over the operation of the movement. A lack of leverage within the wider political scene, combined with hostility from their male colleagues, led the Ladies' Land League to pursue a radical strategy, turning to peasant women, whom they believed to be their true allies. They faced growing repression for inciting tenants to refuse to pay their rents, although, unlike their male colleagues, they were not treated as political prisoners. Later in the century women were also active in promoting cultural nationalism. In 1896, Alice Milligan and Anna Johnson published *Shan Van Vocht* to assist in the promotion of the Irish language. Women were prominent, too, in the Gaelic League, established in 1893. Mary E. Butler, for example, was a member of its executive as well as being an active member of Sinn Fein. When the Inghinidhe na hÉireann (Daughters of Erin) was founded in 1900, with Maud Gonne as its president, it emerged as one of the few organisations which hoped to unite feminist with nationalist aims.[74] Hitherto, an independent women's rights movement had failed to truly flourish. Anna Haslam's Dublin Women's Suffrage Association (1876) was criticised for its moderate aims, whilst the nationalist movement itself tended to be hostile to any moves which prioritised women's needs over those of the great Irish struggle.[75] For Welsh women also, national identity was a source of personal pride and political activity. This was clearly seen in the Welsh women's temperance campaign, whose members refused to organise with the BWTA out of a desire to maintain their own national identity, language and culture.[76]

Conclusion

This period witnessed the zenith of female community authority. Upper- and upper-middle-class women in particular could capitalise upon their social position to carve a niche for female public involvement in areas that had not yet been appropriated by the state. As political and administrative structures became more formalised, women had to realign their political engagement away from informal influence towards participation in organised political activities; although cultural barriers still prevented their full and equal participation. By legitimising female initiatives to claim a public voice, the rhetoric of women's mission for moral reform provided the most radical challenge of the women's rights movement. It enabled feminists to use the spectre of the abused prostitute to assault the entire construction of masculine legal, sexual and political privilege. Yet, women's political involvement cannot be reduced to engagement with this one discourse. They demonstrated complex loyalties to a range of other identities and political languages. Women were independent political actors whose actions are not readily reducible to broad generalisations.

12

FAMILIES, RELATIONSHIPS AND HOME LIFE

Introduction

The years 1860–1900 witnessed a remarkable number of changes in the premises and discourses of family life. Women's growing access to employment opportunities and increased involvement in philanthropic and political life meant that traditional understandings of gendered roles within marriage were potentially threatened. In this light, the continuing acceptance of traditional structures of family life in most sectors is striking. Nevertheless, women do not appear to have simply acquiesced in patriarchal modes of family life. Middle-class and elite women demonstrated an ability to accommodate their own needs, as well as new ideas concerning relationships, mothering and consumer needs, within conventional formulations of married life and family responsibilities.

Courtship

At the highest levels of society social exclusivity, combined with the tradition of lavish private entertainment, facilitated the continuance of a restricted marriage market. The tight rules of social etiquette (in which women tended to be the chief arbiters) with its rituals of card-leaving and the like, helped to seal the privileged from intrusion by the socially inferior. Marriages were considered appropriate, however, with the upper middle classes, whose wealth was an important factor for the landed classes in an age of agricultural depression. The growing exclusivity of the upper middle classes facilitated such marriages, as did the cultural overlap between the richest bankers and industrialists and

172

the landed classes.[1] Consequently, among both the landed classes and the upper middle classes there was clear adhesion to the importance of a good match. Barbara Caine discovered that many of the sisters of Beatrice Webb were 'inclined rather to an eighteenth-century view that marriage should be based on rational considerations rather than mere sentiment'. Other women might choose spouses for the social position and influence they brought, as Pat Jalland discovered in her study of nineteenth-century political wives.[2]

For the bulk of the middle classes, changes in leisure patterns, including the growing popularity of theatres, tennis, seaside holidays and dances, greatly widened the field of potential marriage partners. This may have made affective motives for marriage more likely, although sensitivities over social status remained.[3] Many contemporaries were certainly disquieted by the apparent freedom in pre-marriage relations, remarking upon the 'fastness' of the young – their proclivity to smoke, flirt and to call one another by their Christian names.[4]

Such unease was voiced by Eliza Lynn Linton in her vituperative article on the 'Girls of the Period' (1868) which ignited a heated debate on the modern manners of young women. Linton poured scorn on young women for their preoccupation with dyed hair and make-up. She depicted them as callous and self-centred, accusing them of jettisoning notions of romantic love and nurturant motherhood for hard-headed calculations of a prosperous marriage. Most contemporaries recognised the article for what is was – a piece of journalistic satire from a known controversialist. Yet the article, as the ensuing debate indicated, exposed some of the veins of anxiety which ran through mid-Victorian attitudes towards female sexuality and marriage. One of these arose from the fact that middle-class men were marrying at increasingly late ages, typically in their very late twenties. This was largely a consequence of the growing emphasis upon consumerism which constrained men to postpone marriage until they were in a position to support a high standard of living. It was feared that as a consequence of this delay, women were becoming increasingly anxious (and thus correspondingly brazen) in their attempts to attract a husband.[5]

Marriage

Linton's article and the debates it aroused signalled the contemporary assumption that women played an active role in the courtship process.

Victorian feminists such as Mona Caird, however, suggested that once married, women became their husbands' vassals, caught in a relationship of 'sexual feudalism'.[6] Feminist novels interested in exploring alternative, egalitarian concepts of marriage abounded in the 1880s and 1890s, and committed feminists attempted to construct new models of marriage. The suffragette, Emmeline Pethick-Lawrence, had an apartment of her own, an anniversary present from her husband, to allow her to work or relax without interruption.[7] The feminist concerns regarding conventional marriage have been largely shared by modern historians. The conclusion of F. M. L. Thompson, that (upper-middle-class) wives 'remained unemancipated, strong or at least unrebellious believers in the dutiful and subordinate role to which their upbringing had conditioned them', is typical.[8]

The perpetuation of male authority within marriage is not surprising, given that most women remained economically dependent upon their husbands; educationally disadvantaged in comparison to them and without political rights. When, in 1891, Mrs Jackson took her estranged husband to court for kidnapping and forcibly detaining her, she only won her case on appeal. Chillingly, her victory outraged both *The Times* and her local community.[9] Subtle psychological influences further encouraged the growth of autocratic male personality types. As John Tosh has suggested: 'The character gap between the stern father and the loving mother made it extremely difficult for a growing boy to accommodate feelings of tenderness and affection in his masculine self-image.'[10] In the courtship and marriage of the Potter sisters, a number of the men involved exhibited a striking tendency towards domination. Beatrice Potter (later Webb), was forced to admit that Joseph Chamberlain would, 'refuse me all freedom of thought in my intercourse with him' and she would have had to 'subordinate all my life, mental and physical' to his career. Among her brothers-in-law, Willie Cripps was cruelly authoritarian towards his wife and children; and Robert Holt condoned the brutal assault of one his sons upon his daughter.[11] It is perhaps not surprising that in many cases, the much-vaunted companionate marriage was probably effected by the wife's willingness to subordinate her wishes to those of her husband. One particularly dutiful upper-class woman, Lady Boileau, subjected herself to a daily examination as to her behaviour towards her husband: 'Have I resisted with all my strength all desire to *defend* myself even if I should not have seen my fault...Have I tried in *everything* to consult his wishes?'[12] Such evidence is a telling example of the extent to which cultural ideals of femininity could be internalised by some individual women. This was an aspect of contemporary womanhood which particularly alarmed feminists of the day, who noted the 'servile, imitative, pliant' characters of wives.[13]

Contemporary proscriptions of companionate domesticity also masked other facets of Victorian marriage. Evolving constructions of elite and middle-class masculinities could complicate male responses to the conjugal home. The rise of the public school, the cult of sport, and imperial expansion all provided the opportunities for the evolution of new masculinities with distinct priorities. The image of the quiet, Evangelical man of fine sensibilities of the 1830s and 1840s had been replaced by the concept of 'Christian manliness', with its associations of muscular and intrepid manhood.[14] As a result, historians of masculinity, such as John Tosh and David Roberts, have detected a process of increasing alienation from domestic concerns, with men seeking out male-only spaces such as the club. As Jane Lewis has observed, 'Men sought women's society but not their companionship'.[15]

These generalisations, whilst valuable, do mask other, contrary trends. It has been pointed out, for example, that the private manners of the upper class were becoming more accommodating to female participation, as practices such as women retiring after dinner became less marked.[16] More tellingly, the studies of Tosh and Roberts are both based upon the family memoirs of notable public figures and are not necessarily typical of a wide social strata. A. J. Hammerton's analysis of divorce proceedings (following the 1857 Act) and autobiographies provides broader evidence of family dynamics and of changing public attitudes towards marriage. Importantly, Hammerton illustrates that although judges maintained that wives should submit to their husbands, there was a discernible shift in what they were prepared to consider as 'unreasonable behaviour' on the part of husbands. Gradually, as the nature of petitioning wives' complaints widened, a consensus emerged in the divorce courts concerning the probity of a companionate view of marriage. Husbands should not overstep the exercise of their authority, and wives should not be expected to put up with abusive or extreme authoritarian behaviour. In 1870 the case of Kelly versus Kelly established the important precedent that non-violent cruelty might be sufficient to warrant a divorce decree.[17]

Despite the fact that it was much harder for women to seek divorce, they were evidently becoming less tolerant of excessive authoritarianism and ill-treatment, filing about 41 per cent of all divorce petitions.[18] Whilst divorce remained highly exceptional (and impossible in Ireland), salacious details of matrimonial breakdown were avidly followed in the press, laying bare the fault-lines within contemporary marriages. This forced a public recognition that the Victorian ideal of marriage could be riven with conflict, bitterness and violence. Elaine Showalter suggested that these emotions were tapped into by stupendously successful authors of sensationalist fiction such as Mrs Henry Wood and Mary E. Braddon. Their novels, which told of the dull inanity of middle-class domesticity and the lure of sexual passion, spoke to the emotional needs of women whose expectations of personal fulfilment were growing ever higher.[19]

In some families, of course, patriarchal authority had never been permitted to shine forth very brightly. Relationships in which the wife dominated the husband, were undoubtedly a feature of Victorian life, as in every society; and the image of the hen-pecked husband provided humorous copy for music hall artists. Equally, many husbands had enormous respect for their wives' judgement. When Archibald Tait was offered the archbishopric of York he declined the post on his wife's advice.[20] Countless other relationships were built upon mutual consideration and devotion. Within such marriages male agendas were still prioritised, but this did not necessarily imply that female interests were always relinquished. Theresa Cripps, married in 1881, worked hard to support the political ambitions of her husband, Alfred, whom she adored. This, however, did not prevent her from finding expression for long-held philanthropic ambitions by organising schemes for domestic and technical education in Buckingham.[21] Indeed, the willingness of so many Victorian men to allow their wives to play an active role in philanthropic and political life suggests a considerable degree of flexibility and respect within contemporary marriages. (It must also have made a powerful impact upon their daughters' perceptions of women's community authority and managerial skills.) Equally, the courage, social and personal skills which women demonstrated in their public life warn us against reducing their personal lives to any simplistic formula of female submission.

For those in the middle class, women's authority within the home could be heightened by their role in upholding the values of morality, propriety and 'decency'. Those who emigrated to the colonies tended to replicate such behaviour, particularly in India where the expatriate community reified British social attitudes. In the pioneer societies however, there was greater potential to challenge traditional proprieties.

Catherine Parr Traill, who emigrated to Canada with her sister and their husbands, was delighted to report that, 'having shaken off the trammels of Grundyism we laugh at the absurdity of those who voluntarily forge afresh and hug their chains.' In Africa, too, where the families of colonial administrators were in evidence from the 1880s, the challenging environment reduced adherence to British social customs.[22]

Women's experience of family life was further diversified by the varying degrees of economic power which they might exert. As Chapter 10 illustrated, many sectors of the lower middle class continued to expect that wives would contribute to the family income. Amongst some occupational groups, notably teachers, this could result in women continuing to work – even with young children at home.[23] It seems unlikely, however, that this should have resulted in any greater degree of marital equality. Most probably looked upon their earnings within the context of the family economy, and did not assume that such money would result in greater personal independence. By contrast, those from wealthy families frequently had financial security established for them in their own right. William Gladstone ensured that any property acquired by his daughters after their marriage would not come under the control of their husbands.[24] Indeed, M. J. Peterson claims that, 'Victorian women were not controlled by their late fathers' or husbands' trusts; rather, they were empowered by them and were at liberty to use inherited monies as they chose'.[25]

Further research is required to more fully substantiate Peterson's assertion. Yet, even if such practices were not wholly representative, the financial situation of elite women was clearly extremely favourable when compared to women of the middle classes, the vast majority of whom ceased paid employment outside the home upon their marriage. It was the fate of these women which so enraged contemporary feminists. Portrayals of the parasitic wife, wholly dependent upon her husband for her economic survival, began to recur in feminist literature.[26]

Despite such pessimism, it was during this period that the first major steps were taken to improve the legal position of married women. In 1870 the Married Women's Property Act was passed. It applied only to England, Ireland and Wales, with Scottish women having to wait until 1877 for reform. The 1870 Act granted wives the ownership and control of their earnings, some specified kinds of inherited property and specially registered investments.[27] This Act, which originally arose out of a concerted feminist campaign, only emerged after an extensive mauling in the House of Lords. The resultant legislation was poorly drafted and often inconsistent. Feminists continued to campaign hard for further legislation – and in 1881 a far more extensive act was passed in Scotland, and then, a year later, in the rest of Britain. These acts entitled women to retain any real and personal property they acquired either before or after marriage and gave women responsibilities for the support of their families. The legislation did not grant women the right of full testamentary capacity (although this was redressed in 1893) and in certain situations a husband remained responsible for his wife's torts (civil injuries). Yet rather than adopting the feminists' demand for legal equality between husband and wife; the framers of the bill merely extended the language of equity to cover the protection of women's property. Consequently, feminist historians point to the use of 'restraint on anticipation' clauses, by which women could be denied the full powers over their property.[28] Nevertheless, contemporary campaigners appear to have been delighted with the outcome of their lobbying. '[E]ven those who have most actively worked for it,' celebrated one feminist journal, '...could scarcely have contemplated so triumphant a conclusion to their unceasing efforts.'[29]

If feminist activists appear to have been satisfied with the outcome of the legislation, so too, according to Leonore Davidoff were creditors. Davidoff makes the point that such reform was necessary because of women's role as 'primary consumers'.[30] Whether the reforms were passed because of the pressure of feminist agitation; the demands of creditors; or more broadly, the wider impulse to rationalise the existing anomalies between common law and equity, it is certainly true that women played a vital role as consumers. This period saw an explosion in retailing and the rise of new forms of shopping, in particular, the department store. Shopping was increasingly viewed as a leisure activity, and one which was particularly associated with women. By the 1880s female consumers were actively encouraged through the provision of refreshment rooms, cloakrooms and public transport. It could be argued that the targeting of female consumers (through advertising, for example) intensified the pressure upon women to conform to particular images of female behaviour and appearance. But others have argued that these developments heralded a new freedom for women. It now became acceptable to traverse the urban space alone (albeit with the persistent nuisance of sexual harassment) and to explore new pleasures and tastes.[31]

Mounting consumerism had other profound, if indirect, consequences for women. The boom in retail markets, the rise in the lifestyles of the middle classes and the growth of public schools and higher education necessitated high levels of expenditure. This was jeopardised by the economic depression of the 1870s, requiring financial retrenchment among these strata. One result, it has been suggested, was the decision to limit the number of children so that financial resources might be concentrated upon a smaller family unit. Certainly, the birth rate fell dramatically during this period. Those (English couples) who married between 1861–9 had an average of 6.16 children, compared to 4.13 children for those who married between 1890–9.[32] J. A. Banks has emphasised the role of the husband in taking this ultimately financial decision,[33] but this has been refuted by Patricia Branca, Michael Mason and Angus McLaren. They note the growing availability of 'female' methods of contraception, including the use of pessaries, the douche, the cap and the sponge. Historians of the American experience have referred to such practices as 'domestic feminism', arguing that it enabled women to exert control over their domestic situation and reproductive behaviour. Branca, who argues that middle-class incomes were precarious throughout this period, believes that the resort to birth-control signifies not only women's embrace of their sexuality, but may be viewed alongside women's growing use of chloroform and cosmetics – as part of a desire to take control over their bodies.[34]

The problem with Branca's argument is that it posits a somewhat anachronistic equation between women's embrace of their sexuality and female emancipation. Many campaigners, including the pioneer doctor, Elizabeth Blackwell, did emphasise the importance of female sexuality and a minority, such as the Legitimation League (1893), championed the cause of free unions.[35] But, as Chapter 11 noted, ideas of sexual chastity were central to the main plank of feminist reform during the late Victorian period. Consequently, Simon Szreter concludes in his magisterial study that the fall in the birth rate was due largely to marriage postponement, abstinence and coitus interruptus. Although some cultural currents (not least eugenicism) were emphasising women's 'national duty' to bear children,[36] Szreter observes that the decision to limit one's family was assisted by what he terms a 'culture of abstinence'. The social purity movement; the outrage over the Contagious Diseases Acts; and the moral imperatives of Evangelical Christianity all contributed to a culture which privileged sexual restraint over indulgence. (Although the apparently high levels of prostitution in these years may well be explicable within the context of sexual restraint within marriage.)[37]

This is not to say, of course, that women could not enjoy satisfying sex lives. At the turn of the century, Molly Trevelyan recorded in her diary the nights of 'wonderful love' spent with her husband, Charles.[38] But, it seems likely that among the middle classes, barrier methods, which were widely, if discreetly advertised in the contemporary press, were more likely to be used by those engaging in extra-marital sex. Rose Dobbs avoided pregnancy for three years following the death of her first husband, during which time she had an active sex life. On her remarriage, she conceived within a year.[39] Anecdotal evidence suggests that contraceptives were also widely used among the aristocracy. Mary Drew complained to her father, William Gladstone in 1886 that, 'What is called "the American sin" [contraception] is now almost universally practised in the upper classes.'[40] Indeed, aristocratic couples marrying in the 1880s produced an average of only two or three children up to the First World War.[41]

Motherhood

Despite the dramatic decline in the numbers of children born to each woman, motherhood remained a central experience for the majority. Gradual, if limited, recognition that motherhood warranted some rights over children was given in the Custody of Infants Act (1873) and the Guardianship of Infants Act (1886).[42] For most women, more significant were the changes in the management of childbirth and the perception of motherhood which occurred during this period. Doctors' growing use of obstetrical instruments and interventionist procedures during labour was accompanied by a gradual diminution in the role of the midwife in middle and upper-class confinements. However, doctors' poor hygiene, ensured that maternal mortality (usually through puerperal fever) remained alarmingly high throughout these years. In England and Wales maternal deaths per 1000 live births fluctuated between 4.6 and 5.1 in the years 1865 to 1904.[43] It would be inaccurate, though, to present an ineluctable trend towards the disempowerment of women during childbirth. Upper-middle-class women, were discerning in their choice and use of doctors, whom they regarded as their social subordinates;[44] and as already noted, women were increasingly demanding the use of chloroform. Female birthing traditions, such as the passing down of gowns worn during labour and notes on their confinements, also mitigated against the loss of female control.[45]

Equally important was the persistence of female traditions of family support which provided women with satisfying emotional relationships. Lady Antrim, for example, was simply bereft when her daughter left to marry, 'every day seems to make the pain of having parted with Sybil deeper', she lamented.[46] These emotional links were often expressed by practical assistance and could become a vital resource during pregnancy.[47] It was the absence of such kinship support which could make the isolation of colonial wives in India, where strict social hierarchies were observed, so acute. This was so for Maria Adelaide Cust, whose high status (her husband was the Commissioner and Superintendent of the Amritsar Division in the Punjab) made it extremely difficult for her to develop social networks.[48]

The existence of a rich, female culture to assist with the exigencies of labour and motherhood was at odds with the views of many contemporary commentators, who complained that the modern woman was too distracted by the charms of consumerism, or too brainwashed by the feminist movement, to take maternal responsibilities seriously. Eliza Lynn Linton, again captured the mood in her 1868 essay, 'Modern Mothers', in which she likened them to 'Junos sitting on the top of Mount Olympus, making occasional gracious and benign descents, but practically too far removed for useful interference'.[49] This image of the removed mother has been rejected by Jessica Gerard. She stresses the close and loving relationships which parents formed with their offspring. Emma Toulmin stayed in bed with her newborn babies for three or four weeks after the birth, a practice, Gerard observes, which would greatly enhance the formation of mother/infant bonds. Meanwhile, more relaxed ideas of parenting were encouraging parents to enjoy their children, even if they did not personally perform many of the daily child-care chores.[50] Others have pointed out that the use of hired staff enabled mothers to practice new, assiduous child-care methods, which exhorted positive discipline, attention to the individual, and empathy.[51] Many were strongly influenced by the child-study movement – as witnessed in Maggie Hobhouse's practice of keeping a 'Children's Book' in which she documented the minutiae of her children's development.[52]

Nevertheless, attempts to oversee and manage their children's progress could be counterpoised by other tendencies which directly militated against female domestic authority. Families in this strata tended to adhere to patrilineal educational patterns; boys were usually sent to the school attended by their fathers – a fact which most mothers were forced to accept.[53] More fundamentally, most women did themselves encourage a gendered domestic hierarchy. M. V. Hughes recalled of her London childhood, 'I came last in all distribution of food at table, treats of sweets and so on. I was expected to wait on the boys, run messages, fetch things left upstairs, and never grumble, let alone refuse.'[54] Such socialisation was reinforced by other culture pressures, contemporary girls' fiction for example, with popular writers such as Charlotte Yonge and E. T. Meade reiterating social stereotypes of women's domestic roles.[55] However, according to Carol Dyhouse, a new generation of women who came to adulthood in the 1880s, were beginning to question such gender-preferential treatment, a fact which could fuel mother/daughter conflicts.[56]

No doubt, despite these tensions, most women continued to find a high degree of satisfaction in the care of their families; but for many, particularly those in the lower middle class, the realities of domestic responsibilities with little paid help would have made for frustrating, tedious lives. Jane Lewis paints a scenario of days filled with 'housework, washing, cooking, quarrels with the maid, crying children and financial problems'. Lewis goes on to note the significant problems of mental and physical health experienced by contemporary women.[57] Certainly, it was during this period that the health of middle- and upper-class women came under growing scrutiny by the medical profession; and a scientific trend to define women in terms of their reproductive organs intensified. The menarche, pregnancy, childbirth, breast-feeding and the menopause were all perceived as physiological crises which could trigger hysteria and neurasthenia (an ill-defined syndrome which encompassed a range of depressive-type symptoms). The obstetrician, Dr Bliss, talked of 'the gigantic power and influence of the ovaries over the whole animal economy of woman'.[58]

It is possible that women's reproductive problems could explain some of the symptoms of weakness and depression observed in numerous women. Pat Jalland has pointed out that women tended to keep occurrences such as miscarriage, secret. Beatrice Clarke, for example, was always described by her family as weak and nervous. A confidential letter, however, revealed that this was because of complications following a miscarriage.[59] Also, the fact that medical science validated and expected female invalidism meant that some were likely to subconsciously reproduce this behaviour, particularly during times of stress.

In a pioneering essay, Carroll Smith-Rosenberg argued that American women might adopt invalidism as a reaction to the subordinate and restricted nature of their lives. It enabled them to express their discontent and to abandon their duties as wives and mothers. (Hence Florence Nightingale's pertinent observation that, 'A married woman was heard to wish that she could break a limb that she might have a little time to herself.'[60])

However, the articulation of medical theories which stressed women's vulnerability may equally be read as a conservative backlash against their increasing educational and employment attainments, for the concentration upon women's illness was at odds with the experience of the majority. Privileged women had always had the opportunity for invigorating exercise, such as horse-riding and walking; and it was male, not female, depression which exercised countless families.[61] As the century wore on, the growing popularity of physical education in the new girls' schools, combined with fashions for tennis and cycling, enhanced women's access to physical exercise. By the end of the century, it was women's health which was most striking to many observers – a factor which advertisements for colonial emigration were quick to exploit.[62]

Single Women and Old Age

For a growing number of women, neither marriage nor motherhood were possible. By the 1890s approximately one in six women would remain unmarried.[63] W. R. Greg had famously made the point in his 1862 article, 'Why are Women Redundant?' For Greg, the problem of 'surplus women', as they were unsympathetically termed, could be alleviated by shipping half a million of them out to the colonies![64] Medical opinion could be equally pessimistic about the fate of single women. Prominent physicians tended to dwell upon the deviance and harm supposedly arising from celibacy, while the press often portrayed spinsters as unnatural, barren and selfish. Certainly there were those, such as Evelyn Murray, who became depressed and drug-dependent, disillusioned with what they held to be the futility of their lives. Most unmarried women were expected to act as housekeepers to elderly parents or bachelor brothers – making them extremely vulnerable when death or marriage relieved them of their duties. As Angie Acland wrote to her brother, on the death of their father in 1900, 'I feel an old woman now that my only object in life is gone.'[65]

Yet for those dedicated to their work (paid or unpaid) and who enjoyed a reasonable income, spinsterhood could be an attractive alternative to marriage, promising greater independence. Eileen Yeo has argued that single women contributed to the forging of a discourse of the 'virgin' or 'social mother'. This potentially enabling concept argued for the importance of women's mothering qualities in such fields as social work and philanthropy.[66] Significantly, a new generation of career women were emerging who made a conscious decision to stay single. These included the educationists Dorothea Beale and Frances Buss, as well as Florence Nightingale.[67] Others, particularly by the 1880s, were choosing to remain single from an ideological opposition to marriage. Contemporaries were sensitive to the existence of an 'anti-marriage league': reports of the 'new woman' who campaigned for women's rights and economic dependence; rejected marriage and enjoyed the modern social freedoms symbolised by the bicycle were typically portrayed as a worrying development.[68]

Feminists, however, attempted to reclaim the image of the single woman from hostile contemporary stereotypes. They rejected the subordination which they believed was inherent in heterosexual unions and embraced chastity as a means of exploring the moral superiority of women. Only a minority advocated the free love which so scandalised mainstream opinion – as in the publication of Grant Allen's, *The Woman Who Did* in 1895. More typically, Elizabeth Wolstenholme Elmy and Frances Swiney dwelt upon women's sexual abuse at the hands of their husbands; whilst Henrietta Muller argued that, 'in rejecting the personal or grosser forms of love, a woman only leaves herself more free to give a larger, holier and deeper love to those who need it most.' Such arguments at times spilled into the eugenicist debate. Were women spared the necessity of marrying, it was asserted, those who did choose to do so would be able to marry the fittest males, thus ensuring the production of strongly, healthy children.[69]

Consequently, as Martha Vicinus argues, women forged an empowering vision of celibacy, with many recreating their own ritualistic forms of institutional life in religious communities, colleges and schools. For women such as these, female relationships were paramount and many developed 'romantic friendships': intense emotional and often physical relations – in a culture which did not yet label, and therefore did not necessarily stigmatise lesbianism.[70]

Even for those who did marry, the threat or realisation of widowhood must have posed considerable financial and personal distress, with those in the middle and lower middle classes presumably in the most precarious position. The economic consequences of widowhood for women awaits further research. However, attention has recently been paid to the devastating impact which the loss of a husband could have upon a woman's sense of identity, even to a publicly active feminist, such as Millicent Garrett Fawcett.[71]

Similarly, little work has yet been done on the implications of old age for the female population. At times, medical science extolled the menopause as the healthiest era in a woman's life, now that she was free from the destabilising effects of menstruation. Living in an age which laid such emphasis upon motherhood, the end of childbearing doubtless had profound implications for Victorian women, although for many, the release from reproduction must have been an enormous relief. Barbara Caine has postulated that the lack of prescriptive literature as to the appropriate behaviour of post-menopausal woman, may signal that this was a time of new possibilities for women. Despite the obvious physiological problems ageing brought, this was certainly true of those who enjoyed economic independence, and was particularly apparent among elderly landed women, who could continue to exert familial and social influence.[72]

Conclusion

During the second half of the nineteenth century, the availability of divorce and contraception, the impact of feminist campaigning and the possibility of alternative life-styles for women as spinsters, all posed challenges to the traditional marriage. Burgeoning consumerism and leisure opportunities, as well as enhanced opportunities in politics, philanthropy and employment also encouraged a heightened sense of self-awareness and confidence among women. However, as previous chapters have stressed, such developments were mediated through existing perceptions of gender difference, a factor which may have helped to ensure the stability of existing gender relations. The patriarchal model of marriage altered but slowly, and it is only right at the end of this period that families appear to have been more willing to challenge extreme manifestations of patriarchal authority and that separation and divorce lost some of its stigma.[73] Although the vast majority remained true to traditional ideas of family life, the growing complexity of life-style decisions as cultural shifts began to make their impact is striking. Even a highly progressive women such as Maria Sharpe, a member of the radical Men and Women's Club, wrestled with ideas of a free love union or celibate spinsterhood, before sacrificing her career and independence for a life of conventional marriage and motherhood.[74]

CONCLUSION

The years covered in this book encompass major shifts and changes in the lives of women. Material benefits such as progress in public health, a decline in family sizes and higher standards of living vastly improved the quality of life for many. Meanwhile, greater access to educational provision, both at the secondary and tertiary level, combined with new openings in many employment sectors, significantly widened opportunities, particularly for those in the upper working and middle classes. Equally, by the end of the period, major legislative advances had been achieved, not least the 1882 Married Women's Property Act. Such triumphs were considerably indebted to the feminist movement, which, by this date, had become influential and highly organised (if still diverse). Women had also been brought closer into the ambit of formal party politics, as the Women's Liberal Federation, in particular, testifies. All these developments were of immense significance to the lives, opportunities and aspirations of contemporary women.

However, it would be equally misguided to construct a simple, linear notion of progress. The divisive nature of gender relations and the backlash against female employment, following the First World War, illustrate this clearly.[1] In the nineteenth century, as we have seen, advances in women's position were mediated through specific, gendered ideologies. This was particularly evident with regard to the education provided for working-class girls, but also in the nature of 'white-collar' employment offered to upper-working- and middle-class women. However, in the case of white-collar work, the proliferation of discourses concerning women's gendered capabilities may have been essential in diffusing potential gender tensions (consider the bitterness occasioned in early nineteenth-century working-class communities

when women's labour was perceived as a threat to male employment).
It is important to remember, of course, that most working women were
not able to take advantage of new employment opportunities. Working-
class women remained clustered in traditionally female occupations,
and a significant proportion were dependent upon highly exploitative
'sweated' work within their own homes.

Women of the highest social classes also remained largely prohibited
(by dint of social custom) from exploring the world of paid employment
in any significant numbers. Those who did work remained highly
ambivalent about their financial remuneration. Nevertheless, in some
fields, most notably in nursing, upper-class women discovered that the
meanings of class weighed heavily in their favour. However, in nursing,
as in philanthropy and local politics, the social influence of upper-class
women was, by the end of the period, on the wane. In an increasingly
democratic society, the authority claimed by the aristocracy was ever
weakening. Gradually, a society was emerging in which meritocratic
procedures and the implementation of standardised bureaucracies weakened the traditional influence of landed power. Whilst the upper classes
may have lost out from these developments, in some areas – notably
philanthropy and politics – middle-class women were quick to benefit.
The emergence of political societies and an increase in organised
(rather than personal) philanthropy were eagerly exploited by this
class. Nevertheless, for middle-class women, as for their working-class
contemporaries, involvement in contemporary politics remained highly
problematic. Their engagement hinged upon certain notions of femininity and female behaviour, and even in the Independent Labour
Party, where women had equal membership with men, it proved enormously difficult to make any impact upon the movement's organisational structure.

Similar class diversity is discernible in women's experiences of family
life. Although this period is popularly characterised as one in which the
nuclear family was paramount, this model only applied to a relatively
small proportion of middle-class people. In the upper classes, the family
had wider connotations of dynastic connections and aspirations; whilst
for substantial sections of the working classes, particularly during the
earlier period, the concept of the extended family was vital in structuring networks of kinship support. For the lower middle class, family life,
far from being a haven of purely affective concerns, could be closely
imbricated with the economic well-being of its members. Women, as we
have seen, played a significant part in maintaining family businesses

and boosting family income – a factor which future investigation may well reveal to belie the current orthodoxy concerning the separation of home from business life by the middle of the century. Nevertheless, despite women's centrality to family life across the classes, patriarchal assumptions remained woven into nineteenth-century masculinities, making truly egalitarian relationships, even by the end of the century, the exception and rarely the norm.

However, despite the qualifications and hesitations one may have in tracing a concept of 'progress' for nineteenth-century women, this study has emphasised the importance of understanding the motivations, experiences and aspirations of women themselves: to look, indeed, at the construction of nineteenth-century femininities. As we have seen, there is no simple relationship between representation and reality. Women experienced and interpreted discursive and rhetorical phenomena in many different and complex ways. The rearticulation of gender difference in such fields as clerical work, for example, may well have served to ease many women's reconciliation to new roles and identities as working women. Yet, at the same time, it may have proved frustrating for women at the top of the ladder, wishing for more responsibility. Similarly, the intensification of debates concerning the importance of women's domestic role may have been welcomed by the better-off sectors of the upper working class, providing as it did ideological justification for their decision that the family economy was best served by their full-time commitment to the home. For those unable to afford such a choice, however, such discussions no doubt added to the many domestic and economic pressures under which they were already labouring.

At other times, contemporary discourse appears to be wholly against the grain of women's experiences. One might cite the incongruency of the depiction of the energetic and publicly active Ellen Courtauld as an 'Angel in the House' (see pp. 59–60). Linda Colley's argument, that the language of women's domestic sphere was a reactive response to women's increasing public activity, seems particularly pertinent in this context. But it was also much more than that. The same woman that embraced opportunities for intervention in public debates, such as anti-slavery, or busied herself with local community projects, may have simultaneously welcomed the fact that she was relieved from the extra duties of assisting in her husband's business, or, as a farmer's wife, be spared the onerous responsibilities of catering for large numbers of live-in farm servants. Equally, women's contribution to charitable and civic projects may have enhanced their self-esteem and led them to look upon their domestic responsibilities with reforming vigour. As has been noted, women's domestic role was closely associated with wider cultural developments: the role of motherhood; heightened attention to the home as a site of consumerism; and a belief that the domestic sphere was crucial in structuring society's commitment to religion or propriety. Women appear to have felt that their importance in the home was vital for the success of these wider social goals.

What emerges from such an approach is that women were active constituents of late Hanoverian and Victorian culture. This is evident, for example, in their articulation of imperialist ideologies; in their primary role in establishing the contours of Victorian respectability; and in their importance in constructing community values. Indeed, one of the central justifications for studying women's history lies not merely in its excavation of the lives and experiences of over half of the population; but that it also illuminates and reorientates our understanding of nineteenth-century culture and society itself. For, as Gisela Bock aptly puts it, 'Women's history concerns not merely half of humankind, but all of it.'[2]

NOTES

Introduction

1. Sheila Rowbotham, *Hidden From History* (London: Pluto Press, 1973).
2. See, for example, Martha Vicinus (ed.), *Suffer and Be Still: Women in the Victorian Age* (London: Methuen, 1972); and Vicinus (ed.), *A Widening Sphere: Changing Roles of Victorian Women* (Bloomington and London: Indiana University Press, 1977).
3. For good overviews of these discussions, see Jane Rendall, 'Uneven Developments: Women's History, Feminist History and Gender History in Great Britain', in Karen Offen, Ruth Roach Pierson and Jane Rendall (eds), *Writing Women's History: International Perspectives* (Basingstoke: Macmillan – now Palgrave, 1991), pp. 45–57; and June Hannam, 'Women, History and Protest', in Diana Richardson and Victorian Robinson (eds), *Introducing Women's Studies: Feminist Theory and Practice* (Basingstoke: Macmillan – now Palgrave, 1991), pp. 303–23.
4. Joan Kelly, *Women, History and Theory: The Essays of Joan Kelly* (Chicago and London: University of Chicago Press, 1984), especially ch. 1.
5. Leonore Davidoff and Catherine Hall, *Family Fortunes: Men and Women of the English Middle Class 1780–1850* (London: Routledge, 1987).
6. J. W. Scott, *Gender and the Politics of History* (New York: Columbia University Press, 1988); Denise Riley, *'Am I That Name?' Feminism and the Category of 'Women' in History* (Basingstoke: Macmillan – now Palgrave, 1988); Mary Poovey, *Uneven Developments: The Ideological Work of Gender in Mid-Victorian England* (Chicago: University of Chicago Press, 1988).
7. For useful debates on the role of poststructuralism in women's history, see Joan Hoff, 'Gender as a Postmodern Category of Paralysis', *Women's History Review*, 3 (1994), pp. 149–68; S. Kingsley Kent, 'Mistrials and Diatribulations: A Reply to Joan Hoff'; C. Ramazanoglu, 'Unravelling Postmodern Paralysis: A Response to Joan Hoff'; Joan Hoff, 'A Reply to My Critics', *Women's History Review*, 5 (1996), pp. 5–30.
8. See, for example, the discussion in Rendall, 'Uneven Developments', especially p. 53.

9. Judith M. Bennett, 'Review Essay: History that Stands Still: Women's Work in the European Past', *Feminist Studies*, 14 (1988), pp. 269–83; Bridget Hill, 'Women's History: A Study in Change, Continuity or Standing Still?', *Women's History Review*, 2, no. 2 (1993), pp. 5–22; Judith M. Bennett, 'Women's History: A Study in Continuity and Change: A Reply to Bridget Hill', *Women's History Review*, 2, no. 2 (1993), pp. 173–90. For debates on the family wage, see also p. 38 below.

10. Carol E. Morgan, 'Gender Constructions and Gender Relations in Cotton and Chain-Making in England: A Contested and Varied Terrain', *Women's History Review*, 6, no. 3 (1997), pp. 376–8. In talking of a 'new revisionism', I am also thinking of stimulating (albeit diverse) recent essays such as Joanna Bourke, 'Housewifery in Working-Class England 1860–1914', *Past and Present*, 143 (1994), pp. 167–97; Henrietta Twycross-Martin, 'Woman Supportive or Woman Manipulative? The "Mrs Ellis" Woman', in Clarissa Campbell Orr (ed.), *Wollstonecraft's Daughters: Womanhood in England and France* (Manchester: Manchester University Press, 1996), pp. 109–20; Michelle de Larrabeiti, 'Conspicuous Before the World: the Political Rhetoric of the Chartist Women', in Eileen Yeo (ed.), *Radical Femininity: Women's Self-Representation in the Public Sphere* (Manchester: Manchester University Press, 1998), pp. 112–13; Shani D'Cruze, ' "Care, Diligence and 'Usfull [sic] Pride": Gender, Industrialisation and the Domestic Economy, *c*. 1770 to *c*. 1840', *Women's History Review*, 3, no. 3 (1994), pp. 31–45; and Margot Finn, 'Women, Consumption and Coverture in England, *c*. 1760–1860', *Historical Journal*, 3, no. 39 (1996), pp. 703–22.

11. For discussion on these points, see Gisela Bock, 'Challenging Dichotomies: Perspectives on Women's History', in Offen, Pierson and Rendall (eds), *Writing Women's History*, ch. 1.

12. A. J. Vickery, 'Golden Ages to Separate Spheres: A Review of the Categories and Chronology of English Women's History', *Historical Journal*, 36, no. 2 (1993), pp. 383–414.

13. Ann Oakley, *Housewife* (Harmondsworth: Penguin, 1974).

14. Bourke, 'Housewifery in Working-Class England 1860–1914'.

15. Finn, 'Women, Consumption and Coverture in England'.

PART I WORKING-CLASS WOMEN, 1800–1860

1 Work

1. Useful overviews of this historiography may be found in Judith Bennett, ' "History that Stands Still": Women's Work in the European Past', *Feminist Studies*, 14 (1988), pp. 269–83; and Amanda Vickery, 'The Neglected

Century: Writing the History of Eighteenth Century Women', *Gender and History*, 3, no. 2 (1991), pp. 211–19.

2. Jane Humphries, 'Enclosures, Common Rights and Women: The Proletarianization of Families in the Late Eighteenth and Early Nineteenth Centuries', *Journal of Economic History*, 50 (1990), pp. 17–42.

3. See Bridget Hill, *Women, Work and Sexual Politics in Eighteenth Century England* (London: UCL, 1994, first published 1989), ch. 5; Raphael Samuel, 'Village Labour', in Raphael Samuel (ed.), *Village Life and Labour* (London: Routledge and Kegan Paul, 1975), pp. 10–12.

4. For an overview of women's declining opportunities, see K. D. M. Snell, *Annals of the Labouring Poor: Social Change and Agrarian England, 1660–1900* (Cambridge: Cambridge University Press, 1985), ch. 1.

5. Eve Hostettler, 'Gourlay Steell and the Sexual Division of Labour', *History Workshop Journal*, 4 (1977), pp. 95–8; Jennie Kitteringham, 'Country Work Girls in Nineteenth-Century England', in Samuel (ed.), *Village Life and Labour*, pp. 73–138, the quote is from p. 92.

6. Sally Alexander, 'Women's Work in Nineteenth-Century London: A Study of the Years 1820–60s', (1976) reprinted in Sally Alexander, *Becoming a Woman: And other Essays in 19th and 20th Century Feminist History* (London: Virago, 1994), pp. 52–3.

7. Kitteringham, 'Country Work Girls'; Barbara W. Robertson, 'In Bondage: The Female Farm Worker in South-East Scotland', in Eleanor Gordon and Esther Breitenbach (eds), *The World is Ill-Divided: Women's Work in Scotland in the Nineteenth and Early Twentieth Centuries* (Edinburgh: Edinburgh University Press, 1990), pp. 117–19.

8. E. F. Richards, 'Women in the British Economy since about 1700: An Interpretation', *History*, 59 (1974), p. 342 n.; David Williams, *The Rebecca Riots: A Study in Agrarian Discontent* (Cardiff: University of Wales Press, 1955), pp. 100–1.

9. Deborah Valenze, *The First Industrial Woman* (Oxford: Oxford University Press, 1995), p. 42.

10. Ibid., ch. 3; Leonore Davidoff, 'The Role of Gender in the "First Industrial Nation": Farming and the Countryside in England, 1780–1850', in Leonore Davidoff, *Worlds Between: Historical Perspectives on Gender and Class* (Cambridge: Polity Press, 1991), p. 193.

11. Hill, *Women, Work and Sexual Politics*, pp. 125–9.

12. Louise A. Tilly and Joan W. Scott, *Women, Work and Family* (New York and London: Routledge, 1989, first published 1978), p. 80.

13. Jessica Gerard, *Country House Life: Family and Servants, 1815–1914* (Oxford: Blackwell, 1994), pp. 39–42.

14. Leonore Davidoff, '"Mastered for Life": Servants and Wives in Victorian and Edwardian England', in Davidoff, *Worlds Between*, pp. 18–40, the quote is from p. 22.

15. Michael Anderson, 'The Social Implications of Demographic Change', in F. M. L. Thompson (ed.), *The Cambridge Social History of Britain, 1750–1950* (Cambridge: Cambridge University Press, 1990), 3 vols, ii, p. 63.

16. Shani D'Cruze, *Crimes of Outrage: Sex, Violence and Victorian Working Women* (London: UCL, 1998), pp. 88–95.

17. Pamela Sharpe, *Adapting to Capitalism: Working Women in the English Economy, 1700–1850* (Basingstoke: Macmillan – now Palgrave, 1995), pp. 101–16.

18. For a fine overview, see Maxine Berg, 'Women's Work, Mechanisation and the Early Phases of Industrialisation in England', in Patrick Joyce (ed.), *The Historical Meanings of Work* (Cambridge: Cambridge University Press, 1987), pp. 64–98.

19. Snell, *Annals of the Labouring Poor*, ch. 6.

20. Maxine Berg, 'What Difference Did Women's Work Make to the Industrial Revolution?', *History Workshop Journal*, 35 (1993), pp. 22–44.

21. Berg, 'Women's Work, [and] Mechanisation', p. 82; Maxine Berg, *The Age of Manufactures 1700–1820: Industry, Innovation and Work in Britain* (London: Routledge, 1994, 2nd edn), p. 151.

22. A concise treatment of the position of women within protoindustry may be found in Pat Hudson, 'Proto-Industrialization in England', in Sheilagh C. Ogilvie and Markus Cerman (eds), *European Protoindustrialization* (Cambridge: Cambridge University Press, 1996), pp. 49–60.

23. Malcolm I. Thomis and Jennifer Grimmett, *Women in Protest 1800–1850* (London: Croom Helm, 1982), pp. 72–3.

24. Jane Gray, 'Gender and Plebeian Culture in Ulster', *Journal of Interdisciplinary History*, 24, no. 2 (1993), p. 266; Mary Cullen, 'Breadwinners and Providers: Women in the Household Economy of Labouring Families, 1835–6', in Maria Luddy and Cliona Murphy (eds), *Women Surviving: Studies in Irish Women's History in the 19th and 20th Centuries* (Dublin: Poolbeg Press, 1989), pp. 85–117.

25. See J. J. Lee, 'Women and the Church Since the Famine', in Margaret MacCurtain and Donncha Ó Corráin (eds), *Women in Irish Society: The Historical Dimension* (Westport, Connecticut: Greenwood Press, 1979), pp. 37–45.

26. Berg, *The Age of Manufactures*, pp. 142–53.

27. Sarah Horrell and Jane Humphries, 'Women's Labour Force Participation and the Transition to the Male Breadwinner Family, 1790–1865', *Economic History Review*, 48 (1995), pp. 89–117; Richards, 'Women in the British Economy', pp. 337–57.

28. Sharpe, *Adapting to Capitalism*, p. 42.

29. Meg Gomersall, *Working-Class Girls in Nineteenth-Century England: Life, Work and Schooling* (Basingstoke: Macmillan – now Palgrave, 1997), pp. 57, 115–7.

30. Jane McDermid, '"Intellectual Instruction is Best Left to a Man": The Feminisation of the Scottish Teaching Profession in the Second Half of the

Nineteenth Century', *Women's History Review*, 6, no. 1 (1997), pp. 95–6; Pinchbeck, *Women Workers*, pp. 232–5.

31. Valenze, *The First Industrial Woman*, pp. 117–18.

32. Pamela Horn, *Victorian Countrywomen* (Oxford: Basil Blackwell, 1991), pp. 193, 196–7.

33. Patricia Hollis (ed.), *Women in Public 1850–1900: Documents of the Victorian Women's Movement* (London: George Allen and Unwin, 1979), p. 46.

34. Gray, 'Gender and Plebeian Culture in Ulster', p. 266.

35. Judy Lown, *Women and Industrialisation: Gender at Work in Nineteenth-Century England* (Cambridge: Polity Press, 1990), p. 33.

36. Pat Hudson, *The Industrial Revolution* (London: Edward Arnold, 1992), p. 229.

37. Lown, *Women and Industrialisation*, p. 107.

38. Valenze, *First Industrial Woman*, p. 90.

39. Patrick Joyce, *Work, Society and Politics: The Culture of the Factory in Later Victorian England* (London: Methuen, 1980), p. 113.

40. Anna Clark, *The Struggle for the Breeches: Gender and the Making of the British Working Class* (London: Rivers Oram Press, 1995), p. 208.

41. Elizabeth K. Helsinger, Robin Lauterbach Sheets and William Veeder (eds), *The Woman Question: Society and Literature in Britain and America 1837–1883* (Chicago and London: University of Chicago Press, 1983), 3 vols, ii, pp. 122–3.

42. Ibid., ii, p. 123.

43. Nicholas Rogers, *Crowds, Culture and Politics in Georgian Britain* (Oxford: Clarendon Press, 1998), p. 234.

44. Clark, *The Struggle for the Breeches*, ch. 11.

45. Patrick Joyce warns against exaggerating this trend, however: *Work, Society and Politics*, pp. 55, 112.

46. Jan Lambertz, 'Sexual Harassment in the Nineteenth-Century English Cotton Industry', *History Workshop Journal*, 19 (1985), pp. 29–61.

47. Clark, *The Struggle for the Breeches*, pp. 239–40.

48. These developments are clearly charted in Carol E. Morgan, 'Women, Work and Consciousness in the Mid-Nineteenth-Century English Cotton Industry', *Social History*, 17 (1992), pp. 23–41.

49. Clark, *The Struggle for the Breeches*, p. 241.

50. Pinchbeck, *Women Workers and the Industrial Revolution*, p. 201.

51. Sophie Hamilton, 'Images of Femininity in the Royal Commissions of the 1830s and 1840s', in Eileen Janes Yeo (ed.), *Radical Femininity: Women's Self-Representation in the Public Sphere* (Manchester: Manchester University Press, 1998), pp. 79–105; Robert Gray, 'Factory Legislation and the Gendering of Jobs in the North of England, 1830–60', *Gender and History*, 5 (1993), pp. 70–5.

52. Gomersall, *Working-Class Girls*, p. 74.

53. Angela V. John, *By the Sweat of Their Brow: Women Workers at Victorian Coal Mines* (London: Croom Helm, 1980), ch. 1.
54. Pinchbeck, *Women Workers and the Industrial Revolution*, p. 266.
55. Hamilton, 'Images of Femininity', pp. 89–93.
56. Harriet Bradley, *Men's Work, Women's Work: A Sociological History of the Sexual Division of Labour in Employment* (Cambridge: Polity Press, 1989), p. 107.
57. Cited in Jane Humphries, 'Protective Legislation, the Capitalist State and Working-Class Men: The Case of the 1842 Mines Regulation Act', *Feminist Review*, no. 7 (1981), p. 26.
58. John, *By the Sweat of their Brow*, pp. 52–60.
59. Tilly and Scott, *Women, Work and Family*, p. 80 and *passim*.
60. Duncan Bythell, *The Sweated Trades: Outwork in Nineteenth Century Britain* (London: Batsford Academic, 1978), pp. 145–6.
61. Alexander, 'Women's Work in Nineteenth-Century London', pp. 23–33.
62. E. P. Thompson and Eileen Yeo (eds), *The Unknown Mayhew: Selections from the Morning Chronicle 1849–50* (London: Merlin Press, 1971), pp. 147–52; Helen Rogers, '"The Good Are Not Always Powerful, Nor the Powerful Always Good": The Politics of Women's Needlework in Mid-Victorian London', *Victorian Studies*, 40 (1997), pp. 589–623.
63. Alexander, 'Woman's Work', pp. 23, 33–8.
64. Ibid., pp. 3–55; Tilly and Scott, *Women, Work and Family*, for example, pp. 87, 125; Bridget Hill, 'Women, Work and the Census', *History Workshop Journal*, 35 (1993), pp. 78–94.
65. Leonore Davidoff, 'The Separation of Home and Work? Landladies and Lodgers in Nineteenth and Twentieth Century England', in Sandra Burman (ed.), *Fit Work for Women* (London and Canberra: Croom Helm, 1979), pp. 64–97.
66. Davidoff, 'Mastered for Life', p. 31.
67. Gray, 'Factory Legislation and the Gendering of Jobs', p. 63.
68. Enid Gauldie, *Cruel Habitations: A History of Working-Class Housing 1780–1918* (London: George Allen and Unwin, 1974), ch. 5.
69. Morgan, 'Women, Work and Consciousness', pp. 35–6.
70. Valenze, *The First Industrial Woman*, *passim*.

2 Politics, Community and Protest

1. Nicholas Rogers, *Crowds, Culture and Politics in Georgian Britain* (Oxford: Clarendon Press, 1998), p. 243.
2. This was a feature of the Rebecca Riots and the Highland Riots, for example. See Malcolm I. Thomis and Jennifer Grimmett, *Women in Protest, 1800–1850* (London: Croom Helm, 1982), pp. 138–46.

3. Rogers, *Crowds, Culture and Politics*, pp. 219–22; Linda Colley, *Britons: Forging the Nation 1707–1837* (New Haven and London: Yale University Press, 1992), pp. 237–8. For a pessimistic assessment of women's political potential, see Sally Alexander, 'Women, Class and Sexual Difference in the 1830s and 1840s: Some Reflections on the Writing of Feminist History', (1983) reprinted in Sally Alexander, *Becoming a Woman and Other Essays in 19th and 20th Century Feminist History* (London: Virago, 1994), pp. 97–125.

4. Anna Clark, *The Struggle for the Breeches: Gender and the Making of the British Working Class* (London: Rivers Oram Press, 1995), pp. 34–9.

5. John Bohstedt, 'Gender, Household and Community Politics: Women in English Riots 1790–1810', *Past and Present*, no. 120 (1988), pp. 88–122; Rogers, *Crowds, Culture and Politics*, p. 216.

6. Thomis and Grimmett, *Women in Protest*, pp. 51–2; David J. V. Jones, *Rebecca's Children: A Study of Rural Society, Crime and Protest* (Oxford: Clarendon Press, 1989).

7. E. F. Richards, 'Patterns of Highland Discontent, 1790–1860', in R. Quinault and J. Stevenson (eds), *Popular Protest and Public Order, 1790–1920* (London: George Allen and Unwin, 1974), pp. 106, 97.

8. E. P. Thompson, 'The Moral Economy of the English Crowd in the Eighteenth Century', *Past and Present*, 50 (1971), p. 116.

9. See John Bohstedt, 'The Myth of the Feminine Food Riot: Women as Proto-Citizens in English Community Politics, 1790–1810', in Harriet B. Applewhite and Darline G. Levy (eds), *Women and Politics in the Age of the Democratic Revolution* (Ann Arbor: The University of Michigan Press, 1993), pp. 21–60, and Bohstedt, 'Gender, Household and Community Politics'.

10. Thompson, 'The Moral Economy of the English Crowd', pp. 76–136.

11. Bohstedt, 'Gender, Household and Community Politics', especially pp. 88–93.

12. Thomis and Grimmett, *Women in Protest*, pp. 32, 39.

13. Ibid., pp. 43–4.

14. Rogers, *Crowds, Culture and Politics*, p. 232; Thomis and Grimmett, *Women in Protest*, p. 36.

15. J. Stevenson, 'Food Riots in England, 1792–1818', in Quinault and Stevenson, *Popular Protest and Public Order*, p. 49.

16. See Deborah Valenze, 'Cottage Religion and the Politics of Survival', in Jane Rendall (ed.), *Equal or Different: Women's Politics, 1800–1914* (Oxford: Blackwell, 1987), pp. 31–56 and Deborah Valenze, *Prophetic Sons and Daughters: Female Preaching and Popular Religion in Industrial England* (Princeton: Princeton University Press, 1985); Clark, *The Struggle for the Breeches*, pp. 94–9.

17. See, for example, Bohstedt, 'Gender, Household and Community Politics', p. 122.

18. Maria Luddy (ed.), *Women in Ireland 1800–1918* (Cork: Cork University Press, 1995), p. 245; Thomis and Grimmett, *Women in Protest*, pp. 29–31.

19. Luddy, *Women in Ireland*, pp. 246–7; Logue, *Popular Disturbances in Scotland*, pp. 199–203.
20. Valenze, 'Cottage Religion and the Politics of Survival', pp. 33–4.
21. Rogers, *Crowds, Culture and Politics*, pp. 219–20.
22. David J. V. Jones, *Before Rebecca: Popular Protests in Wales, 1793–1835* (London: Penguin, 1973), p. 128.
23. For a good overview, see Thomis and Grimmet, *Women in Protest*, pp. 88–102.
24. Ibid., pp. 100–1.
25. Rogers, *Crowds, Culture and Politics*, p. 242.
26. James Epstein, 'Understanding the Cap of Liberty: Symbolic Practice and Social Conflict in Early Nineteenth-Century England', *Past and Present*, 122 (1989), pp. 75–118.
27. See, for example, Rogers, *Crowds, Culture and Politics*, p. 241.
28. Quoted in Thomis and Grimmet, *Women in Protest*, p. 92.
29. E. and R. Frow, 'Women in the Early Radical and Labour Movement', *Marxism Today*, 12, no. 4 (1968), p. 106.
30. Ruth and Edmund Frow, *Political Women 1800–1850* (London: Pluto Press, 1989), p. 31.
31. See, for example, Catherine Hall, 'The Tale of Samuel and Jemima: Gender and Working-Class Culture in Early Nineteenth-Century England', (1986) reprinted in Catherine Hall, *White, Male and Middle-Class: Explorations in Feminism and History* (Cambridge: Polity Press, 1992), especially pp. 124–9.
32. Joan Perkin, *Women and Marriage in Nineteenth Century England* (Chicago: Lyceum, 1989), p. 39.
33. Thomis and Grimmett, *Women in Protest*, pp. 102–3.
34. Clark, *The Struggle for the Breeches*, pp. 164–74 (the quote is from p. 174).
35. Frow and Frow, *Political Women*, pp. 35–8, 40–1.
36. Thomis and Grimmett, *Women in Protest*, p. 104; see also Iain McCalman, 'Females, Feminism and Free Love in an Early Nineteenth Century Radical Movement', *Labour History*, 38 (1980), pp. 1–25.
37. Helen Rogers, *Women and the People: Authority, Authorship and the Radical Tradition in Nineteenth-Century England* (Aldershot: Ashgate, 2000), p. 84.
38. Churching was an Anglican ritual performed upon women to 'cleanse' them after childbirth. Frow and Frow, *Political Women*, ch. 4 (the quote is taken from p. 63); Thomis and Grimmett, *Women in Protest*, pp. 106–9. For Eliza Sharples, see Helen Rogers, '"The Prayer, the Passion and the Reason" of Eliza Sharples: Freethought, Women's Rights and Republicanism, 1832–52', in Eileen Yeo (ed.), *Radical Femininity: Women's Self-Representation in the Public Sphere* (Manchester: Manchester University Press, 1998), pp. 52–78.
39. Frow and Frow, *Political Women*, pp. 50–5 (the quote is taken from p. 51).
40. The fullest exposition of Owenism and women's role within it may be found in Barbara Taylor, *Eve and the New Jerusalem, Socialism and Feminism in the*

Nineteenth Century (London: Virago, 1983). See also Frow and Frow, *Political Women*, ch. 6.

41. Frow and Frow, *Political Women*, pp. 95–6.
42. See Clark, *The Struggle for the Breeches*, pp. 186–7.
43. See the story of the Manea Fen community, Taylor, *Eve and the New Jerusalem*, pp. 254–8.
44. Ibid., p. 248 and the rest of ch. 8 for a full account of women's experiences in the communities.
45. Ibid., pp. 162–7.
46. Clark, *The Struggle for the Breeches*, pp. 108–11; J. F. C. Harrison, *The Second Coming: Popular Millenarianism 1780–1850* (London: Routledge and Kegan Paul, 1979), p. 110.
47. David Jones, 'Women and Chartism', *History*, 68 (1983), pp. 10–13.
48. Clark, *Struggle for the Breeches*, p. 227; Dorothy Thompson, *The Chartists* (London: Temple Smith, 1984), p. 141.
49. Thompson, *The Chartists*, pp. 135, 137–9.
50. Jutta Schwarzkopf, *Women in the Chartist Movement* (Basingstoke: Macmillan – now Palgrave, 1991), p. 89.
51. Cited in Frow and Frow, *Political Women*, p. 198.
52. Clark, *The Struggle for the Breeches*, pp. 229–30.
53. For women's contribution to Chartist culture, see Michelle de Larrabeiti, 'Conspicuous Before the World: The Political Rhetoric of the Chartist Women', in Yeo, *Radical Femininity*, pp. 112–13; Eileen Yeo, 'Will the Real Mary Lovett Please Stand Up? Chartism, Gender and Autobiography', in Malcolm Chase and Ian Dyck (eds), *Living and Learning: Essays in Honour of J. F. C. Harrison* (Aldershot: Scolar Press, 1996), p. 178; Jones, 'Women and Chartism', p. 9.
54. Thompson, *The Chartists*, p. 148.
55. Dorothy Thompson, 'Women and Nineteenth-Century Radical Politics', in Juliet Mitchell and Ann Oakley (eds), *The Rights and Wrongs of Women* (Harmondsworth: Penguin, 1976), pp. 121–3; Clark, *The Struggle for the Breeches*, pp. 191–2; Schwarzkopf, *Women in the Chartist Movement*, p. 199.
56. Schwarzkopf, *Women in the Chartist Movement*, p. 226.
57. Ibid. But see Jones, 'Women and the Chartists', pp. 1–5 for a brief overview of some of the radical voices on women within Chartism.
58. Jones, 'Women and Chartism', pp. 15, 17.
59. Anna Clark, 'The Rhetoric of Chartist Domesticity: Gender, Language and Class in the 1830s and 1840s', *Journal of British Studies*, 31 (1992), pp. 74–6.
60. Thompson, 'Women and Nineteenth-Century Radical Politics', pp. 135–8.
61. Jones, 'Women and Chartism', pp. 13–14.
62. Schwarzkopf, *Women in the Chartist Movement*, p. 254.
63. Thompson, *The Chartists*, p. 150.

64. Schwarzkopf, *Women in the Chartist Movement*, p. 262.

65. Quoted in de Larrabeiti, 'Conspicuous Before the World', p. 122.

66. Matthew Cragoe, '"And Jenny Rules the Roost": Women and Electoral Politics, 1832–1868', in Kathryn Gleadle and Sarah Richardson (eds), *Women in British Politics, 1760–1860: The Power of the Petticoat* (Basingstoke: Macmillan – now Palgrave, 2000), pp. 153–68; Jones, 'Women and Chartism', p. 16; Luddy, *Women in Ireland*, pp. 247–8.

3 Families, Relationships and Home Life

1. Rita M. Rhodes, *Women and the Family in Post-Famine Ireland: Status and Opportunity in a Patriarchal Society* (London: Garland, 1992), p. 3.

2. David J. V. Jones, *Rebecca's Children: A Study of Rural Society, Crime and Protest* (Oxford: Clarendon Press, 1989), p. 104.

3. John E. Archer, 'Under Cover of Night: Arson and Animal Maiming', in G. E. Mingay (ed.), *The Unquiet Countryside* (London: Routledge, 1989), pp. 65–77; E. J. Hobsbawm and George Rudé, *Captain Swing* (London: Lawrence and Wishart, 1969).

4. F. M. L. Thompson, *The Rise of Respectable Society: A Social History of Victorian Britain, 1830–1900* (London: Fontana Press, 1988), pp. 181–91.

5. David Vincent, *Bread, Knowledge and Freedom, A Study of Nineteenth-Century Working-Class Autobiography* (London: Europa Publications, 1981), ch. 3.

6. See Hilary Land, 'The Family Wage', *Feminist Review*, 6 (1980), pp. 55–77; and Michele Barrett and Mary McIntosh, 'The 'Family Wage', in E. Whitelegg et al., *The Changing Experience of Women* (Oxford: Oxford University Press, 1982), pp. 71–87.

7. Anna Clark, *The Struggle for the Breeches: Gender and the Making of the British Working Class* (London: Rivers Oram Press, 1995).

8. Leonore Davidoff, '"Mastered for Life": Servants and Wives in Victorian and Edwardian England', in Leonore Davidoff, *Worlds Between: Historical Perspectives on Gender and Class* (Cambridge: Polity Press, 1995), p. 21.

9. Judy Lown, *Women and Industrialisation: Gender at Work in Nineteenth-Century England* (Cambridge: Polity Press, 1990), pp. 43–5.

10. Clark, *The Struggle for the Breeches*, p. 40.

11. Ivy Pinchbeck, *Women Workers and the Industrial Revolution, 1750–1850* (London: Virago, 1981, first published 1930), p. 313.

12. Neil McKendrick, 'Home Demand the Economic Growth: A New View of the Role of Women and Children in the Industrial Revolution', in Neil McKendrick (ed.), *Historical Perspectives: Studies in English Thought and Society, in Honour of J. H. Plumb* (London: Europa Publications, 1974), pp. 152–210. But see also Mariana Valverde, 'The Love of Finery: Fashion and the Fallen

Woman in Nineteenth Century Social Discourse', *Victorian Studies*, 32, no. 2 (1989), pp. 169–88.

13. Louise A. Tilly and Joan W. Scott, *Women, Work and Family* (London and New York: Routledge, 1989, first published 1978), pp. 115–16.

14. J. Mark-Lawson and A. Witz, 'From Family Labour to Family Wage? The Case of Women's Labour in Nineteenth-Century Coalmining', *Social History*, 13 (1988), pp. 151–74.

15. Lown, *Women and Industrialisation*, pp. 144–5, 85–6.

16. John R. Gillis, *For Better, For Worse: British Marriages, 1600 to the Present* (Oxford: Oxford University Press, 1985), pp. 121–4.

17. Ibid., p. 121.

18. Jones, *Rebecca's Children*, p. 38. Clark, *The Struggle for the Breeches*, pp. 45–6, but Methodists remained hostile to the practice, ibid., pp. 105–7.

19. Gillis, *For Better, For Worse*, pp. 190–209.

20. Michael Anderson, 'The Social Implications of Demographic Change', in F. M. L. Thompson (ed.), *The Cambridge Social History of Britain 1750–1950* (Cambridge: Cambridge University Press, 1990), 3 vols, ii, p. 36.

21. Hans Medick, 'The Proto-Industrial Family Economy: The Structural Function of Household and Family During the Transition From Peasant Society to Industrial Capitalism', *Social History*, 1 (1976), pp. 313–14.

22. Gillis, *For Better, For Worse*, p. 127.

23. Pat Thane, 'Women and the Poor Law in Victorian and Edwardian England', *History Workshop Journal*, 6 (1978), p. 32; Anna Clark, *Women's Silence. Men's Violence: Sexual Assault in England 1770–1845* (London: Pandora, 1987), pp. 83–9.

24. Jones, *Rebecca's Children*, pp. 269–70.

25. David Levine, 'Industrialization and the Proletarian Family in England', *Past and Present*, no. 107 (1985), pp. 180, 183–4.

26. Pat Hudson, 'Protoindustrialization in England', in Sheilagh C. Ogilvie and Markus Cerman (eds), *European Protoindustrialization* (Cambridge: Cambridge University Press, 1996), pp. 49–60.

27. Margaret Hewitt, *Wives and Mothers in Victorian Industry* (London: Rockliff, 1958), ch. 5.

28. E. P. Thompson and Eileen Yeo (eds), *The Unknown Mayhew: Selections from the Morning Chronicle 1849–50* (London: Merlin Press, 1971), see, for example, pp. 148, 160.

29. Gillis, *For Better, For Worse*, p. 165.

30. Shani D'Cruze, ' "Care, Diligence and 'Usfull [sic] Pride": Gender, Industrialisation and the Domestic Economy, c.1770 to c.1840', *Women's History Review*, 3, no. 3 (1994), pp. 31–45.

31. Quoted in Eric Richards, 'Women in the British Economy Since about 1700: An Interpretation', *History*, 59 (1974), p. 341.

32. Robert E. Kennedy Jr, *The Irish: Emigration, Marriage and Fertility* (Los Angeles: University of California Press, 1973), p. 52.

33. Mary Cullen, 'Breadwinners and Providers: Women in the Household Economy of Labouring Families, 1835–6', in Maria Luddy and Cliona Murphy (eds), *Women Surviving: Studies in Irish Women's History in the Nineteenth and Twentieth Centuries* (Dublin: Poolbeg Press, 1989), p. 113.

34. Deborah Valenze, *Prophetic Sons and Daughters: Female Preaching and Popular Religion in Industrial England* (Princeton: Princeton University Press, 1985), p. 254.

35. Medick, 'The Proto-Industrial Family Economy', pp. 291–315, especially p. 312.

36. Deborah Valenze, *The First Industrial Woman* (Oxford: Oxford University Press, 1995), p. 126.

37. Amanda Vickery, 'The Neglected Century: Writing the History of Eighteenth-Century Women', *Gender and History*, 3, no. 2 (1991), pp. 213–14.

38. John Bohstedt, 'Gender, Household and Community Politics: Women in English Riots 1790–1810', *Past and Present*, no. 120 (1988), pp. 88–122, especially pp. 95, 121; Medick, 'The Proto-Industrial Family Economy', p. 313.

39. J. J. Lee, 'Women and the Church Since the Famine', in Margaret MacCurtain and Donncha Ó Corráin (eds), *Women in Irish Society: The Historical Dimension* (Westport, Connecticut: Greenwood Press, 1979), pp. 37–9.

40. John Burnett (ed.), *Useful Toil, Autobiographies of Working People from the 1820s to the 1920s* (London: Allen Lane, 1976), p. 61.

41. Cullen, 'Breadwinners and Providers', pp. 112–13; Gillis, *For Better, For Worse*, p. 199.

42. Gillis, *For Better, For Worse*, p. 182.

43. See Nancy Tomes, 'A Torrent of Abuse: Crimes of Violence Between Working-Class Men and Women in London, 1840–75', *Journal of Social History*, 11 (1978), pp. 328–45.

44. Clark, *Struggle for the Breeches*, pp. 71–83.

45. Ibid., pp. 104–5.

46. Gillis, *For Better, For Worse*, pp. 130, 151–2.

47. Clark, *The Struggle for the Breeches*, p. 69, Perkin, *Women and Marriage*, p. 158.

48. Clark, *The Struggle for the Breeches*, *passim*, but see, for example, p. 34.

49. Cited in Elizabeth K. Helsinger, Robin Lauterbach Sheets and William Veeder (eds), *The Woman Question Society and Literature in Britain and America 1837–1883* (Chicago and London: University of Chicago Press, 1983), 3 vols, ii, pp. 123–4. Similar observations were made of women in the metal trades, see Pinchbeck, *Women Workers*, p. 273.

50. Lown, *Women and Industrialisation*, pp. 74–82.

51. Clark, *The Struggle for the Breeches*, pp. 257–8.

52. Vincent, *Bread, Knowledge and Freedom*, p. 44.
53. June Purvis, *Hard Lessons: The Lives and Education of Working Women in Nineteenth-Century England* (Cambridge: Polity Press, 1989), p. 3.
54. Leonore Davidoff, 'The Family in Britain', in Thompson, *Cambridge Social History of Britain*, ii, p. 90.
55. Joan Perkin, *Women and Marriage in Nineteenth-Century England* (Chicago: Lyceum, 1989), p. 117.
56. See, for example, Leah Leneman, *Alienated Affections: The Scottish Experience of Divorce and Separation, 1684–1830* (Edinburgh: Edinburgh University Press, 1998), pp. 328–30.
57. For full details, see Mary Lyndon Shanley, *Feminism, Marriage and the Law in Victorian England 1850–1895* (London: I. B. Tauris), ch. 1.
58. Anderson, 'The Social Implications', p.1. In Ireland the population was devastated in the mid-1840s by the famine and emigration.
59. Maxine Berg, 'Women's Work, Mechanisation and The Early Phases of Industrialisation in England', in Patrick Joyce (ed.), *The Historical Meanings of Work* (Cambridge: Cambridge University Press, 1987), p. 76.
60. Richards, 'Women in the British Economy since about 1700', p. 346.
61. Michael Anderson, *Family Structure in Nineteenth Century Lancashire*, (Cambridge: Cambridge University Press, 1971), ch. 6; Hewitt, *Wives and Mothers*, ch. 2.
62. See Hewitt, *Wives and Mothers*, p. 10; 'The employment of the wife dissolves the family utterly . . .', Friedrich Engels, *The Condition of the Working Class in England* (London: Granada, 1969, first published 1845), p. 172.
63. Elizabeth Gaskell, *Mary Barton* (1848). See Susan Morgan, *Sisters in Time: Imagining Gender in Nineteenth-Century British Fiction* (Oxford: Oxford University Press, 1989), ch. 4.
64. See Clark, *The Struggle for the Breeches*, pp. 253–5 and *passim*.
65. Anderson, *Family Structure*, pp. 141–6; Cruze, 'Care, Diligence and 'Usfull Pride'.

PART II MIDDLE-CLASS AND UPPER-CLASS WOMEN, 1800–1860

4 Work

1. Quoted in Leonore Davidoff and Catherine Hall, *Family Fortunes: Men and Women of the Middle Class 1780–1850* (London: Routledge, 1987), p. 315; see also *Family Fortunes*, ch. 3 for a rich discussion of domestic ideology.
2. Jessica Gerard, *Country House Life: Family and Servants, 1815–1914* (Oxford: Blackwell, 1994), pp. 130–6; K. D. Reynolds, *Aristocratic Women and Political Society in Victorian Britain* (Oxford: Clarendon Press, 1998), pp. 28–42;

Amanda Vickery, *The Gentleman's Daughter: Women's Lives in Georgian England* (New Haven and London: Yale University Press, 1998), ch. 4.

3. Patricia Branca, *Silent Sisterhood: Middle-Class Women in the Victorian Home* (London: Croom Helm, 1977), p. 40 and *passim*.

4. Margaret Bryant, *The Unexpected Revolution: A Study in the History of the Education of Women and Girls in the Nineteenth Century* (London: University of London Institute of Education, 1979), p. 30.

5. See Leonore Davidoff, 'The Rationalization of Housework', in Leonore Davidoff, *Worlds Between: Historical Perspectives on Gender and Class* (Cambridge: Polity Press, 1995), pp. 73–102.

6. See A. James Hammerton, *Emigrant Gentlewomen: Genteel Poverty and Female Emigration, 1830–1914* (London: Croom Helm, 1979), ch. 1.

7. See Reynolds, *Aristocratic Women and Political Society*, pp. 190–1.

8. Patricia Hollis (ed.), *Women in Public 1850–1900: Documents of the Victorian Women's Movement* (London: George Allen and Unwin, 1979), p. 45.

9. June Purvis, *A History of Women's Education in England* (Milton Keynes: Open University Press, 1991), p. 66ff.

10. Kathryn Hughes, *The Victorian Governess* (London: Hambledon Press, 1993).

11. M. Smith, *Autobiography of Mary Smith, Schoolmistress and Nonconformist: A Fragment of a Life, with Letters from Jane Welsh Carlyle and Thomas Carlyle*, ed. George Coward (London: Bemrose and Sons, 1892), 2 vols.

12. See Martha Vicinus, *Independent Women: Work and Community for Single Women, 1850–1920* (London: Virago Press, 1985) ch. 5 for a stimulating account of the professional subculture which developed in the new schools.

13. For full details, see Anne Summers, *Angels and Citizens: British Women as Military Nurses 1854–1914* (London: Routledge and Kegan Paul, 1988), chs 1–2.

14. Vicinus, *Independent Women*, ch. 3.

15. Sally Alexander, 'Women's Work in Nineteenth-Century London', (1976) reprinted in Sally Alexander, *Becoming a Woman: And Other Essays in 19th and 20th Century Feminist History* (London: Virago Press, 1994), p. 28.

16. Useful material on these issues may be found in Elizabeth K. Helsinger, Robin Lauterbach Sheets and William Veeder (eds), *The Woman Question: Society and Literature in Britain and America 1837–1883*, (Chicago and London: University of Chicago Press, 1983), 3 vols, iii, chs 1–2.

17. Joanna Trollope, *Britannia's Daughters: Women of the British Empire* (London: Pimlico, 1994; first published Hutchinson, 1983), p. 93–4.

18. Quoted in Dominic David Alessio, 'Domesticating "the Heart of the Wild": Female Personifications of the Colonies 1886–1940', *Women's History Review*, 6, no. 2 (1997), p. 249. See also Hammerton, *Emigrant Gentlewomen*.

19. Marion Amies, 'The Victorian Governess and Colonial Ideals of Womanhood', *Victorian Studies*, 31 (1988), pp. 537–65.

20. For full details on Gillies, see Charlotte Yeldham, *Margaret Gillies RWS, Unitarian Painter of Mind and Emotion 1803–1887* (Lampeter: Edwin Mellor Press, 1997).

21. Kathryn Gleadle, *The Early Feminists: Radical Unitarians and the Emergence of the Women's Rights Movement, 1831–51* (Basingstoke: Macmillan – now Palgrave, 1995), p. 92.

22. Philippa Levine, *Victorian Feminism, 1850–1900* (London: Hutchinson, 1987), pp. 82–90. The quote is from p. 89.

23. Reynolds, *Aristocratic Women and Political Society*, pp. 60, 54–5.

24. Quoted in Joan Perkin, *Women and Marriage in Nineteenth-Century England* (Chicago: Lyceum Books, 1989), p. 78.

25. See the excellent discussion in Reynolds, *Aristocratic Women and Political Society*, pp. 45–7, 91–100.

26. Bridget Hill, 'Women, Work and the Census', *History Workshop Journal*, 35 (1993), p. 82; Catherine Hall, 'Strains in the "Firm of Wife, Children and Friends": Middle-Class Women and Employment in Early-Nineteenth-Century England', in Catherine Hall, *White Male and Middle-Class: Explorations in Feminism and History* (Cambridge: Polity Press, 1992), p. 176.

27. Hall, 'Strains in the "Firm of Wife, Children and Friends"', pp. 185–7.

28. Theodore Koditschek, *Class Formation and Urban-Industrial Society, Bradford, 1750–1850* (Cambridge: Cambridge University Press, 1990), p. 210.

29. Hall, 'Strains in the "Firm of Wife, Children and Friends"', pp. 186–7.

30. Davidoff and Hall, *Family Fortunes*, pp. 279–89.

31. Koditschek, *Class Formation and Urban-Industrial Society*, p. 189.

32. A. James Hammerton, *Cruelty and Companionship: Conflict in Nineteenth-Century Married Life* (London and New York: Routledge, 1992), pp. 84, 114.

33. Jane Robinson, *Angels of Albion: Women of the Indian Mutiny* (London: Viking, 1996), p. 237.

34. M. Jeanne Peterson, *Family, Love and Work in the Lives of Victorian Gentlewomen* (Bloomington and Indianapolis: Indiana University Press, 1989), pp. 165–6.

35. Ivy Pinchbeck, *Women Workers and the Industrial Revolution, 1750–1850* (London: Virago, 1981, first published 1930), pp. 33–5.

36. See, for example, Davidoff and Hall, *Family Fortunes*, p. 289.

37. L. Davidoff, 'The Role of Gender in the "First Industrial Nation": Farming and the Countryside in England, 1780–1850', in Davidoff, *Worlds Between*, p. 196.

38. Pamela Horn, *Victorian Countrywomen* (Oxford: Basil Blackwell, 1991), p. 112.

39. Judy Lown, *Women and Industrialisation: Gender at Work in Nineteenth Century England* (Cambridge: Polity Press, 1990), pp. 29, 102, 146, 149, 164.

40. Ruth Watts, *Gender, Power and the Unitarians in England 1760–1860* (London and New York: Longman, 1998), pp. 71–2, 88.

41. Koditschek, *Class Formation and Urban-Industrial Society*, pp. 550–1.

42. Angela V. John, 'Beyond Paternalism: The Ironmaster's Wife in the Industrial Community', in Angela V. John (ed.), *Our Mothers' Land: Chapters in Welsh Women's History, 1830–1939* (Cardiff: University of Wales Press, 1991), p. 48.

43. Quoted in Pamela Horn, *Ladies of the Manor: Wives and Daughters in Country-House Society, 1830–1918* (Stroud: Alan Sutton, 1991), pp. 184–5; Reynolds, *Aristocratic Women and Political Society*, p. 63.

44. John, 'Beyond Paternalism', pp. 43–68. The quotes are taken from pp. 47 and 44.

45. Anna Clark, *The Struggle for the Breeches: Gender and the Making of the British Working Class* (London: Rivers Oram Press, 1995), p. 19; Reynolds, *Aristocratic Women and Political Society*, p. 120.

46. Quoted in Pinchbeck, *Women Workers*, p. 315.

47. Davidoff and Hall, *Family Fortunes*, pp. 209–13; 275–9, 280.

48. Penelope Lane, 'Women in the Regional Economy: The East Midlands, 1700–1830', (Unpublished PhD Thesis, University of Warwick, 1999), chs 2 and 3; Koditschek, *Class Formation and Urban-Industrial Society*, p. 222.

49. Edgar Johnson, *Charles Dickens: His Tragedy and Triumph* (Harmondsworth: Penguin, 1980, first published 1952), p. 30.

50. Hannah Barker, 'Women and Business in Eighteenth Century Manchester', unpublished paper delivered at 'On the Town: Women and Urban Life in Eighteenth Century England, 1660–1820', conference held at the University of Leicester, 29 May 1999.

51. Ibid., and Perkin, *Women and Marriage*, p. 15.

52. Alexander, 'Women's Work', p. 28.

53. Pamela Sharpe and Stanley D. Chapman, 'Women's Employment and Industrial Organisation: Commercial Lace Embroidery in Early Nineteenth-Century Ireland and England', *Women's History Review*, 5, no. 3 (1996), pp. 332, 338.

54. Davidoff and Hall, *Family Fortunes*, pp. 297–8.

55. Peterson, *Family, Love and Work*, pp. 139–43.

56. Fiona Bowie, Deborah Kirkwood and Shirley Ardener (eds), *Women and Missions: Past and Present: Anthropological and Historical Perceptions* (Oxford: Berg Publishers, 1993), chs 2–4.

57. Ruth Watts, *Gender, Power and the Unitarians in England 1760–1860* (London: Longman, 1998), pp. 43–56.

58. There is a substantial literature on the work of Mary Carpenter. For a summary, see Watts, *Gender, Power and the Unitarians*, pp. 174–8; and Seth Koven, 'Borderlands: Women, Voluntary Action, and Child Welfare in Britain, 1840–1914', in Seth Koven and Sonya Michel (eds), *Mothers of a New World: Maternalist Politics and the Origins of Welfare States* (London and New York: Routledge, 1993), pp. 96–106.

59. Koven, 'Borderlands', pp. 102–6.

60. F. K. Prochaska, *Women and Philanthropy in Nineteenth-Century England* (Oxford: Clarendon Press, 1980), pp. 175–6.

61. See Hill, 'Women, Work and the Census' for a discussion of some of these implications.

5 Politics, Community and Protest

1. The classic account is Catherine Hall, 'The Early Formation of Victorian Domestic Ideology', (1979) reprinted in Catherine Hall, *White, Male and Middle Class: Explorations in Feminism and History* (Cambridge: Polity Press, 1992), pp. 75–93.

2. See, for example, Leonore Davidoff and Catherine Hall, *Family Fortunes: Men and Women of the English Middle Class 1780–1850* (London: Routledge, 1987), especially p. 19.

3. Linda Colley, *Britons: Forging the Nation 1707–1837* (London and New Haven: Yale University Press, 1992), pp. 254–62. The quotes are from pp. 254 and 261.

4. F. K. Prochaska, *Women and Philanthropy in Nineteenth-Century England* (Oxford: Clarendon Press, 1980), p. 36.

5. Ann Summers, '"A Home from Home": Women's Philanthropic Work in the Nineteenth Century', in S. Burman (ed.), *Fit Work for Women* (London: Croom Helm, 1979), p. 39.

6. Kathryn Sutherland, 'Hannah More's Counter-Revolutionary Feminism', in Kelvin Everest (ed.), *Revolution in Writing: British Literary Responses to the French Revolution* (Milton Keynes and Philadelphia: Open University Press, 1991), pp. 27–63.

7. Prochaska, *Women and Philanthropy*, p. 25.

8. Ruth Watts, *Gender, Power and the Unitarians in England 1760–1860* (London and New York: Longman, 1998), pp. 166–70.

9. Kenneth Corfield, 'Elizabeth Heyrick: Radical Quaker', in Gail Malmgreen (ed.), *Religion in the Lives of English Women* (London: Croom Helm, 1986), pp. 41–67.

10. Prochaska, *Women and Philanthropy*, ch. 5.

11. See Martha Vicinus, *Independent Women: Work and Community For Single Women, 1850–1920* (London: Virago, 1985), ch. 2.

12. Prochaska, *Women and Philanthropy*, pp. 30–1, 50–1 and *passim*.

13. K. D. Reynolds, *Aristocratic Women and Political Society in Victorian Britain* (Oxford: Clarendon Press, 1998), pp. 102–10.

14. Jessica Gerard, *Country House Life: Family and Servants, 1815–1914* (Oxford: Blackwell, 1994), pp. 122–3; Peter Mandler, 'From Almack's to Willis's: Aristocratic Women and Politics, 1815–1867', in Amanda Vickery (ed.),

Women, Privilege and Power: British Women and Politics, 1780–1998 (Stanford: Stanford University Press, 2001).

15. Such practices were strongly endorsed by leading proponents of philanthropy, such as Hannah More. See the activities of the Stanley girls in her *Coelebs in Search of a Wife* (1809).

16. Reynolds, *Aristocratic Women and Political Society*, pp. 87–9. See pp. 80–91 for women and religious patronage.

17. Elaine Chalus, ' "That Epidemical Madness": Women and Electoral Politics in the Late Eighteenth Century', in Hannah Barker and Elaine Chalus (eds), *Gender in Eighteenth-Century England: Roles, Representations and Responsibilities* (London and New York: Longman, 1997), p. 156.

18. Reynolds, *Aristocratic Women and Political Society*; Elaine Chalus, 'That Epidemical Madness'; Amanda Foreman, *Georgiana Duchess of Devonshire* (London: HarperCollins, 1998).

19. Pat Jalland, *Women, Marriage and Politics, 1860–1914* (Oxford: Clarendon Press, 1986), p. 205.

20. P. J. Jupp, 'The Roles of Royal and Aristocratic Women in British Politics, *c.* 1782–1832', in Mary O' Dowd and Sabine Wichert (eds), *Chattel, Servant or Citizen: Women's Status in Church, State and Society* (Belfast: Institute of Irish Studies, Queen's University, 1995), pp. 106–7.

21. Reynolds, *Aristocratic Women and Political Society*, pp. 132–9; Sarah Richardson, 'The Role of Women in Electoral Politics', *Northern History*, 32 (1996), pp. 133–51.

22. Reynolds, *Aristocratic Women*, p. 141.

23. Richardson, 'The Role of Women in Electoral Politics', p. 145.

24. Foreman, *Georgiana Duchess of Devonshire*, chs 23–4.

25. Leonore Davidoff, *The Best Circles: Society, Etiquette and the Season* (London: Croom Helm, 1973), p. 26; K. D. Reynolds, 'Politics without Feminism. The Victorian Political Hostess,' in Clarissa Campbell Orr (ed.), *Wollstonecraft's Daughters: Womanhood in England and France* (Manchester and New York: Manchester University Press, 1996), 94–108.

26. Jupp, 'The Roles of Royal and Aristocratic Women', p. 113.

27. Reynolds, *Aristocratic Women*, pp. 191–2, 210–12.

28. Jane Robinson, *Angels of Albion: The Women of the Indian Mutiny*, (London: Viking, 1996), p. 90. See also Reynolds, *Aristocratic Women and Political Society*, p. 120.

29. Leonore Davidoff, 'The Role of Gender in the "First Industrial Nation": Farming and the Countryside in England, 1780–1850', in Leonore Davidoff, *Words Between, Historical Perspectives on Gender and Class* (Cambridge: Polity Press, 1991), p. 190; Davidoff and Hall, *Family Fortunes*, pp. 135–7.

30. Elaine Chalus, ' " . . . & if I were in Parliament": Women, Electoral Privilege and Practice in the Eighteenth Century'; and Matthew Cragoe, ' "Jenny

rules the roost": Women and Electoral Politics, 1821–1868', in Kathryn Gleadle and Sarah Richardson (eds), *Women and British Politics, 1760–1860: The Power of the Petticoat*. (Basingstoke: Macmillan – now Palgrave, 2000), pp. 19–38 and 153–68.

31. These themes are explored in Kathryn Gleadle, 'Women and Politics in the British Nonconformist Enlightenment, 1780–1830', in Vickery (ed.), *Women, Privilege and Power*; and Sarah Richardson, ' "Well-Neighboured Houses": The Political Networks of Elite Women, 1780–1860,' in Gleadle and Richardson, *Women in British Politics*, pp. 56–73.

32. Ruth and Edmund Frow (eds), *Political Women 1800–1850* (London: Pluto Press, 1989), pp. 2–15.

33. Helen Rogers, ' "The Prayer, The Passion and the Reason" of Eliza Sharples: Freethought, Women's Rights and Republicanism, 1832–52', in Eileen Yeo (ed.), *Radical Femininity: Women's Self-Representation in the Public Sphere* (Manchester: Manchester University Press, 1998), pp. 52–78. The quote is on p. 53.

34. The activities of such women emerges clearly in Frow and Frow, *Political Women*, ch. 3.

35. Susanna Saxton, for example, secretary of the Manchester Female Reformers, ibid., pp. 18–19.

36. See Dolores Dooley, 'Anna Doyle Wheeler', in Mary Cullen and Maria Luddy (eds), *Women, Power and Consciousness in 19th Century Ireland* (Dublin: Attic Press, 1995), pp. 19–53.

37. Barbara Taylor, *Eve and the New Jerusalem: Socialism and Feminism in the Nineteenth Century* (London: Virago Press, 1983), pp. 72–3.

38. Kathryn Gleadle, ' "Our Several Spheres": Middle-Class Women and the Feminisms of Early Victorian Radicalism', in Gleadle and Richardson (eds), *Women in British Politics*, pp. 136–9.

39. Jutta Schwarzkopf, *Women in the Chartist Movement* (Basingstoke: Macmillan – now Palgrave, 1991), *passim*.

40. Simon Morgan, 'Domestic Economy and Political Agitation: Women and the Anti-Corn Law League 1839–1846', in Gleadle and Richardson (eds), *Women in British Politics*, pp. 115–33.

41. Alex Tyrell, 'Women's Mission and Pressure Group Politics in Britain, (1825–60)', *Bulletin of the John Rylands University Library*, 63 (1980), p. 221.

42. Ibid., pp. 193–210.

43. Corfield, 'Elizabeth Heyrick'; the term 'moral radicalism' is developed in Louis and Rosemary Billington, ' "A Burning Zeal for Righteousness": Women in the British Anti-Slavery Movement 1820–1860', in Jane Rendall (ed.), *Equal or Different: Women's Politics, 1800–1914* (Oxford: Basil Blackwell, 1987), pp. 82–111; Clare Midgley, *Women Against Slavery: The British Campaigns 1780–1870* (London: Routledge, 1992), pp. 103–18.

44. Midgley, *Women Against Slavery*, p. 53.

45. Clare Midgley, 'Slave Sugar Boycotts, Female Activism and the Domestic Base of British Anti-Slavery Culture', *Slavery and Abolition*, 17, no. 3 (1996), pp. 137–62.

46. Vron Ware, *Beyond the Pale: White Women, Racism, and History* (London: Verso, 1992), pp. 72–3.

47. Midgley, *Women Against Slavery*, pp. 17, 45, 62–71.

48. Ibid., p. 116.

49. Ibid., pp. 158–72.

50. This emerges clearly in the letters edited by Clare Taylor, *British and American Abolitionists: An Episode in Transatlantic Understanding* (Edinburgh: Edinburgh University Press, 1974), *passim*.

51. Tyrell, 'Women's Mission', p. 202.

52. Jill Liddington, *The Long Road to Greenham: Feminism and Anti-Militarism in Britain since 1820* (London: Virago, 1989), ch. 1; Tyrell, 'Woman's Mission', p. 218; Elizabeth Isichei, *Victorian Quakers* (Oxford: Oxford University Press, 1970), p. 108.

53. Lillian Lewis Shiman, ' "Changes are Dangerous": Women and Temperance in Victorian England', in Malmgreen (ed.), *Religion in the Lives of English Women*, pp. 195–7. See also Tyrell, 'Women's Mission', pp. 219–21; Jane Rendall, *The Origins of Modern Feminism: Women in Britain, France and the United States, 1780–1860* (Chicago: Lyceum Books, 1985), pp. 254–6.

54. Gleadle, 'Our Several Spheres', pp. 136–9.

55. Rendall, *Origins of Modern Feminism*, p. 217.

56. Gleadle, *The Early Feminists*.

57. Ibid., pp. 177–82.

58. Lee Holcombe, *Wives and Property: Reform of the Married Women's Property Law in Nineteenth-Century England* (Toronto and Buffalo: University of Toronto Press, 1983), pp. 58–62.

59. Philippa Levine, *Feminist Lives in Victorian England. Private Roles and Public Commitment* (Oxford: Basil Blackwell, 1990).

60. Sally Alexander, *Becoming a Woman: And Other Essays in 19th and 20th Century Feminist History* (London: Virago, 1994), pp. 129, 139.

6   Families, Relationships and Home Life

1. For a classic treatment of these themes see Catherine Hall, 'The Early Formation of Victorian Domestic Ideology', (1979) in Catherine Hall, *White, Male and Middle Class: Explorations in Feminism and History* (Cambridge: Polity Press, 1992), pp. 75–93.

2. Lawrence Stone, *The Family, Sex and Marriage in England 1500–1800* (Harmondsworth: Penguin, 1990, first published 1977), especially chs 6, 8–9.

3. F. M. L. Thompson, *English Landed Society in the Nineteenth Century* (London: Routledge and Kegan Paul, 1963), p. 100.

4. Judith Schneid Lewis, *In the Family Way: Childbearing in the British Aristocracy, 1760–1860* (New Brunswick, New Jersey: Rutgers University Press, 1986), ch. 1. See also Jessica Gerard, *Country House Life: Family and Servants, 1815–1914* (Oxford: Blackwell, 1994), ch. 4.

5. Amanda Vickery, *The Gentleman's Daughter: Women's Lives in Georgian England* (New Haven, Connecticut and London: Yale University Press, 1998), pp. 39–58; see also K. D. Reynolds, *Aristocratic Women and Political Society in Victorian Britain* (Oxford: Clarendon Press, 1998), *passim*.

6. Thompson, *English Landed Society*, pp. 99, 18.

7. Stana Nenadic, 'Middle-Rank Consumers and Domestic Culture in Edinburgh and Glasgow 1720–1840', *Past and Present*, no. 145 (1994), pp. 122–54.

8. Leonore Davidoff and Catherine Hall, *Family Fortunes: Men and Women of the English Middle Class, 1780–1850* (London: Routledge, 1987), pp. 219–22. See also pp. 99–106 for the importance of religious communities.

9. Lewis, *In the Family Way*, pp. 122–3; Davidoff and Hall, *Family Fortunes*, p. 335.

10. Lewis, *In the Family Way*, *passim*, but especially pp. 193–217.

11. John Hawkins Miller, '"Temple and Sewer": Childbirth, Prudery and Victoria Regina', in Anthony S. Wohl (ed.), *The Victorian Family: Structure and Stresses* (London: Croom Helm, 1978), pp. 23–43.

12. Patricia Branca, *Silent Sisterhood: Middle-Class Women in the Victorian Home* (London: Croom Helm, 1975), p. 85.

13. Ibid., pp. 102–3; Davidoff and Hall, *Family Fortunes*, pp. 335–8; Lewis, *In the Family Way*, pp. 209–13.

14. Michael Brooks, 'Love and Possession in a Victorian Household; The Example of the Ruskins', in Wohl (ed.), *The Victorian Family*, pp. 89–92.

15. For an initial consideration of how radical women might attempt to encourage progressivism in their children, see Kathryn Gleadle, 'Women and Politics in the British Nonconformist Enlightenment, 1780–1830', in Amanda Vickery (ed.), *Women, Privilege and Power: British Women and Politics, 1780–1998* (Stanford: Stanford University Press, 2001).

16. See Theodore Koditschek, *Class Formation and Urban–Industrial Society, Bradford, 1750–1850* (Cambridge: Cambridge University Press, 1990), pp. 188–9.

17. Lewis, *In the Family Way*, ch. 2; Gerard, *Country House Life*, p. 75.

18. Leonore Davidoff, *The Best Circles: Society, Etiquette and the Season* (London: Croom Helm, 1973), p. 53.

19. Gerard, *Country House Life*, pp. 71–2.

20. Pat Jalland and John Hooper (eds), *Women from Birth to Death: The Female Life Cycle in Britain 1830–1914* (Brighton: Harvester Press, 1986), pp. 304, 275; Vickery, *The Gentleman's Daughter*, p. 98.

21. Barbara Caine, *Destined to be Wives: The Sisters of Beatrice Webb* (Oxford: Clarendon Press, 1986), p. 31.
22. Elizabeth K. Helsinger, Robin Lauterbachs Sheets and William Veeder (eds), *The Woman Question: Society and Literature in Britain and America, 1837–1883* (Chicago and London: University of Chicago Press, 1983), 3 vols, ii, pp. 136–40.
23. For a critique of the historiography see A. J. Vickery, 'Golden Ages to Separate Spheres: A Review of the Categories and Chronology of English Women's History', *Historical Journal*, 36, no. 2 (1993), pp. 383–414.
24. Henrietta Twycross-Martin, 'Woman Supportive or Woman Manipulative? The "Mrs Ellis" Woman', in Clarissa Campbell Orr (ed.), *Wollstonecraft's Daughters: Womanhood in England and France* (Manchester: Manchester University Press, 1996), pp. 109–20.
25. Nenadic, 'Middle-Rank Consumers and Domestic Culture', pp. 136–7.
26. Koditschek, *Class Formation and Urban–Industrial Society*, ch. 8.
27. Jalland and Hooper, *Women from Birth to Death*, pp. 304–9.
28. Davidoff, *The Best Circles*, pp. 39–40.
29. Joanna Trollope, *Britannia's Daughters: Women of the British Empire* (London: Pimlico, 1994, first published 1983), p. 46.
30. Caroline Cornwallis, *Selections from the Letters of Caroline Frances Cornwallis* (London: Trubner and Co, 1864), p. 20.
31. Kathryn Gleadle, *The Early Feminists: Radical Unitarians and the Emergence of the Women's Rights Movement, c. 1831–51* (Basingstoke: Macmillan – now Palgrave, 1995), pp. 21–32.
32. See Joan Perkin, *Women and Marriage in Nineteenth-Century England* (Chicago: Lyceum Books, 1989), pp. 89–94.
33. Lewis, *In the Family Way*, ch. 1, p. 167; Gerard, *Country House Life*, p. 108.
34. Perkin, *Women and Marriage*, pp. 215–18.
35. Davidoff and Hall, *Family Fortunes*, p. 152.
36. In Scotland divorce was easier to obtain. R. A. Houston, 'Women in the Economy and Society of Scotland 1500–1800', in R. A. Houston and I. D. Whyte (eds), *Scottish Society 1500–1800* (Cambridge: Cambridge University Press, 1989), p. 132. The Act was never passed in Ireland, see David Fitzpatrick, 'Divorce and Separation in Modern Irish History', *Past and Present*, 114 (1987), pp. 172–96.
37. Mary Landon Shanley, ' "One Must Ride Behind": Married Women's Rights and the Divorce Act of 1857', *Victorian Studies*, 25 (1982), p. 364.
38. Ibid., p. 366.
39. Michael Mason, *The Making of Victorian Sexuality* (Oxford: Oxford University Press, 1995), pp. 195–205.
40. Jill Liddington, *Land, Gender and Authority: The Ann Lister Diaries 1833–36* (London: Rivers Oram Press, 1998); Gleadle, *The Early Feminists*, pp. 112–13; T. Wemyss Reid, *The Life of the Right Honourable William Edward Forster*

(London: Chapman Hall, 1888), 2 vols, i, pp. 47–8; Elizabeth Mavor, *The Ladies of Llangollen: A Study in Romantic Friendship* (Harmondsworth: Penguin, 1971).

41. Lewis, *In the Family Way*, p. 37.
42. Reynolds, *Aristocratic Women and Political Society*, p. 6.
43. Quoted in Perkin, *Women and Marriage*, p. 79.
44. Trollope, *Britannia's Daughters*, p. 123.
45. Matthew Cragoe, '"Jenny Rules the Roost": Women and Electoral Politics, 1832–1868', in Kathryn Gleadle and Sarah Richardson (eds), *Women in British Politics, 1760–1860: The Power of the Petticoat* (Basingstoke: Macmillan – now Palgrave, 2000), p. 158; Elaine Chalus, '"But His Wife Governed". Women and the Politics of Influence in Eighteenth Century Politics', paper delivered at the conference, 'On the Town: Women and Urban Life in Eighteenth Century England, 1660–1820', University of Leicester, 29 May 1999.
46. See, for example, Shanley, 'One Must Ride Behind', pp. 374–5.
47. Quoted in Koditschek, *Class Formation and Urban–Industrial Society*, p. 225.
48. Davidoff and Hall, *Family Fortunes*, p. 323.
49. For an outline of middle-class female education, see Carol Dyhouse, *Girls Growing Up in Late Victorian and Edwardian England* (London: Routledge and Kegan Paul, 1981), ch. 2.
50. Gerard, *Country House Life*, pp. 53, 103.
51. Vickery, *The Gentleman's Daughter*, chs 6–7. For the empowering possibilities in female correspondence networks, see Marjorie Reeves, *Pursuing the Muses: Female Education and Nonconformist Culture, 1700–1900* (London, 1997).
52. For full details of married women's legal position, see Lee Holcombe, *Wives and Property: Reform of the Married Women's Property Law in Nineteenth-Century England* (Toronto and Buffalo: University of Toronto Press, 1983), chs 2 and 3.
53. Melanie Tebbutt, *Making Ends Meet: Pawnbroking and Working-Class Credit* (Leicester: Leicester University Press, 1983), p. 42.
54. Margaret Forster, *Significant Sisters: The Grassroots of Active Feminism 1839–1939* (Harmondsworth, Penguin, 1984), ch. 1.
55. Fitzpatrick, 'Divorce and Separation', p. 178.
56. Reynolds, *Aristocratic Women and Political Society*, p. 113.
57. Branca, *Silent Sisterhood*, p. 9.
58. Perkin, *Women and Marriage*, p. 13.
59. Hammerton, *Cruelty and Companionship*, p. 114.
60. Gleadle, *The Early Feminists*, pp. 117–24.
61. Maxine Berg, 'Women's Property in Eighteenth-Century England', *Journal of Interdisciplinary History*, 2, no. 24 (1993), pp. 233–50, quote from p. 234.

62. Davidoff and Hall, *Family Fortunes*, pp. 209–13, 275–9; Mary Poovey, *Uneven Developments: The Ideological Work of Gender in Mid-Victorian England* (London and Chicago: University of Chicago Press, 1988), pp. 71–2.
63. Margot Finn, 'Women, Consumption and Coverture in England, *c.* 1760–1860', *Historical Journal*, 3, no. 39 (1996), pp. 703–22, the quote is p. 707.
64. Vickery, *Gentleman's Daughter*, chs 5, 7.
65. Pat Jalland, *Death in the Victorian Family* (Oxford: Oxford University Press, 1996), ch. 11.

PART III WORKING-CLASS WOMEN, 1860–1900

7 Work

1. Quoted in Eric Richards, 'Women in the British Economy Since about 1700: An Interpretation', *History*, 59 (1974), p. 351.
2. Elizabeth Roberts, *Women's Work, 1840–1940* (Basingstoke: Macmillan – now Palgrave, 1988), p. 22. The equivalent rates in Scotland were 28 per cent in 1871, 27 per cent in 1891, and 24 per cent in 1911.
3. For a clear account of the factors affecting women's work, the analysis of Tilly and Scott remains extremely useful: Louise A. Tilly and Joan W. Scott, *Women, Work and Family* (London and New York; Routledge, 1989, first published 1978), pt 2.
4. Ellen Jordan, 'Female Unemployment in England and Wales, 1851–1911: An Examination of the Census Figures for 15–19 Year Olds', *Social History*, 13 (1988), pp. 175–90.
5. Joanna Bourke, *Husbandry to Housewifery: Women, Economic Change and Housework in Ireland, 1890–1914* (Oxford: Clarendon, 1993).
6. Quoted in Jane Lewis, *Women in England 1870–1950: Social Divisions and Social Change* (Hemel Hempstead: Harvester Wheatsheaf, 1984), p. 50.
7. Joanna Bourke, 'Housewifery in Working-Class England, 1860–1914', *Past and Present*, 143 (1994), pp. 167–97.
8. Quoted in Meg Gomersall, *Working-Class Girls in Nineteenth Century England: Life, Work and Schooling* (Basingstoke: Macmillan – now Palgrave, 1997), p. 40.
9. See Dot Jones, 'Counting the Cost of Coal: Women's Lives in the Rhondda, 1811–1911', in Angela V. John (ed.), *Our Mothers' Land: Chapters in Welsh Women's History, 1830–1939* (Cardiff: University of Wales Press, 1991), pp. 109–33.
10. Ann Oakley, *Housewife* (Harmondsworth: Penguin, 1974), pp. 43–56.

11. Eleanor Gordon, *Women and the Labour Movement in Scotland 1850–1914* (Oxford: Clarendon Press, 1991), p. 22; see also Edward Higgs, 'Women, Occupation and Work in the Nineteenth-Century Census', *History Workshop Journal*, 23 (1987), pp. 59–80.

12. Ellen Ross, *Love and Toil: Motherhood in Outcast London, 1870–1918* (Oxford: Oxford University Press, 1993), p. 45.

13. Sally Alexander, 'Women's Work in Nineteenth-Century London: A Study of the Years 1820–60s', (1976) reprinted in Sally Alexander, *Becoming a Woman: And other Essays in 19th and 20th Century Feminist History* (London: Virago, 1994), pp. 42–5; Melanie Tebbutt, *Making Ends Meet: Pawnbroking and Working-Class Credit* (Leicester: Leicester University Press, 1983), pp. 51–66; Clare Midgley, 'Ethnicity, "race" and Empire', in June Purvis (ed.), *Women's History: Britain, 1850–1945: An Introduction* (London: UCL Press, 1995), pp. 248–9.

14. The discussion on homework is indebted to Duncan Bythell, *The Sweated Trades: Outwork in Nineteenth-Century Britain* (London: Batsford Academic, 1978); Pamela Horn, *Victorian Countrywomen* (Oxford: Basil Blackwell, 1991), ch. 7; Belinda Westover, ' "To Fill the Kids' Tummies": The Lives and Work of Colchester Tailoresses, 1880–1918', in Leonore Davidoff and Belinda Westover (eds), *Our Work, Our Lives, Our Worlds: Women's History and Women's Work* (Basingstoke: Macmillan – now Palgrave, 1986), pp. 54–75; Shelley Pennington and Belinda Westover, *A Hidden Workforce: Homeworkers in England, 1850–1985* (Basingstoke: Macmillan – now Palgrave, 1989); and James A. Schmeichen, *Sweated Industries and Sweated Labor: The London Clothing Trades, 1860–1914* (Urbana: University of Illinois Press, 1984).

15. Quoted in Barbara Drake, *Women in Trade Unions* (London: Virago, 1984, first published 1920), p. 31.

16. Pennington and Westover, *A Hidden Workforce*, pp. 104–5; see also Drake, *Women in Trade Unions*, ch. 2.

17. Sonya O. Rose, *Limited Livelihoods: Gender and Class in Nineteenth-Century England* (London: Routledge, 1992), pp. 96–9, 98–9.

18. Patricia E. Malcolmson, 'Laundresses and the Laundry Trade in Victorian England', *Victorian Studies*, 24 (1981), pp. 439–62.

19. Judith R. Walkowitz, *Prostitution and Victorian Society: Women, Class and the State* (Cambridge: Cambridge University Press, 1980), ch. 1; Lucy Bland, *Banishing the Beast: English Feminism and Sexual Morality 1885–1914* (Harmondsworth: Penguin, 1985), pp. 95–123; F. K. Prochaska, *Women and Philanthropy in Nineteenth-Century England* (Oxford: Clarendon Press, 1980), ch. 6; Linda Nead, *Myths of Sexuality: Representations of Women in Victorian Britain* (Oxford: Basil Blackwell, 1988), chs 3–5.

20. Roberts, *Women's Work*, p. 34.

21. Drake, *Women and Trade Unions*, pp. 27–8.

22. Jenny Morris, 'The Characteristics of Sweating: The Late Nineteenth-Century London and Leeds Tailoring Trade', in Angela V. John (ed.), *Unequal Opportunities: Women's Employment in England 1800–1918* (Oxford: Basil Blackwell, 1986), pp. 94–121.

23. Nancy Osterud, 'Gender Divisions and the Organization of Work in the Leicester Hosiery Industry'; and Felicity Hunt, 'Opportunities Lost and Gained', in ibid, pp. 45–68 and pp. 71–93. The quote is from p. 87.

24. Harriet Bradley, *Men's Work, Women's Work: A Sociological History of the Sexual Division of Labour in Employment* (Cambridge: Polity Press, 1989), p. 165.

25. Rose, *Limited Livelihoods*, p. 28.

26. Angela V. John, *By the Sweat of their Brow: Women Workers At Victorian Coal Mines* (London: Routledge and Kegan Paul, 1984), pp. 176–84.

27. Gordon, *Women and the Labour Movement*, pp. 156–61. See Jill Liddington and Jill Norris, *One Hand Tied Behind Us: The Rise of the Women's Suffrage Movement* (London: Virago, 1978), ch. 5 for the differing status of jobs within the textile factories.

28. Jutta Schwarzkopf, 'Gendering Exploitation: The Use of Gender in the Campaign Against Driving in Lancashire Weaving Sheds, 1886–1903', *Women's History Review*, 7, no. 4 (1998), pp. 449–73.

29. Harold Benenson, 'The "Family Wage" and Working Women's Consciousness in Britain, 1880–1914', *Politics and Society*, 19 (1991), p. 91.

30. Carol E. Morgan, 'Gender Constructions and Gender Relations in Cotton and Chain-Making in England: A Contested and Varied Terrain', *Women's History Review*, 6, no. 3 (1997), pp. 376–8.

31. Richard Whipp, 'Kinship, Labour and Enterprise: The Staffordshire Pottery Industry 1890–1920', in Pat Hudson and W. R. Lee (eds), *Women's Work and the Family Economy in Historical Perspective* (Manchester: Manchester University Press, 1990), pp. 192–3.

32. Jill Norris, ' "Well Fitted for Females": Women in the Macclesfield Silk Industry', in J. A. Jowitt and A. J. McIvor (eds), *Employers and Labour in the English Textile Industries* (London and New York: Routledge, 1988), p. 198; Gordon, *Women in the Labour Movement*, p. 154.

33. Margaret Hewitt, *Wives and Mothers in Victorian Industry* (London: Rockliff, 1958), p. 178.

34. Drake, *Women in Trade Unions*, p. 30; Liddington and Norris, *One Hand Tied Behind Us*, p. 84.

35. Gordon, *Women and the Labour Movement*, pp. 152–3, ch. 5.

36. Joanna Bornat, ' "What About That Lass of Yours Being in the Union?": Textile Workers and Their Union in Yorkshire, 1888–1922', in Davidoff and Westover, *Our Work, Our Lives*, pp. 76–98.

37. Benenson, 'The Family Wage', p. 73.

38. See Chapter 11.

39. Liddington and Norris, *One Hand Tied Behind Us*, pp. 96–7.

40. Patricia Hollis (ed.), *Women in Public 1850–1900: Documents of the Victorian Women's Movement* (London: George Allen and Unwin, 1979), p. 53.

41. Gordon, *Women and the Labour Movement*, p. 26.

42. For the economic activities of Irish migrant women, see Midgley, 'Ethnicity, "race" and Empire', pp. 253–5.

43. Raphael Samuel, 'Village Labour', in Raphael Samuel (ed.), *Village Life and Labour* (London: Routledge and Kegan Paul, 1975), p. 21.

44. These details are taken from Jennie Kitteringham, 'Country Work Girls in Nineteenth-Century England', in Samuel, *Village Life*, pp. 73–138 and Horn, *Victorian Countrywomen*, pp. 144–63; Barbara W. Robertson, 'In Bondage: The Female Farm Worker in South-East Scotland', in Eleanor Gordon and Esther Breitenbach (eds), *The World is Ill-Divided: Women's Work in Scotland in the Nineteenth and Early Twentieth Centuries* (Edinburgh: Edinburgh University Press, 1990), pp. 117–35.

45. Karen Sayer, *Women of the Fields: Representations of Rural Women in the Nineteenth Century* (Manchester: Manchester University Press, 1995), pp. 127–35.

46. For further details of such organisations, see Prochaska, *Women and Philanthropy*, pp. 148–55.

47. Quoted in Juliet Gardiner (ed.), *The New Woman: Women's Voices 1880–1918* (London: Collins and Brown, 1993), p. 129.

48. Leonore Davidoff, ' "Mastered for Life": Servant and Wife in Victorian and Edwardian England', (1974) reprinted in Leonore Davidoff, *Worlds Between: Historical Perspectives on Gender and Class* (Cambridge: Polity Press, 1995), p. 22; Edward Higgs, 'Domestic Service and Household Production', in John (ed.), *Unequal Opportunities*, pp. 130–5.

49. Burnett, *Useful Toil*, p. 187.

50. This issue is raised, for example, in Brian Harrison, 'For Church, Queen and Family: The Girls' Friendly Society, 1874–1920', *Past and Present*, 61 (1973), p. 117.

51. Higgs, 'Domestic Service', p. 135.

52. Horn, *Victorian Countrywomen*, pp. 142–3.

53. Liz Stanley (ed.), *The Diaries of Hannah Cullwick* (London: Virago, 1984).

54. Margaret Llewelyn Davies (ed.), *Life as We Have Known It by Co-operative Working Women* (New York and London: W. W. Norton, 1975, first published 1931), p. 4.

55. Carol Dyhouse, *Girls Growing Up in Late Victorian and Edwardian England* (London: Routledge and Kegan Paul, 1981), ch. 3; Anna Davin, *Growing Up Poor: Home, School and Street in London 1870–1914* (London: Rivers Oram, 1996), pt 2.

56. Tilly and Scott, *Women, Work and Family*, p. 156.

57. Ellen Mappen, *Helping Women at Work: The Women's Industrial Council, 1889–1914* (London: Hutchinson, 1985), pp. 132–3.

58. Lewis, *Women in England*, pp. 165–6.

59. Bradley, *Men's Work, Women's Work*, p. 181.
60. Lee Holcombe, *Victorian Ladies at Work: Middle-Class Working Women in England and Wales, 1850–1914* (Newton Abbot: David and Charles, 1973), pp. 117–22; Elizabeth Roberts, *A Woman's Place: An Oral History of Working-Class Women 1890–1940* (Oxford: Basil Blackwell, 1984), p. 47.
61. Meta Zimmeck, ' "Jobs for the Girls": The Expansion of Clerical Work for Women, 1850–1914', in John (ed.), *Unequal Opportunities*, pp. 158–61.
62. Holcombe, *Victorian Ladies at Work*, p. 154.
63. Zimmeck, 'Jobs for the Girls', pp. 153–78.
64. Hollis (ed.), *Women in Public*, p. 45.
65. Tilly and Scott, *Women, Work and Family*, p. 160.
66. Frances Widdowson, 'Educating Teacher – Women and Elementary Teaching in London, 1900–1914', in Davidoff and Westover (eds), *Our Work, Our Lives*, pp. 99–123.
67. Quote in Horn, *Victorian Countrywomen*, p. 209.
68. Hollis (ed.), *Women in Public*, p. 45.
69. F. K. Prochaska, *Women and Philanthropy in Nineteenth-Century England* (Oxford: Clarendon Press, 1980), pp. 126–9.
70. Ross, *Love and Toil*, pp. 120–2.
71. Oakley, *Housewife*, p. 55.

8 Politics, Community and Protest

1. See Chapter 2.
2. Brian Harrison, 'Class and Gender in Modern British Labour History', *Past and Present*, 124 (1989), pp. 121–58.
3. See Eugenio F. Biagini and Alastair J. Reid (eds), *Currents of Radicalism: Popular Radicalism, Organized Labour and Party Politics in Britain 1850–1914* (Cambridge: Cambridge University Press, 1991), particularly the introduction; Jon Lawrence, 'Popular Radicalism and the Socialist Revival in Britain', *Journal of British Studies*, 31 (1992), pp. 163–86.
4. See Elizabeth Roberts, *A Woman's Place: An Oral History of Working-Class Women 1890–1940* (Oxford: Basil Blackwell, 1984), pp. 187–94.
5. Rosemary A. N. Jones, 'Women, Community and Collective Action: The "Ceffyl Pren" Tradition', in Angela V. John (ed.), *Our Mothers' Land: Chapters in Welsh Women's History, 1830–1939* (Cardiff: University of Wales Press, 1991), pp. 17–41.
6. Maria Luddy (ed.), *Women in Ireland 1800–1918* (Cork: Cork University Press, 1995), p. 245.
7. Angela V. John, *By the Sweat of Their Brow: Women Workers at Victorian Coal Mines* (London: Routledge and Kegan Paul, 1984), p. 126.

8. Eric Richards, *A History of the Highland Clearances: Agrarian Transformation and the Evictions, 1746–1886* (London: Croom Helm, 1982), pp. 486–90.

9. Janet K. Tebrake, 'Irish Peasant Women in Revolt: The Land League Years', *Irish Historical Studies*, 28, no. 109 (1992), pp. 63–80.

10. Luddy, *Women in Ireland*, pp. 304–19.

11. Sandra Stanley Holton, *Suffrage Days: Stories from the Women's Suffrage Movement* (London and New York: Routledge, 1996), p. 61.

12. Matthew Cragoe, '"Jenny Rules the Roost": Women and Electoral Politics, 1832–1868', in Kathryn Gleadle and Sarah Richardson (eds), *Women in British Politics, 1760–1860: The Power of the Petticoat* (Basingstoke: Macmillan – now Palgrave, 2000). Working women's support for the Liberal party awaits research, although see Jane Rendall, 'Who was Lily Maxwell? Women's Suffrage and Manchester Politics, 1866–1867', in June Purvis and Sandra Stanley Holton (eds), *Votes for Women* (London: Routledge, 2000), pp. 57–83.

13. Judith R. Walkowitz, *Prostitution and Victorian Society: Women, Class and the State* (Cambridge: Cambridge University Press, 1980), p. 144.

14. Cited in Gerry Maguire, *Conservative Women: A History of Women and the Conservative Party, 1874–1997* (London: Macmillan – now Palgrave, 1998), pp. 32 and 36.

15. Michael Savage, *The Dynamics of Working-Class Politics: The Labour Movement in Preston, 1880–1940* (Cambridge: Cambridge University Press, 1987), pp. 53–5.

16. Maria Bottomley, 'Women and Industrial Militancy', in J. A. Jowitt and A. J. McIvor (eds), *Employers and Labour in the English Textile Industries* (London and New York: Routledge, 1988), pp. 171–86.

17. Joanna Bornat, '"What About That Lass of Yours Being in the Union?": Textile Workers and Their Union in Yorkshire, 1888–1922', in Leonore Davidoff and Belinda Westover (eds), *Our Work, Our Lives, Our Worlds: Women's History and Women's Work* (Basingstoke: Macmillan – now Palgrave, 1986), pp. 92–5.

18. Joanna Bornat, 'Lost Leaders: Women, Trade Unionism and the Case of the General Union of Textile Workers, 1875–1914', in Angela V. John (ed.), *Unequal Opportunities: Women's Employment in England, 1800–1918* (Oxford: Basil Blackwell, 1986), pp. 207–34.

19. Roberts, *A Woman's Place*, p. 49.

20. Karen Hunt, *Equivocal Feminists: The Social Democratic Federation and the Woman Question, 1884–1911* (Cambridge: Cambridge University Press, 1996), p. 268; Bornat, 'Lost Leaders', p. 218.

21. Karen Sayer, 'Field-Faring Women: The Resistance of Women Who Worked in the Fields of Nineteenth-Century England', *Women's History Review*, 2, no. 2 (1995), p. 188; Richard Whipp, 'Kinship, Labour and Enterprise: The Staffordshire Pottery Industry, 1890–1920', in Pat Hudson and W. R. Lee (eds),

Women's Work and the Family Economy in Historical Perspective (Manchester: Manchester University Press, 1990), p. 199.

22. Melanie Tebbutt, *Making Ends Meet: Pawnbroking and Working-Class Credit* (Leicester: Leicester University Press, 1983), pp. 40–1.

23. Quoted in Jill Liddington and Jill Norris, *One Hand Tied Behind Us: The Rise of the Women's Suffrage Movement* (London: Virago, 1978), p. 142.

24. Ibid., see particularly pp. 77–83, 143–51.

25. Leah Leneman, *A Guid Cause: The Women's Suffrage Movement in Scotland* (Aberdeen: Aberdeen University Press, 1991), pp. 23–4.

26. This paragraph draws upon June Hannam, ' "In the Comradeship of the Sexes Lies the Hope of Progress and Social Regeneration": Women in the West Riding ILP *c*.1890–1914', in Jane Rendall (ed.), *Equal or Different: Women's Politics, 1800–1914* (Oxford: Basil Blackwell, 1987), pp. 214–38.

27. Hunt, *Equivocal Feminists*, p. 225.

28. Liddington and Norris, *One Hand Tied Behind Us*, pp. 130–2.

29. Eleanor Gordon, *Women and the Labour Movement in Scotland 1850–1914* (Oxford: Clarendon Press, 1991), pp. 264–5.

30. Liddington and Norris, *One Hand Tied Behind Us*, pp. 122–4, 132–4.

31. Jill Liddington, *The Life and Times of a Respectable Rebel: Selina Cooper (1864–1946)* (London: Virago, 1984), pp. 35–8.

32. Liddington and Norris, *One Hand Tied Behind Us*, pp. 117–18.

33. F. Reid, 'Socialist Sunday Schools in Britain, 1892–1939', *International Review of Social History*, 11 (1966), pp. 20–4.

34. Edward Royle, 'Owenism and the Secularist Tradition: The Huddersfield Secular Society and Sunday School', in Malcolm Chase and Ian Dyck (eds), *Living and Learning, Essays in Honour of J. F. C. Harrison* (Aldershot: Scolar Press, 1996), especially pp. 211–14.

35. Quoted in Liddington and Norris, *One Hand Tied Behind Us*, p. 122.

36. See Lawrence, 'Popular Radicalism', especially p. 178.

37. See Hunt, *Equivocal Feminists*. The quotation is from p. 215.

38. Quoted in ibid., p. 84.

39. A full analysis of the WCG may be found in Gillian Scott, *Feminism and the Politics of Working Women: The Women's Co-operative Guild, 1880s to the Second World War* (London: University College London, 1988).

40. Alistair Thomson, ' "Domestic Drudgery Will be a Thing of the Past": Co-operative Women and the Reform of Housework', in Stephen Yeo (ed.), *New Views of Co-operation* (London: Routledge, 1988), pp.108–27.

41. Jean Gaffin, 'Women and Co-operation', in Lucy Middleton (ed.), *Women in the Labour Movement: The British Experience* (London: Croom Helm, 1977), p. 114; Thomson, 'Domestic Drudgery will be a Thing of the Past', pp. 114–15; Liddington and Norris, *One Hand Tied Behind Us*, pp. 136–7.

42. Kathryn Gleadle, *The Early Feminists: Radical Unitarians and the Emergence of the Women's Rights Movement, c.1831–51* (Basingstoke: Macmillan – now Palgrave, 1995), pp. 49–52, 98–9.

43. Gordon, *Women and the Labour Movement*, p. 268.

44. Scott, *Feminism and the Politics of Working Women*, pp. 103–4.

45. Margaret Llewelyn Davies, *Life as We have Known It* (London and New York, W. W. Norton, 1975, first published 1931), pp. 47–8.

46. See Liddington and Norris, *One Hand Tied Behind Us*, pp. 137–40; Patricia Hollis, *Ladies Elect: Women in English Local Government, 1865–1914* (Oxford: Clarendon Press, 1987), pp. 241–6; Hannam, 'In the Comradeship of the Sexes', pp. 221–3; Hunt, *Equivocal Feminists*, p. 267; Gordon, *Women in the Labour Movement*, p. 265.

47. See Hollis, *Ladies Elect*, p. 246.

48. Pat Thane, 'Women in the British Labour Party and the Construction of State Welfare, 1906–1939', in Seth Koven and Sonya Michel (eds), *Mothers of a New World: Maternalist Politics and the Origins of Welfare States* (London and New York: Routledge, 1993), pp. 343–77.

49. Leonore Davidoff, '"Mastered for Life": Servants and Wives in Victorian and Edwardian England', in Leonore Davidoff, *Worlds Between: Historical Perspectives on Gender and Class* (Cambridge: Polity Press, 1995), pp. 32–3, 39n.

50. Brian Harrison, 'For Church, Queen and Family: The Girls' Friendly Society, 1874–1920', *Past and Present*, 61 (1973), pp. 121–38.

51. F. K. Prochaska, 'A Mother's Country; Mothers' Meetings and Family Welfare in Britain, 1850–1950' *History*, 74 (1989), pp. 379–99.

52. Cited in Davies, *Life as We have Known It*, p. 40.

53. The following discussion of the Primrose League is drawn from Martin Pugh, *The Tories and the People, 1880–1935* (Oxford: Basil Blackwell, 1985); Maguire, *Conservative Women*, ch. 2; Beatrix Campbell, *The Iron Ladies: Why do Women Vote Tory* (London: Virago, 1987), ch. 1.

54. Gareth Stedman Jones, 'Working-Class Culture and Working-Class Politics in London, 1870–1900: Notes on the Remaking of a Working Class', in Gareth Stedman Jones, *Languages of Class: Studies in English Working Class History 1832–1982* (Cambridge: Cambridge University Press, 1983), pp. 179–238; Jon Lawrence, 'Class and Gender in the Making of Urban Toryism, 1880–1914', *English Historical Review*, 108 (1993), pp. 629–52.

55. Pugh, *The Tories and the People*, pp. 49–51.

56. Holton, *Suffrage Days*, p. 52.

9 Families, Relationships and Home Life

1. Gareth Stedman Jones, 'Working-Class Culture and Working-Class Politics in London, 1870–1900: Notes on the Remaking of a Working Class', in Gareth Stedman Jones, *Languages of Class: Studies in English Working Class History 1832–1982* (Cambridge: Cambridge University Press, 1983), pp. 179–238.

2. David Levine, 'Industrialization and the Proletarian Family in England', *Past and Present*, 107 (1985), p. 181.

3. Nancy Tomes, 'A "Torrent of Abuse": Crimes of Violence Between Working-Class Men and Women in London, 1840–1875', *Journal of Social History*, 11 (1978), pp. 328–45.

4. Ann Oakley, *Housewife* (Harmondsworth: Penguin, 1974), p. 43.

5. John Burnett (ed.), *Useful Toil: Autobiographies of Working People from the 1820s to the 1920s* (London: Allen Lane, 1976), p. 75.

6. Pamela Horn, *Victorian Countrywomen* (Oxford: Basil Blackwell, 1991), p. 131.

7. Linda Mahood, *The Magdalenes: Prostitution in the Nineteenth Century* (London: Routledge, 1990), pp. 70–1.

8. Ellen Ross, *Love and Toil: Motherhood In Outcast London, 1870–1918* (Oxford: OUP, 1993), p. 67; David R. Green and Alan G. Parton, 'Slums and Slum Life: Victorian England: London and Birmingham at Mid-Century', in Martin Gaskell (ed.), *Slums* (Leicester: Leicester University Press, 1990), p. 28; Rita M. Rhodes, *Women and the Family in Post-Famine Ireland: Status and Opportunity in a Patriarchal Society* (London: Garland, 1992), p. 272.

9. Jose Harris, *Private Lives, Public Spirit: Britain 1870–1914* (Harmondsworth: Penguin, 1993), p. 69; Maria Luddy (ed.), *Women in Ireland 1800–1918: A Documentary History* (Cork: Cork University Press, 1995), pp. 22–5; 27–30.

10. Joanna Bourke, *Husbandry to Housewifery: Women, Economic Change and Housework in Ireland, 1890–1914* (Oxford: Clarendon Press, 1993), p. 273.

11. Iris Minor, 'Working-Class Women and Matrimonial Law Reform, 1890–1914', in D. E. Martin and D. Rubinstein (eds), *Ideology and the Labour Movement: Essays Presented to John Saville* (London: Croom Helm, 1979), pp. 113–14.

12. Horn, *Victorian Countrywomen*, p. 28.

13. Michael Mason, *The Making of Victorian Sexuality* (Oxford: Oxford University Press, 1995), pp. 84–6.

14. Cited in Margaret Llewelyn Davies, *Maternity: Letters from Working Women Collected by the Women's Co-operative Guild*, (London: Virago, 1978, first published 1915), p. 89.

15. Harold Benenson, 'The "Family Wage" and Working Women's Consciousness in Britain, 1880–1914', *Politics and Society*, 19 (1991), p. 79.

16. Quoted in Margaret Llewelyn Davies (ed.), *Life as We Have Known It By Co-operative Working Women* (London and New York: W. W. Norton, 1975, first published 1931), p. 38.

17. For further discussion, see Margot Finn, 'Working-Class Women and the Context for Consumer Control in Victorian Country Courts', *Past and Present*, 161 (1998), pp. 116–54.

18. Melanie Tebbutt, *Making Ends Meet: Pawnbroking and Working-Class Credit* (Leicester: Leicester University Press, 1983), p. 34; Ross, *Love and Toil*, pp. 81–4.

19. Ross, *Love and Toil*, pp. 37–9; Elizabeth Roberts, *A Woman's Place: An Oral History of Working-Class Women 1890–1940* (Oxford: Basil Blackwell, 1984), p. 29.

20. Cited in Davies, *Maternity*, p. 20.

21. Roberts, *A Woman's Place*, p. 40; Ross, *Love and Toil*, pp. 31–6.

22. Richard Whipp, 'Kinship, Labour and Enterprise in the Staffordshire Pottery Industry, 1890–1920', in Pat Hudson and W. R. Lee (eds), *Women's Work and the Family Economy in Historical Perspective* (Manchester: Manchester University Press, 1990), p. 196. See also the case of Dundee jute workers: Michael Savage, *The Dynamics of Working-Class Politics: The Labour Movement in Preston, 1880–1940* (Cambridge: Cambridge University Press, 1987), pp. 54–5.

23. Pat Thane, 'Women and the Poor Law in Victorian and Edwardian England', *History Workshop Journal*, 6 (1978), pp. 24–5.

24. Quoted in Davies, *Maternity*, p. 23. See also Laura Oren, 'The Welfare of Women in Laboring Families in England, 1860–1950', in Mary S. Hartman and Lois Banner (eds), *Clio's Consciousness Raised: New Perspectives on the History of Women* (London: Harper and Row, 1974), pp. 226–44.

25. Lynn Jamieson, 'Limited Resources and Limiting Conventions. Working-Class Mothers and Daughters in Urban Scotland, *c.* 1890–1925', in Jane Lewis (ed.), *Labour and Love: Women's Experience of Home and Family, 1950–1940* (Oxford: Basil Blackwell, 1986), pp. 49–69.

26. Cited in Roberts, *A Woman's Place*, p. 112.

27. Green and Parton, 'Slums and Slum Life', pp. 51–2; Alan O' Day, 'Varieties of Anti-Irish Behaviour in Britain, 1846–1922', in Panikos Panayi (ed.), *Racial Violence in the Nineteenth and Twentieth Centuries* (London: Leicester University Press, 1996), pp. 26–43.

28. Anna Davin, *Growing Up Poor: Home, School and Street in London, 1870–1914* (London: Rivers Oram Press, 1996), pp. 29–38.

29. Ibid., pp. 38–43; Diana Gittins, 'Marital Status, Work and Kinship, 1850–1930', in Lewis (ed.), *Labour and Love*, pp. 259–60, 262.

30. Cited in Dyhouse, *Feminism and the Family*, p. 135. See also the sad case of Mrs O cited in Maud Pember Reeves, *Round About a Pound a Week* (London: Virago, 1979, first published 1913), pp. 161–4.

31. For the importance of the WCG to women of this class, see the contributions to Davies, *Life as We Have Known It*. Anna Davin is particularly sensitive to the subtle variations in life-style among various strata of the working class, see her *Growing Up Poor*, *passim*.

32. Roberts, *A Woman's Place*, p. 116.

33. Rickie Burman, ' "She Looketh Well to the Ways of Her Household"': The Changing Role of Jewish Women in Religious Life, *c*. 1880–1930', in Gail Malmgreen (ed.), *Religion in the Lives of English Women, 1760–1930* (London and Sydney: Croom Helm, 1986), pp. 234–59.

34. P. E. Malcolmson, 'Laundresses and the Laundry Trade in Victorian England', *Victorian Studies*, 24 (1981), p. 460; Benenson, 'The Family Wage', p. 78.

35. Eleanor Gordon, *Women and the Labour Movement in Scotland 1850–1914* (Oxford: Clarendon Press, 1991), pp. 164–5.

36. Jamieson, 'Limited Resources and Limiting Conventions'.

37. Roberts, *A Woman's Place*, p. 193.

38. Reeves, *Round About a Pound*, pp. 17–20.

39. Joan Perkin, *Women and Marriage in Nineteenth-Century England* (Chicago: Lyceum, 1989), section II, especially p. 131.

40. Peter Bailey, 'Will the Real Bill Banks Please Stand Up? Towards a Role Analysis of Mid-Victorian Working-Class Respectability', *Journal of Social History*, 12 (1979), pp. 36–53; Davin, *Growing Up Poor*, p. 70.

41. An interesting discussion of marital conflict may be found in Joanna Bourke, 'Housewifery in Working-Class England 1860–1914', *Past and Present*, 43 (1994), pp. 188–96.

42. Shani D'Cruze, *Crimes of Outrage: Sex, Violence and Victorian Working Women* (London: UCL, 1998), p. 68.

43. Perkin, *Women and Marriage*, pp. 116, 174; Tomes, 'A Torrent of Abuse'.

44. See Ross, *Love and Toil*, p. 84.

45. Iris Minor, 'Working-Class Women and Matrimonial Law Reform, 1890–1914', in D. E. Martin and D. Rubinstein (eds), *Ideology and the Labour Movement: Essays Presented to John Saville* (London: Croom Helm, 1979), p. 106; Tomes, 'A Torrent of Abuse', p. 340.

46. Minor, 'Working-Class Women and Matrimonial Law Reform', pp. 103–24; see also Thane, 'Women and the Poor Law', pp. 29–51.

47. Gail Savage, ' "The Wilful Communication of a Loathsome Disease"': Marital Conflict and Venereal Disease in Victorian England', *Victorian Studies*, 34 (1990), pp. 44–5; Carol Dyhouse, *Feminism and the Family in England 1880–1939* (Oxford: Basil Blackwell, 1989), p. 152.

48. Cited in Davies, *Maternity*, p. 121.

49. Elizabeth Roberts, *A Woman's Place*, p. 82.

50. Ibid., pp. 41, 104.

51. Eve Hostettler, ' "Making Do": Domestic Life Among East Anglian Labourers, 1890–1910', in Leonore Davidoff and Belinda Westover (eds),

Our Work, Our Lives, Our Worlds: Women's History and Women's Work (Basingstoke: Macmillan – now Palgrave, 1986), pp. 37–8.

52. Ross, *Love and Toil*, p. 101.

53. Angus McLaren, *Birth Control in Nineteenth-Century England* (New York: Holmes and Meier, 1978), p. 219.

54. J. A. Banks, *Prosperity and Parenthood: A Study of Family Planning among the Victorian Middle Classes* (London: Routledge and Kegan Paul, 1954).

55. For an overview of these approaches, see R. I. Woods, 'Approaches to the Fertility Transition in Victorian England', *Population Studies*, 41, (1987), pp. 283–311.

56. See, for example, Karl Ittman, *Work, Gender and Family in Victorian England* (Basingstoke: Macmillan – now Palgrave, 1995).

57. Similar conclusions have been drawn for the period 1900–39. Diana Gittins, for example, in *Fair Sex: Family Size and Structure, 1900–1939* (London: Hutchinson, 1982) notes that women's relationship to the socio-economic system was a critical factor in birth control decisions.

58. McLaren, *Birth Control*; Mason, *The Making of Victorian Sexuality*, pp. 57–60.

59. Roberts, *A Woman's Place*, pp. 83–103.

60. See, for example, Davies, *Maternity*, pp. 27–8, 59–60, 65–6, 67, 95, 115.

61. Gittins, *The Fair Sex*, p. 153; Ross, *Love and Toil*, p. 102.

62. Ross, *Love and Toil*, pp. 104–6; McLaren, *Birth Control*, p. 246.

63. Ann Oakley, 'Wisewoman and Medicine Man: Changes in the Management of Childbirth', in Juliet Mitchell and Ann Oakley (eds), *The Rights and Wrongs of Women* (Harmondsworth: Penguin, 1976), pp. 42–4.

64. Rhodes, *Women and the Family*, pp. 95–6.

65. The classic account of this movement is Anna Davin, 'Imperialism and Motherhood', *History Workshop Journal*, 5 (1978), pp. 9–65.

66. Lara V. Marks, *Model Mothers: Jewish Mothers and Maternity Provision in East London, 1870–1939* (Oxford: Clarendon Press, 1994).

67. Ross, *Love and Toil*, p. 182.

68. Linda Mahood, 'Family Ties: Lady Child-Savers and Girls of the Street 1850–1925', in Esther Breitenbach and Eleanor Gordon (eds), *Out of Bounds: Women in Scottish Society 1800–1945* (Edinburgh: Edinburgh University Press, 1992), p. 55.

69. Carol Dyhouse, 'Working-Class Mothers and Infant Mortality in England, 1895–1914', (1979) reprinted in C. Webster (ed.), *Biology, Medicine and Society 1840–1940* (Cambridge: Cambridge University Press, 1981), pp. 83–4, 92–3.

70. Cited in Dyhouse, 'Working-Class Mothers', p. 89.

71. See ibid.; and Davin, 'Imperialism and Motherhood'.

72. Jane Lewis, *The Politics of Motherhood. Child and Maternal Welfare in England 1900–1939* (London: Croom Helm, 1980), ch. 2.

73. Davin, *Growing Up Poor*, p. 53.

226 Notes

74. Cited in Dyhouse, 'Working-Class Mothers', p. 96.
75. Whipp, 'Kinship, Labour and Enterprise', p. 196.
76. Roberts, *A Woman's Place*, p. 107.

PART IV MIDDLE-CLASS AND UPPER-CLASS WOMEN, 1860–1900

10 Work

1. Ellen Jordan, *The Women's Movement and Women's Employment in Nineteenth-Century Britain* (London and New York: Routledge, 1999), pp. 195–7.
2. Details of these developments may be found in June Purvis, *A History of Women's Education in England* (Milton Keynes: Open University Press, 1991), pp. 75–92; Jane McDermid, 'Women and Education', in June Purvis (ed.), *Women's History: Britain, 1850–1945* (London: UCL, 1995), pp. 109–11; Maria Luddy (ed.), *Women in Ireland, 1800–1918: A Documentary History* (Cork: Cork University Press, 1995), pp. 89–92.
3. Carol Dyhouse, *Girls Growing Up in Late Victorian and Edwardian England* (London: Routledge and Kegan Paul, 1981), ch. 2, the quotes are from pp. 73 and 92; Sara Delamont, 'The Contradictions in Ladies' Education', in Sara Delamont and Lorna Duffin (eds), *Nineteenth-Century Woman: Her Cultural and Physical World* (London: Croom Helm, 1978), pp. 134–63.
4. Ruth Watts, *Gender, Power and the Unitarians in England 1760–1860* (London: Longmans, 1998), p. 156.
5. The discussion on universities draws on Carol Dyhouse, *No Distinction of Sex? Women in British Universities 1870–1939* (London: UCL, 1995), *passim*.
6. Delamont, 'The Contradictions in Ladies' Education', pp. 134–63, the quote is from p. 157; Barbara Caine, *Victorian Feminists* (Oxford: Oxford University Press, 1992), ch. 3.
7. Anne Digby, 'Women's Biological Straitjacket', in Susan Mendus and Jane Rendall (eds), *Sexuality and Subordination: Interdisciplinary Studies of Gender in the Nineteenth Century* (London and New York: Routledge, 1989), pp. 208–15.
8. Dyhouse, *No Distinction of Sex*, p. 12; Luddy, *Women in Ireland*, pp. 90–1.
9. Dyhouse, *No Distinction of Sex*, p. 192.
10. Ibid., Martha Vicinus, *Independent Women: Work and Community for Single Women, 1850–1920* (London: Virago, 1985), ch. 4; Janet Howarth and Mark Curthoys, 'The Political Economy of Women's Higher Education in Late 19th and Early 20th Century Britain', *Social History*, 60 (1987), pp. 108–31.
11. Dyhouse, *No Distinction of Sex*, pp. 18–21.
12. Vicinus, *Independent Women*, p. 177.

13. Rita McWilliams-Tullberg, 'Women and Degrees at Cambridge University, 1862–97', in Martha Vicinus (ed.), *A Widening Sphere, Changing Roles of Victorian Women* (Bloomington: Indiana University Press, 1977), p. 125.

14. Lee Holcombe, *Victorian Ladies at Work: Middle-Class Working Women in England and Wales 1850–1914* (Newton Abbot: David and Charles, 1973), p. 34.

15. Juliet Gardiner (ed.), *The New Woman: Women's Voices 1880–1918* (London: Collins and Brown, 1993), pp. 81–2; Vicinus, *Independent Women*, ch. 5.

16. Frances Widdowson, 'Educating Teacher – Women and Elementary Teaching in London, 1900–1914', in Leonore Davidoff and Belinda Westover (eds), *Our Work, Our Lives, Our Worlds: Women's History and Women's Work* (Basingstoke: Macmillan – now Palgrave, 1986), pp. 99–123.

17. Joyce Senders Pedersen, 'Some Victorian Headmistresses: A Conservative Tradition of Social Reform', *Victorian Studies*, 29 (1981), pp. 463–88.

18. Holcombe, *Victorian Ladies at Work*, p. 45.

19. Elizabeth Roberts, *A Woman's Place: An Oral History of Working-Class Women 1890–1940* (Oxford: Basil Blackwell, 1984), pp. 29, 35. The pressures on teachers are brought out in Anna Davin, *Growing Up Poor: Home, School and Street in London 1870–1914* (London: Rivers Oram Press, 1996), pt. 2.

20. M. Jeanne Peterson, *Family, Love and Work in the Lives of Victorian Gentlewomen* (Bloomington and Indianapolis: Indiana University Press, 1989), pp. 139–45.

21. Dyhouse, *No Distinction of Sex*, pp. 136–7, 100.

22. Pat Jalland, *Women, Marriage and Politics, 1860–1914* (Oxford: Clarendon Press, 1986), p. 283.

23. Peterson, *Family, Love and Work*, p. 147.

24. Vicinus, *Independent Women*, p. 149; Dyhouse, *No Distinction of Sex*, p. 138 and ch. 6.

25. Levine, *Victorian Feminism*, p. 96.

26. Catriona Blake, *The Charge of the Parasols: Women's Entry to the Medical Profession* (London: The Women's Press, 1990), p. 69. This paragraph follows *The Charge of the Parasols, passim*.

27. Antoinette Burton, 'Contesting the Zenana: The Mission to Make "Lady Doctors" for India', 1874–85', *Journal of British Studies*, 35 (1995), pp. 368–97.

28. Anne Summers, *Angels and Citizens: British Women as Military Nurses 1854–1914* (London: Routledge and Kegan Paul, 1988), chs 5–7.

29. Vicinus, *Independent Women*, ch. 3; Holcombe, *Ladies at Work*, ch. 4.

30. Summers, *Angels and Citizens*, pp. 91, 162, 95–6.

31. Holcombe, *Victorian Ladies at Work*, p. 92.

32. Ibid., pp. 96–102.

33. Pamela Horn, *Victorian Countrywomen* (Oxford: Basil Blackwell, 1991), p. 218; Summers, *Angels or Citizens*, p. 140.

34. Patricia Hollis (ed.), *Women in Public 1850–1900: Documents of the Victorian Women's Movement* (London: George Allen and Unwin, 1979), p. 45.

35. Jane Lewis, *Women in England, 1870–1950* (Hemel Hempstead: Harvester Wheatsheaf, 1984), p. 197.

36. Ellen Jordan, 'The Lady Clerks at the Prudential: The Beginning of Vertical Segregation by Sex in Clerical Work in Nineteenth-Century Britain', *Gender and History*, 8, no. 1 (1996), pp. 65–81.

37. Meta Zimmeck, 'Jobs for the Girls: The Expansion of Clerical Work for Women, 1850–1914', in Angela V. John (ed.), *Unequal Opportunities, Women's Employment in England 1800–1918* (Oxford: Basil Blackwell, 1986), pp. 153–77, quote from p. 165; Holcombe, *Victorian Ladies at Work*, pp. 151, 178–9.

38. Philippa Levine, *Victorian Feminism, 1850–1900* (London: Hutchinson, 1987), pp. 93–6.

39. Holcombe, *Victorian Ladies at Work*, pp. 179–82; see also pp. 152–62.

40. Ibid., p. 103.

41. Hollis (ed.), *Women in Public 1850–1900*, p. 45.

42. Harriet Bradley, *Men's Work, Women's Work: A Sociological History of the Sexual Division of Labour in Employment* (Cambridge: Polity Press, 1989), p. 180.

43. Holcombe, *Victorian Ladies at Work*, ch. 5.

44. Lewis, *Women in England*, p. 194.

45. See Jalland, *Women, Marriage and Politics*, intro; Dyhouse, *Girls Growing Up*, p. 50.

46. Peterson, *Family, Love and Work*, pp. 145–61. For female travellers, see Jane Robinson, *Wayward Women: A Guide to Women Travellers* (Oxford: Oxford University Press, 1990).

47. J. A. Banks and Olive Banks, *Feminism and Family Planning in Victorian England* (Liverpool: Liverpool University Press, 1964), *passim*, but see especially p. 12.

48. Caine, *Destined to be Wives*, p. 109.

49. Edward Higgs, 'Domestic Service and Household Production', in John (ed.), *Unequal Opportunities*, pp. 132–3.

50. Carol Dyhouse, *Feminism and the Family 1880–1939* (Oxford: Basil Blackwell, 1989), ch. 3.

51. A. James Hammerton, *Cruelty and Companionship: Conflict in Nineteenth-Century Married Life* (London and New York: Routledge, 1992), pp. 114–15.

52. Jessica Gerard, *Country House Life: Family and Servants, 1815–1914* (Oxford: Blackwell, 1994), p. 98.

53. Jessica Gerard, 'Lady Bountiful: Women of the Landed Classes and Rural Philanthropy', *Victorian Studies*, 30 (1987), pp. 183–211. The quote is on p. 191.

54. Pamela Horn, *High Society: The English Social Elite, 1880–1914* (Stroud: Alan Sutton, 1992), p. 53.

55. Peterson, *Family, Love and Work*, pp. 166–86; Summers, *Angels or Citizens*, p. 112.

56. Caine, *Destined to be Wives*, p. 97; Peterson, *Family, Love and Work*, p. 151.

57. Shelley Pennington and Belinda Westover, *A Hidden Workforce: Homeworkers in England, 1850–1985* (London: Macmillan – now Palgrave, 1989), pp. 19–21.
58. Horn, *Countrywomen*, p. 186.
59. Ibid., pp. 128–30; Peterson, *Family, Love and Work*, p. 148.
60. Peterson, *Family, Love and Work*, p. 69; Nupur Chaudhuri, 'Memsahibs and Motherhood in Nineteenth-Century Colonial India', *Victorian Studies*, 31 (1988), pp. 534–5.
61. Leonore Davidoff, *The Best Circles: Society, Etiquette and the Season* (London: Croom Helm, 1973), p. 63; Horn, *High Society*, p. 68.
62. Horn, *High Society*, pp. 61, 70.
63. Davidoff, *The Best Circles*, p. 94.
64. Angela V. John, 'Beyond Paternalism: The Ironmaster's Wife in the Industrial Community', in Angela V. John (ed.), *Our Mothers' Land: Chapters in Welsh Women's History, 1830–1939* (Cardiff: University of Wales Press, 1991), p. 54.
65. Peterson, *Family, Love and Work*, p. 137.
66. F. K. Prochaska, *Women and Philanthropy in Nineteenth-Century England* (Oxford: Clarendon Press, 1980), p. 224.
67. Peter Williams, ' "The Missing Link". The Recruitment of Women Missionaries in Some English Evangelical Missionary Societies in the Nineteenth Century', in Fiona Bowie, Deborah Kirkwood and Shirley Ardener (eds), *Women and Missions: Past and Present. Anthropological and Historical Perceptions* (Oxford: Berg Publishers, 1993), p. 43.
68. Catriona Clear, 'The Limits of Female Autonomy: Nuns in Nineteenth-Century Ireland', in Maria Luddy and Cliona Murphy (eds), *Women Surviving, Studies in Irish Women's History in the Nineteenth and Twentieth Centuries* (Dublin: Poolbeg Press, 1989), p. 21.
69. Vicinus, *Independent Women*, ch. 6.

11 Politics, Community and Protest

1. See Jessica Gerard, 'Lady Bountiful: Women of the Landed Classes and Rural Philanthropy', *Victorian Studies*, 30 (1987), pp. 183–211.
2. Pamela Horn, *Victorian Countrywomen* (Oxford: Basil Blackwell, 1991), p. 46.
3. F. K. Prochaska, *Women and Philanthropy in Nineteenth-Century England* (Oxford: Clarendon Press, 1980), p. 144.
4. K. D. Reynolds, *Aristocratic Women and Political Society in Victorian Britain* (Oxford: Clarendon Press, 1998), pp. 118–19; Jessica Gerard, *Country House Life: Family and Servants, 1815–1914* (Oxford: Blackwell, 1994), p. 127.

5. Antoinette M. Burton, 'The White Woman's Burden: British Feminists and "The Indian Woman", 1865–1915'; and Barbara N. Ramusack, 'Cultural Missionaries, Maternal Imperialists, Feminist Allies: British Women Activists in India, 1865–1945', in Nupur Chaudhuri and Margaret Strobel (eds), *Western Women and Imperialism: Complicity and Resistance* (Bloomington and Indiana: Indiana University Press, 1992), pp. 144 and 19–36; Vron Ware, *Beyond the Pale: White Women, Racism, and History* (London: Verso, 1992), pp. 163–4; Nancy Fix Anderson, 'Bridging Cross-Cultural Feminisms: Annie Besant and Women's Rights in England and India, 1874–1933', *Women's History Review*, 3, no. 4 (1994), pp. 563–80.

6. The WPPL became the Women's Trade Union League in 1891 (WTUL); the WIC merged with the Women's Trade Union Association in 1897. Rosemary Feurer, 'The Meaning of "Sisterhood": The British Women's Movement and Protective Labor Legislation, 1870–1900', *Victorian Studies*, 31 (1988), pp. 233–60; Eleanor Mappen, *Helping Women at Work: The Women's Industrial Council, 1889–1914* (London: Hutchinson, 1985); Eleanor Gordon, *Women and the Labour Movement in Scotland 1850–1914* (Oxford: Clarendon Press, 1991), pp. 212–35.

7. Jane Lewis, *Women and Social Action in Victorian and Edwardian England* (Aldershot: Edward Elgar, 1991), *passim*, but see especially pp. 33–4.

8. Prochaska, *Women and Philanthropy*, pp. 171–3.

9. For the social purity movement, see Lucy Bland, *Banishing the Beast: English Feminism and Sexual Morality, 1885–1914* (Harmondsworth: Penguin, 1995), ch. 3; Judith R. Walkowitz, *City of Dreadful Delight: Narratives of Sexual Danger in Late-Victorian London* (London: Routledge, 1992), chs 3–4; Frank Mort, 'Purity, Feminism and the State, Sexuality and Moral Politics, 1880–1914', in M. Langan and B. Schwartz (eds), *Crises in the British State 1880–1914* (London: Hutchinson, 1985), pp. 209–25.

10. Olive Anderson, 'Women Preachers in Mid-Victorian Britain: Some Reflections on Feminism, Popular Religion and Social Change', *Historical Journal*, 3 (1969), pp. 467–84.

11. Lillian Lewis Shiman, ' "Changes are Dangerous": Women and Temperance in Victorian England', in Gail Malmgreen (ed.), *Religion in the Lives of English Women, 1760–1930* (London and Sydney: Croom Helm, 1986), pp. 193–215.

12. For some of the complexities of Booth's view on the woman question, see Elizabeth K. Helsinger, Robin Lauterbach Sheets and William Veeder (eds), *The Woman Question: Society and Literature in Britain and America, 1837–1883* (Chicago and London: University of Chicago Press, 1983), 3 vols, ii, pp. 180–3.

13. For further details, see Patricia Hollis, *Ladies Elect: Women in English Local Government 1865–1914* (Oxford: Clarendon Press, 1987). The following paragraphs draw heavily upon this work.

14. Maria Luddy (ed.), *Women in Ireland, 1800–1918: A Documentary History* (Cork: Cork University Press, 1995), pp. 289–96.

15. Hollis, *Ladies Elect*, p. 2.
16. Ibid., chs 4–5.
17. Ibid., chs 2–3.
18. David Rubinstein, *Before the Suffragettes: Women's Emancipation in the 1890s* (Brighton: Harvester Press, 1986), p. 173.
19. Annmarie Turnbull, ' "So Extremely Like Parliament": The Work of Women Members of the London School Board, 1870–1914', in London Feminist History Group, *The Sexual Dynamics of History: Men's Power, Women's Resistance* (London: Pluto Press, 1983), pp. 120–33; Hollis, *Ladies Elect*, pp. 83–8.
20. Hollis, *Ladies Elect*, p. 177.
21. Ibid., pp. 317–24.
22. Bland, *Banishing the Beast*, pp. 111–15.
23. Hollis, *Ladies Elect*, p. 391.
24. Martin Pugh, *Women and the Women's Movement in Britain, 1914–1959* (Basingstoke: Macmillan – now Palgrave, 1992), pp. 226–30.
25. See, for example, Martha Vicinus, *Independent Women: Work and Community for Single Women, 1850–1920* (London: Virago, 1985), p. 244.
26. G. E. Maguire, *Conservative Women: A History of Women and the Conservative Party, 1874–1997* (London: Macmillan – now Palgrave, 1998), pp. 16–21; Martin Pugh, *The Tories and the People* (Oxford: Basil Blackwell, 1985), pp. 72–80; Reynolds, *Aristocratic Women*, p. 189; Dorothy Thompson, *Outsiders: Class, Gender and Nation* (London: Verso, 1993), ch. 6.
27. Reynolds, *Aristocratic Women*, ch. 5; Pugh, *Tories and the People*, pp. 43–5.
28. Quoted in Reynolds, *Aristocratic Women*, p. 153.
29. Ibid., pp. 175–6.
30. Maguire, *Conservative Women*, pp. 25–6.
31. Pat Jalland, *Women, Marriage and Politics 1860–1914* (Oxford: Clarendon Press, 1986), pp. 204, 98–9.
32. Pugh, *The Tories and the People*, p. 47; Maguire, *Conservative Women*, pp. 21–2.
33. Jalland, *Women, Marriage and Politics*, pp. 204–10.
34. This discussion of the WLF relies upon Linda Walker, 'Party Political Women: A Comparative Study of Liberal Women and the Primrose League 1888–1914', in Jane Rendall (ed.), *Equal or Different: Women's Politics 1800–1914* (Oxford: Basil Blackwell, 1987), pp. 165–91.
35. Jalland, *Women, Marriage and Politics*, pp. 217–18.
36. Walker, 'Party Political Women', pp. 175–7.
37. Cited in Beatrix Campbell, *The Iron Ladies: Why Do Women Vote Tory* (London: Virago, 1987), p. 28.
38. Pugh, *Tories and the People*, p. 50.
39. Walker, 'Party Political Women', p. 185.
40. Quoted in Campbell, *The Iron Ladies*, p. 15.
41. June Hannam, ' "In the Comradeship of the Sexes Lies the Hope of Progress and Social Regeneration": Women in the West Riding ILP

c.1890–1914', in Rendall, (ed.), *Equal or Different?*, pp. 214–38; Jill Lidding-
ton and Jill Norris, *One Hand Tied Behind Us: The Rise of the Women's Suffrage
Movement* (London: Virago, 1978), pp. 129–31. For the SDF, see Karen
Hunt, *Equivocal Feminists: The Social Democratic Federation and the Woman
Question 1884–1911* (Cambridge: Cambridge University Press, 1996).

42. Hannam, 'In the Comradeship of the Sexes', pp. 218, 225.

43. See Liddington and Norris, *One Hand Tied Behind Us*, especially pp.
77–83.

44. Sandra Stanley Holton, *Suffrage Days: Stories from the Women's Suffrage Movement* (London and New York: Routledge, 1996), p. 58.

45. Gillian Scott, *Feminism and the Politics of Working Women: The Women's
Co-operative Guild, 1880s to the Second World War* (London: UCL, 1998),
p. 72; Alistair Thomson, '"Domestic Drudgery Will be a Thing of
the Past": Co-operative Women and the Reform of Housework', in
Stephen Yeo (ed.), *New Views of Co-operation* (London: Routledge, 1988),
pp. 115–16.

46. For an overview of mid-Victorian feminism, see Barbara Caine, *English
Feminism 1780–1980* (Oxford: Oxford University Press, 1997), ch. 3.

47. See Martin Pugh, *The March of the Women: A Revisionist Analysis of the Campaign for Women's Suffrage, 1866–1914* (Oxford: Oxford University Press,
2000), pp. 8–10.

48. Cited in Susan Kingsley Kent, *Sex and Suffrage in Britain 1860–1914* (Lon-
don: Routledge, 1990, first published 1987), p. 14. See also Sheila Jeffreys,
The Spinster and Her Enemies: Feminism and Sexuality 1880–1930 (London:
Pandora, 1985).

49. Pugh, *The March of Women*.

50. Philippa Levine, *Feminist Lives in Victorian England: Private Roles and Public
Commitment* (Oxford: Basil Blackwell, 1990).

51. Leah Leneman, 'The Awakened Instinct: Vegetarianism and the Women's
Suffrage Movement in Britain', *Women's History Review*, 6, no. 2 (1997), pp.
271–87; Mary Ann Elston, 'Women and Anti-Vivisection in Victorian England, 1870–1900', in Nicholas A. Rupke (ed.), *Vivisection in Historical Perspective* (London: Croom Helm, 1987), pp. 259–94.

52. Levine, *Feminist Lives*, pp. 80–7.

53. Full details of the campaign may be found in Judith R. Walkowitz, *Prostitution and Victorian Society* (Cambridge: Cambridge University Press, 1980),
particularly pt II.

54. For the use of melodramatic tropes in the campaign, see Walkowitz, *City of
Dreadful Delight*, pp. 86–93. For a full discussion of the relative importance
of female and male networks of support and friendship and support in the
movement, see Barbara Caine, *Victorian Feminists* (Oxford: Oxford University Press, 1992), ch. 5.

55. Walkowitz, *Prostitution and Victorian Society*, pp. 143–6,133–6.

56. Burton, 'The White Woman's Burden', pp. 139–45.
57. See Lucy Bland, 'Feminist Vigilantes of Late-Victorian England', in Carol Smart (ed.), *Regulating Womanhood: Historical Essays on Marriage, Motherhood and Sexuality* (London and New York: Routledge, 1992), pp. 33–52.
58. Cited in Bland, *Banishing the Beast*, p. 99.
59. For a bleak assessment of Mill's role, see Barbara Caine, 'John Stuart Mill and the English Women's Movement', *Historical Studies*, 18 (1978), pp. 52–67.
60. Sylvia Strauss, *'Traitors to the Masculine Cause': The Men's Campaign for Women's Rights* (Connecticut: Greenwood Press, 1982), pp. 179, 199.
61. For useful debates on these issues, see Angela V. John and Claire Eustance (eds), *The Men's Share? Masculinities, Male Support and Women's Suffrage in Britain 1890–1920* (London: Routledge, 1997); Levine, *Feminist Lives in Victorian England*; Olive Banks, *Becoming a Feminist: The Social Origins of 'First Wave' Feminism* (Brighton: Wheatsheaf, 1986), ch. 6.
62. For further details on the splits which beset the movement, see Sandra Stanley Holton, 'Women and the Vote', in June Purvis (ed.), *Women's History Britain, 1850–1945: An Introduction* (London: UCL Press, 1995), pp. 280–7.
63. Sandra Stanley Holton, *Feminism and Democracy: Women's Suffrage and Reform Politics in Britain 1900–1918* (Cambridge: Cambridge University Press, 1986), p. 18.
64. See Frances Power Cobbe, 'Why Women Desire the Franchise' (1874) reprinted in Jane Lewis (ed.), *Before the Vote was Won: Arguments for and Against Women's Suffrage 1864–1896* (London: Routledge, 1987), pp. 179–83. This was a common argument.
65. Sandra Stanley Holton, 'British Freewomen: National Identity, Constitutionalism and Languages of Race in Early Suffragist Histories', in Eileen Yeo (ed.), *Radical Femininity: Women's Self-Representation in the Public Sphere* (Manchester: Manchester University Press, 1998), pp. 149–71.
66. Sandra Stanley Holton, ' "Now You See It, Now You Don't": The Women's Franchise League and Its Place in Contending Narratives of the Women's Suffrage Movement', in Maroula Joannou and June Purvis (eds), *The Women's Suffrage Movement: New Feminist Perspectives* (Manchester: Manchester University Press, 1998), pp. 15–36.
67. Holton, *Feminism and Democracy*.
68. For an analysis of Dora Montefiore's evolving positions on suffrage, see Karen Hunt, 'Journeying Through Suffrage: The Politics of Dora Montefiore', in Claire Eustance, Joan Ryan and Laura Ugolini (eds), *A Suffrage Reader: Charting Directions in British Suffrage History* (London: Leicester University Press, 2000), pp. 162–76.
69. Pugh, *Tories and the People*, pp. 59–61.
70. For anti-suffragism in this period, see Mrs Humphrey Ward, 'An Appeal Against Female Suffrage' (1889) in Lewis (ed.), *Before the Vote was Won,*

pp. 409–17; Brian Harrison, *Separate Spheres: The Opposition to Women's Suffrage in Britain* (London: Croom Helm, 1978); Pugh, *The March of Women*, pp. 145–67.

71. For an extended discussion of the links between feminism and empire, see Antoinette Burton, *Burdens of History: British Feminists, Indian Women, and Imperial Culture, 1865–1915* (Chapel Hill: University of North Carolina Press, 1994).

72. Jill Liddington, *The Long Road to Greenham: Feminism and Anti-Militarism in Britain since 1820* (London: Virago, 1989), ch. 2.

73. Luddy (ed.), *Women in Ireland*, pp. 322–7.

74. Margaret Ward, *Unmanageable Revolutionaries: Women and Irish Nationalism* (London: Pluto Press, 1989), chs 1–2; Luddy (ed.), *Women in Ireland*, pp. 260–8, 297–304.

75. Luddy (ed.), *Women in Ireland*, pp. 271–3; see also Rosemary Cullen Owens, *Smashing Times: A History of the Irish Women's Suffrage Movement* (Dublin: Attic Press, 1984), ch. 2.

76. Ceridwen Lloyd-Morgan, 'From Temperance to Suffrage?', in Angela V. John (ed.), *Our Mothers' Land: Chapters in Welsh Women's History, 1830–1939* (Cardiff: University of Wales Press, 1991), pp. 135–58.

12 Families, Relationships and Home Life

1. F. M. L. Thompson, *The Rise of Respectable Society: A Social History of Victorian Britain, 1830–1900* (London: Fontana Press, 1988), pp. 105–11.

2. Barbara Caine, *Destined to be Wives: The Sisters of Beatrice Webb* (Oxford: Clarendon Press, 1986), p. 92; Pat Jalland, *Women, Marriage and Politics, 1860–1914* (Oxford: Clarendon Press, 1986), especially p. 91.

3. Thompson, *The Rise of Respectable Society*, pp. 99–105.

4. Michael Mason, *The Making of Victorian Sexuality* (Oxford: Oxford University Press, 1994), pp. 117–23.

5. Elizabeth K. Helsinger, Robin Lauterbach Sheets and William Veeder (eds), *The Woman Question: Society and Literature in Britain and America, 1837–1883* (London and Chicago: University of Chicago Press, 1983), 3 vols, i, ch. 6; J. A. Banks and Olive Banks, *Feminism and Family Planning in Victorian England* (Liverpool: Liverpool University Press, 1964), p. 30.

6. Jose Harris, *Private Lives, Public Spirit: Britain, 1870–1914* (Harmondsworth: Penguin Books, 1994), p. 77.

7. Carol Dyhouse, *Feminism and the Family in England 1880–1939* (Oxford: Blackwell, 1989), p. 41.

8. Thompson, *The Rise of Respectable Society*, p. 63.

9. Jane Lewis, *Women in England, 1870–1950: Sexual Divisions and Social Change* (Hemel Hempstead: Harvester Wheatsheaf, 1984), p. 120.

10. John Tosh, 'Domesticity and Manliness in the Victorian Middle Class: The Family of Edward White Benson', in M. Roper and J. Tosh (eds), *Manful Assertions: Masculinities in Britain Since 1800* (London: Routledge, 1981), p. 65.

11. Caine, *Destined to be Wives*, pp. 79, 136, 155–6.

12. Jessica Gerard, *Country House Life: Family and Servants, 1815–1914* (Oxford: Blackwell, 1994), p. 102.

13. The phrase is Cicely Hamilton's. See Juliet Gardiner (ed.), *The New Woman: Women's Voices 1880–1918* (London: Collins and Brown, 1993), p. 65.

14. Leonore Davidoff and Catherine Hall, *Family Fortunes: Men and Women of the English Middle Class, 1780–1850* (London: Routledge, 1987), pp. 108–13; Hugh McLeod, *Religion and Society in England, 1850–1914* (Basingstoke: Macmillan – now Palgrave 1996), pp. 149–56.

15. Tosh, 'Domesticity and Manliness'; D. Roberts, 'The Paterfamilias and the Victorian Governing Class', in Anthony S. Wohl (ed.), *The Victorian Family: Structure and Stresses* (London: Croom Helm, 1978), pp. 59–81; Lewis, *Women in England*, p. 125.

16. Martin Pugh, *The Tories and the People* (Oxford: Basil Blackwell, 1985), pp. 45–6.

17. A. James Hammerton, *Cruelty and Companionship: Conflict in Nine-teenth-Century Married Life* (London and New York: Routledge, 1992), chs 3–4.

18. Gail Savage, ' "The Wilful Communication of a Loathsome Disease": Marital Conflict and Venereal Disease in Victorian England', *Victorian Studies*, 34 (1990), p. 47.

19. Elaine Showalter, 'Family Secrets and Domestic Subversion: Rebellion in the Novels of the 1860s', in Wohl, *The Victorian Family*, pp. 101–16.

20. M. Jeanne Peterson, *Family, Love and Work in the Lives of Victorian Gentlewomen* (Bloomington and Indianapolis: Indiana University Press, 1989), p. 169.

21. Caine, *Destined to be Wives*, p. 160.

22. Joanna Trollope, *Britannia's Daughters: Women of the British Empire* (London: Pimlico, 1994, first published 1983), pp. 48, 130–1.

23. Diana M. Copelman, ' "A New Comradeship between Men and Women": Family, Marriage and London's Women Teachers, 1870–1914', in Jane Lewis (ed.), *Labour and Love: Women's Experience of Home and Family, 1850–1940* (Oxford: Basil Blackwell, 1986), pp. 175–93.

24. Jalland, *Women, Marriage and Politics*, pp. 60–1.

25. Peterson, *Family, Love and Work*, p. 130.

26. Dyhouse, *Feminism and the Family*, p. 36.

27. For full details, see Lee Holcombe, *Wives and Property: Reform of the Married Women's Property Law in Nineteenth-Century England* (Toronto and London: University of Toronto Press, 1983), ch. 8, pp. 191–3.

28. Ibid., ch. 9.

29. Quoted in Philippa Levine, *Victorian Feminism 1850–1900* (London: Hutchinson, 1987), p. 140.

30. Leonore Davidoff, 'The Family in Britain', in F. M. L. Thompson (ed.), *Cambridge Social History of Britain 1750–1950* (Cambridge: Cambridge University Press, 1990), 3 vols, ii, p. 99.

31. See Erika D. Rappaport, '"The Halls of Temptation": Gender, Politics and the Construction of the Department Store in Late Victorian London', *Journal of British Studies*, 35 (1996), pp. 58–83 and Judith R. Walkowitz, *City of Dreadful Delight: Narratives of Sexual Danger in Late-Victorian London* (London: Virago Press, 1992), pp. 46–52. For women and advertising, see Lori Ann Loeb, *Consuming Angels: Advertising and Victorian Women* (Oxford: Oxford University Press, 1994).

32. John Belchem, *Industrialization and the Working Class: The English Experience, 1750–1900* (London: Scholar Press, 1990).

33. J. A. Banks, *Prosperity and Parenthood: A Study of Family Planning Among the Victorian Middle Classes* (London: Routledge and Kegan Paul, 1954).

34. Patricia Branca, *Silent Sisterhood: Middle-Class Women in the Victorian Home* (London: Croom Helm, 1975), ch. 7; Mason, *The Making of Victorian Sexuality*, pp. 57–61; Angus McLaren, *Birth Control in Nineteenth-Century England* (New York: Holmes and Meier, 1978); Daniel Scott Smith, 'Family Limitation, Sexual Control and Domestic Feminism in Victorian America', in Mary S. Hartmann and Lois Banner (eds), *Clio's Consciousness Raised: New Perspectives on the History of Women* (London: Harper and Row, 1974), pp. 119–36.

35. For an exhaustive discussion of feminist views towards sexuality, see Lucy Bland, *Banishing the Beast: English Feminism and Sexual Morality 1885–1914* (Harmondsworth: Penguin, 1995), especially, ch. 4.

36. Anna Davin, 'Imperialism and Motherhood', *History Workshop Journal*, 5 (1978), pp. 9–65.

37. Simon Szreter, *Fertility, Class and Gender in Britain, 1860–1914* (Cambridge: Cambridge University Press, 1996).

38. Jalland, *Women, Marriage and Politics*, p. 121.

39. Caine, *Destined to be Wives*, pp. 103–8.

40. Cited in Pat Jalland and John Hooper (eds), *Women from Birth to Death: The Female Life Cycle in Britain 1830–1914* (Brighton: Harvester Press, 1986), p. 276.

41. Pamela Horn, *High Society: The English Social Elite, 1880–1914* (Stroud: Alan Sutton, 1992), p. 97.

42. See Holcombe, *Wives and Property*, p. 54.

43. Jalland, *Women, Marriage and Politics*, p. 171.

44. Ibid., pp. 135–6.

45. John Hawkins Miller, '"Temple and Sewer": Childbirth, Prudery and Victoria Regina', in Wohl, *The Victorian Family*, pp. 37–8.

46. Jalland, *Women, Marriage and Politics*, p. 35.

47. See, for example, Caine, *Destined to be Wives*, p. 119.

48. Nupur Chaudhuri, 'Memsahibs and Motherhood in Nineteenth-Century Colonial India', *Victorian Studies*, 31 (1988), pp. 517–35.

49. Quoted in Helsinger, Sheets and Veeder, *The Woman Question*, i, p. 107.

50. Gerard, *Country House Life*, pp. 73, 83–4.

51. Theresa McBride, ' "As the Twig is Bent": The Victorian Nanny', in Wohl, *The Victorian Family*, p. 48; Branca, *Silent Sisterhood*, p. 110.

52. Caine, *Destined to be Wives*, p.124; Harris, *Private Lives*, p. 82.

53. Caine, *Destined to be Wives*, p. 132.

54. Quoted in Dyhouse, *Feminism and the Family*, p. 17.

55. Deborah Gorham, *The Victorian Girl and the Feminine Ideal* (London: Croom Helm, 1982); and Sheila Rowbotham, *Good Girls Make Good Wives: Guidance for Girls in Victorian Fiction* (Oxford: Basil Blackwell, 1989).

56. Dyhouse, *Feminism and the Family*, pp. 22–30.

57. Lewis, *Women in England*, pp. 115–16, 118.

58. Lorna Duffin, 'The Conspicuous Consumptive: Woman as an Invalid', in Sara Delamont and Lorna Duffin (eds), *The Nineteenth-Century Woman: Her Cultural and Physical World* (London: Croom Helm, 1978), p. 35. See also Anne Digby, 'Women's Biological Straitjacket', in Susan Mendus and Jane Rendall (eds), *Sexuality and Subordination: Interdisciplinary Studies of Gender in the Nineteenth Century* (London: Routledge, 1989), pp. 192–220.

59. Jalland, *Women, Marriage and Politics*, p. 168.

60. Florence Nightingale, *Cassandra*, reprinted in Ray Strachey, *The Cause: A Short History of the Women's Movement in Great Britain* (London: Virago, 1978, first published 1928), p. 402.

61. Peterson, *Family, Love and Work*, pp. 63, 116–20.

62. Dominic David Alessio, 'Domesticating "the Heart of the Wild": Female Personifications of the Colonies 1886–1940', *Women's History Review*, 6, no. 2 (1997), p. 260.

63. Bland, *Banishing the Beast*, p. 162.

64. See Helsinger, Sheets and Veeder, *The Woman Question*, ii, pp. 136–9.

65. Jalland, *Women, Marriage and Politics*, ch. 9, see especially pp. 276–9, 262.

66. Eileen Janes Yeo, *The Contest for Social Science: Relations and Representations of Gender and Class* (London: Rivers Oram Press, 1996), pp. 122–4.

67. See Dyhouse, *Feminism and the Family*, p. 10.

68. See the introduction and useful collection of documents in Gardiner (ed.), *The New Woman*.

69. Quoted in Bland, *Banishing the Beast*, p. 166 and ch. 6; Sheila Jeffreys, *The Spinster and Her Enemies: Feminism and Sexuality 1880–1930* (London: Pandora, 1985), pp. 27–45.

70. Martha Vicinus, *Independent Women: Work and Community for Single Women, 1850–1920* (London: Virago, 1985); Bland, *Banishing the Beast*, pp. 168–71.

71. Janet Howarth, 'Mrs Henry Fawcett (1847–1929): The Widow as a Problem in Feminist Biography', in June Purvis and Sandra Stanley Holton (eds), *Votes for Women* (London: Routledge, 2000), pp. 84–108.
72. Jalland and Hooper, *Women from Birth to Death*, pp. 287–303; Caine, *Destined to be Wives*, p. 185; Gerard, *Country House Life*, p. 117.
73. Hammerton, *Cruelty and Companionship*, p. 149.
74. Bland, *Banishing the Beast*, pp. 173–82.

Conclusion

1. Susan Kingsley Kent, *Making Peace: the Reconstruction of Gender in Interwar Britain* (Princeton: Princeton University Press, 1993).
2. Gisela Bock, 'Women's History and Gender History: Aspects of an International Debate', in *Gender and History*, 1, no. 1 (1989), p. 10.

FURTHER READING

This is a select bibliography, designed to highlight the essential texts on this subject. For more detailed works, readers are recommended to consult the notes for each chapter.

General Works

The following books all provide an excellent introduction to the study of nineteenth-century British women:

Helsinger, Elizabeth K., Robin Lauterbach Sheets and William Veeder (eds), *The Woman Question: Society and Literature in Britain and America 1837–1883* (Chicago and London: University of Chicago Press, 1983), 3 vols.

Hollis, Patricia (ed.), *Women in Public 1850–1900: Documents of the Victorian Women's Movement* (London: George Allen and Unwin, 1979).

Lewis, Jane, *Women in England 1870–1950* (Hemel Hempstead: Harvester Wheatsheaf, 1984).

Luddy, Maria (ed.), *Women in Ireland 1800–1918* (Cork: Cork University Press, 1995).

Purvis, June (ed.), *Women's History: Britain, 1850–1945* (London: UCL Press, 1995).

Rendall, Jane, *Women in an Industrializing Society: England 1750–1880* (Oxford: Blackwell, 1990).

Vicinus, Martha (ed.), *Suffer and Be Still: Women in the Victorian Age* (Bloomington and London: Indiana University Press, 1972).

Vicinus, Martha (ed.), *A Widening Sphere: Changing Roles of Victorian Women* (Bloomington and London: Indiana University Press, 1977).

Work and Education

Alexander, Sally, 'Women's Work in Nineteenth-Century London', (1976) reprinted in Sally Alexander, *Becoming a Woman and Other Essays in 19th and 20th Century Feminist History* (London: Virago, 1994), pp. 3–55.
A seminal essay, illuminating the diverse strategies for income generation among working-class metropolitan women.

Bourke, Joanna, 'Housewifery in Working-Class England, 1860–1914', *Past and Present*, 143 (1994), pp. 167–97.
A reassessment of the significance of women's unpaid labour within the home.

Delamont, Sara, 'The Contradictions in Ladies' Education', in Sara Delamont and Lorna Duffin (eds), *Nineteenth Century Woman: Her Cultural and Physical World* (London: Croom Helm, 1978), pp. 134–63.
Highlights clearly the complexities inherent in middle-class educational reform.

Drake, Barbara, *Women in Trade Unions* (London: Virago, 1984, first published 1920).
A classic account of the subject.

Dyhouse, Carol, *No Distinction of Sex? Women in British Universities 1870–1939* (London: UCL, 1995).
The first comprehensive study of women's chequered access to higher education.

Gordon, Eleanor, and Esther Breitenbach (eds), *The World is Ill-Divided: Women's Work in Scotland in the Nineteenth and Early Twentieth Centuries* (Edinburgh: Edinburgh University Press, 1990).
Useful essays on Scottish women's work.

Hall, Catherine, 'Strains in the "Firm of Wife, Children and Friends": Middle-Class Women and Employment in Early-Nineteenth-Century England', in Catherine Hall, *White, Male and Middle-Class: Explorations in Feminism and History* (Cambridge: Polity Press, 1992), pp. 172–202.
The only sustained analysis of the economic activities of early Victorian middle-class women.

Holcombe, Lee, *Victorian Ladies at Work: Middle-Class Working Women in England and Wales 1850–1914* (Newton Abbot: David and Charles, 1973).
Extremely detailed account.

Hughes, Kathryn, *Victorian Governess* (London: Hambledon Press, 1993).
Demonstrates the enormous problems faced by wage-earning genteel women.

John, Angela V. (ed.), *Unequal Opportunities: Women's Employment in England 1800–1918* (Oxford: Basil Blackwell, 1986).
An important book which covers the key areas with thoughtful and detailed contributions.

Peterson, M. Jeanne, *Family, Love and Work in the Lives of Victorian Gentlewomen* (Bloomington and Indianapolis: Indiana University Press, 1989).
An optimistic assessment of the significance of the unpaid work of upper-middle class women.

Pinchbeck, Ivy, *Women Workers and the Industrial Revolution, 1750–1850* (London: Virago, 1981, first published 1930).
A classic account of the impact of industrialisation upon working women.

Purvis, June, *Hard Lessons: The Lives and Education of Working Women in Nineteenth Century England* (Cambridge: Polity Press, 1989).
Particularly interesting for its coverage of adult education.

Reynolds, K. D., *Aristocratic Women and Political Society in Victorian Britain* (Oxford: Clarendon Press, 1998).
Extremely suggestive of the contribution of aristocratic women to the family estate.

Rose, Sonya O., *Limited Livelihoods: Gender and Class in Nineteenth Century England* (London: Routledge, 1992).
An extended analysis of the gendered implications of women's employment.

Tilly Louise A., and Joan W. Scott, *Women, Work and Family* (New York and London: Routledge, 1989 reprint, first published 1978).
An influential study exploring women's work within a familial and social context.

Valenze, Deborah, *The First Industrial Woman* (Oxford: Oxford University Press, 1995).
Particularly strong on the cultural discourses relating to women's work.

Vicinus, Martha, *Independent Women: Work and Community for Single Women, 1850–1920* (London: Virago Press, 1985).
A superb account of the cultural and personal implications of the broadening opportunities for middle-class women from the mid-century.

Politics, Philanthropy and Protest

Bland, Lucy, *Banishing the Beast: English Feminism and Sexual Morality, 1885–1914* (Harmondsworth: Penguin, 1995).
A central text for understanding the agendas of late Victorian feminism.

Caine, Barbara, *Victorian Feminists* (Oxford: Oxford University Press, 1992).
Contains four thoughtful biographical studies of leading Victorian feminists.

Chaudhuri, Nupur, and Margaret Strobel (eds), *Western Women and Imperialism: Complicity and Resistance* (Bloomington and Indiana: Indiana University Press, 1992).

Offers keen insights into the imperial dimensions of women's philanthropic engagement.

Cullen, Mary, and Maria Luddy (eds), *Women, Power and Consciousness in 19th Century Ireland* (Dublin: Attic Press, 1995).
Illuminating series of essays on the activities of Irish women.

Gleadle, Kathryn, and Sarah Richardson (eds), *Women in British Politics, 1760–1860: The Power of the Petticoat* (Basingstoke: Macmillan – now Palgrave, 2000).
A collection of the latest research in the field.

Gordon, Eleanor, *Women and the Labour Movement in Scotland 1850–1914* (Oxford: Clarendon Press, 1991).
A detailed and thought-provoking account.

Hollis, Patricia (ed.), *Ladies Elect: Women in English Local Government 1865–1914* (Oxford: Clarendon Press, 1987).
A comprehensive assessment of women's involvement in local government.

Holton, Sandra Stanley, *Suffrage Days: Stories from the Women's Suffrage Movement* (London and New York: Routledge, 1996).
Sheds new light on little-known figures.

Liddington, Jill, and Jill Norris, *One Hand Tied Behind Us: The Rise of the Women's Suffrage Movement* (London: Virago, 1978).
A highly readable account of working women's contribution to the women's suffrage movement.

Midgley, Clare, *Women Against Slavery: The British Campaigns 1780–1870* (London: Routledge, 1992).
A detailed analysis of this central pressure-group campaign.

Prochaska, F. K., *Women and Philanthropy in Nineteenth-Century England* (Oxford: Clarendon Press, 1980).
A thorough examination of women's philanthropic activities.

Rendall, Jane, *The Origins of Modern Feminism: Women in Britain, France and the United States, 1780–1860* (Chicago: Lyceum Books, 1985).
A superb account of early feminism.

Rendall, Jane (ed.), *Equal or Different: Women's Politics, 1800–1914* (Oxford: Blackwell, 1987).
A key collection of essays, particularly useful for women's involvement in party politics.

Reynolds, K. D., *Aristocratic Women and Political Society in Victorian Britain* (Oxford: Clarendon Press, 1998).
A carefully researched contribution considering all aspects of aristocratic women's public and private authority.

Schwarzkopf, Jutta, *Women in the Chartist Movement* (London: Macmillan – now Palgrave, 1991).
A provocative interpretation which emphasises the reactionary elements within Chartism.

Taylor, Barbara, *Eve and the New Jerusalem: Socialism and Feminism in the Nineteenth Century* (London: Virago Press, 1983).
A pioneering text providing a sophisticated interpretation of women's involvement in the Owenite movement.

Thomis, Malcolm I., and Jennifer Grimmett, *Women in Protest: 1800–1850* (London: Croom Helm, 1982).
Extremely useful overview.

Walkowitz, Judith R., *Prostitution and Victorian Society: Women, Class and the State* (Cambridge: Cambridge University Press, 1980).
An important book, of far-reaching implications, examining women's response to the Contagious Diseases Acts.

Ward, Margaret, *Unmanageable Revolutionaries: Women and Irish Nationalism* (London: Pluto Press, 1989).
A clear introduction to the topic.

Yeo, Eileen, *Radical Femininity: Women's Self-Representation in the Public Sphere* (Manchester: Manchester University Press, 1998).
An interesting collection of essays, which focuses upon the discursive aspects of women's public activity.

Family Life

Branca, Patricia, *Silent Sisterhood: Middle-Class Women in the Victorian Home* (London: Croom Helm, 1975).
Delivers an up-beat assessment of the family lives and domestic activities of middle-class women.

Caine, Barbara, *Destined to be Wives: The Sisters of Beatrice Webb* (Oxford: Clarendon Press, 1986).
An illuminating case-study of an upper-middle-class family.

Clark, Anna, *The Struggle for the Breeches: Gender and the Making of the British Working Class* (London: Rivers Oram Press, 1995).
An ambitious and thought-provoking analysis of the nature of working-class gender relations within the community, the workplace and the family.

Davidoff, Leonore, and Catherine Hall, *Family Fortunes: Men and Women of the English Middle Class, 1780–1850* (London: Routledge, 1987).
An enormously influential study considering the relationship between the rise of the middle class and its gendered dynamics.

Gillis, John R., *For Better, For Worse: British Marriages, 1600 to the Present* (Oxford: Oxford University Press, 1985).
A fascinating survey of British marriages.

Holcombe, Lee, *Wives and Property: Reform of the Married Women's Property Law in Nineteenth-Century England* (Toronto and London: University of Toronto Press, 1983).
>Discusses in full the complexities of married women's legal position.

Jalland, Pat, *Women, Marriage and Politics, 1860–1914* (Oxford: Clarendon Press, 1986).
>A sensitive and moving account of married life among the upper middle classes.

Jalland Pat, and John Hooper (eds), *Women from Birth to Death: The Female Life Cycle in Britain 1830–1914* (Brighton: Harvester Press, 1986).
>An excellent anthology of documents.

Lewis Jane (ed.), *Labour and Love: Women's Experience of Home and Family, 1850–1940* (Oxford: Basil Blackwell, 1986).
>Lively interpretations of family life covering a wide range of issues.

Lewis, Judith Schneid, *In the Family Way: Childbearing in the British Aristocracy, 1760–1860* (New Brunswick, New Jersey: Rutgers University Press, 1986).
>An excellent introduction to the private lives of aristocratic women.

Perkin, Joan, *Women and Marriage in Nineteenth-Century England* (London: Routledge, 1989).
>A useful and accessible introduction to the subject.

Roberts, Elizabeth, *A Woman's Place: An Oral History of Working-Class Women 1890–1940* (Oxford: Basil Blackwell, 1984).
>Excellent oral history providing important insights into the lives of working-class women.

Ross, Ellen, *Love and Toil: Motherhood in Outcast London, 1870–1918* (Oxford: Oxford University Press, 1993).
>A superb account of the exigencies of motherhood in the East End of London.

Vickery, Amanda, *The Gentleman's Daughter: Women's Lives in Georgian England* (New Haven and London: Yale University Press, 1998).
>Illuminating material on elite women at the beginning of the period, particularly with regard to their leisure and domestic activities.

INDEX